ON FREUD'S "SPLITTING OF THE EGO IN THE PROCESS OF DEFENCE"

CONTEMPORARY FREUD
Turning Points and Critical Issues

General Editor: Leticia Glocer Fiorini

On Freud's "Analysis Terminable and Interminable"
edited by Joseph Sandler

Freud's "On Narcissism: An Introduction"
edited by Joseph Sandler, Ethel Spector Person, Peter Fonagy

On Freud's "Observations on Transference-Love"
edited by Ethel Spector Person, Aiban Hagelin, Peter Fonagy

On Freud's "A Child Is Being Beaten"
edited by Ethel Spector Person

On Freud's "Group Psychology and the Analysis of the Ego"
edited by Ethel Spector Person

On Freud's "Mourning and Melancholia"
edited by Leticia Glocer Fiorini, Thierry Bokanowski, Sergio Lewkowicz

On Freud's "The Future of an Illusion"
edited by Mary Kay O'Neil & Salman Akhtar

ON FREUD'S "SPLITTING OF THE EGO IN THE PROCESS OF DEFENCE"

Edited by

Thierry Bokanowski & Sergio Lewkowicz

Foreword by

Elias Mallet da Rocha Barros

CONTEMPORARY FREUD
Turning Points and Critical Issues

Routledge
Taylor & Francis Group
LONDON AND NEW YORK

Part I: Grateful acknowledgement is made to Sigmund Freud Copyrights, Ltd; the Institute of Psycho-Analysis, London; the Hogarth Press; and BASIC BOOKS, a member of Perseus Books Group, for permission to reprint "Splitting of the Ego in the Process of Defence" as published in *The Complete Edition of the Psychological Works of Sigmund Freud, Vol. 23*, trans. and ed. James Strachey. All rights reserved 1957. Reproduced by arrangement with Paterson Marsh Ltd., London. And in *The Collected Papers of Sigmund Freud, Vol. 5*, authorized translation under the supervision of Joan Riviere, published by BASIC BOOKS, Inc., a member of Perseus Books Group, by arrangement with the Hogarth Press, Ltd. and the Institute of Psycho-Analysis, London. Reprinted by permission of BASIC BOOKS, a member of Perseus Books Group. Chapter 9, "Splitting of the Ego and Perversion", is an amended version of L. Carignan, "The Secret Study of a Perverse Transference", *International Journal of Psychoanalysis, 80* (1999): 909–928; reprinted by permission.

First published 2009 by Karnac Books Ltd.

Published 2018 by Routledge
2 Park Square, Milton Park, Abingdon, Oxon OX14 4RN
711 Third Avenue, New York, NY 10017, USA

Routledge is an imprint of the Taylor & Francis Group, an informa business

British Library Cataloguing in Publication Data

A C.I.P. for this book is available from the British Library

ISBN: 978-1-85575-755-4 (pbk)

Edited, designed, and produced by Communication Crafts

CONTENTS

CONTEMPORARY FREUD

IPA Publications Committee

This significant series was founded by Robert Wallerstein and first edited by Joseph Sandler, Ethel Spector Person, and Peter Fonagy, and its important contributions have greatly interested psychoanalysts of different latitudes.

The objective of this series is to approach Freud's work from a present and contemporary point of view. On the one hand, this means highlighting the fundamental contributions of his work that constitute the axes of psychoanalytic theory and practice. On the other, it implies the possibility of getting to know and spreading the ideas of present psychoanalysts about Freud's *oeuvre*, both where they coincide and where they differ.

This series considers at least two lines of development: a contemporary reading of Freud that reclaims his contributions and a clarification of the logical and epistemic perspectives from which he is read today.

Freud's theory has branched out, and this has led to a theoretical, technical, and clinical pluralism that has to be worked through. It has therefore become necessary to avoid a snug and uncritical coexistence of concepts in order to consider systems of increasing complexities that take into account both the convergences and the divergences of the categories at play.

Consequently, this project has involved an additional task—that is, gathering psychoanalysts from different geographical regions representing, in addition, different theoretical stances, in order to be able to show their polyphony. This also means an extra effort for the reader that has to do with distinguishing and discriminating, establishing relations or contradictions that each reader will have to eventually work through.

Being able to listen to other theoretical viewpoints is also a way of exercising our listening capacities in the clinical field. This means that the listening should support a space of freedom that would allow us to hear what is new and original.

In this spirit we have brought together authors deeply rooted in the Freudian tradition and others who have developed theories that had not been explicitly taken into account in Freud's work.

Freud's "Splitting of the Ego" shows his last thoughts especially concerning fetishism and psychosis, and it also enlightens his ideas on the non-unified structure of the ego. He focuses on the question of the relation between the ego and reality and introduces another model different from that of repression and the return of the repressed, by establishing the notion of disavowal as a specific psychic mechanism concerning the ego.

The editors, Thierry Bokanowski and Sergio Lewkowicz, together with the contributors to this volume, accepted the challenge to consider Freudian ideas and their expansions and implications in contemporary psychoanalysis.

Special thanks are due to the editors and to the contributors to this volume, which enriches the Contemporary Freud series.

Leticia Glocer Fiorini
Series Editor

ACKNOWLEDGEMENTS

We are extremely pleased and honoured to present this new volume in the Contemporary Freud series.

Although the idea of splitting was introduced by Freud in his earliest works (1895, *Studies on Hysteria*), the concept had only been theoretically settled by him in much later contributions: in 1927, about fetishism, and finally in 1938, when he describes it as a defence mechanism that modifies the functioning of the ego to a similar extent, but in different ways, in the neuroses, perversions, or psychoses.

For Freud, this specific mechanism is connected with a defence in the face of a perception that traumatizes the ego, a perception partly accepted and partly denied at the same time, which leads, in the mind, to the coexistence of two opposite attitudes, apparently not conflicting, but always linked with the castration complex and bisexuality. For Freud, the conflict takes place between the perception by the ego and the drive. The gap inscribed on the line of the splitting will thereafter be a source of fracture for all successive traumatisms. However, as underlined by Freud, it is not always easy to decide which mechanism occurs—repression? suppression? and/or splitting?—when we are facing someone who adopts two different psychic attitudes, opposite and independent, given that this psychic configuration is based on topographical and structural factors. (In any case, the ego's coherence is never complete, and the two contradictory attitudes occur all the time at various levels.)

Since these advances, these concepts have undergone many developments and many modifications in the psychoanalytic field, leading at the present time to the idea that the splitting mechanism is (as are denial, projective identification, idealization, etc.) normal and is one of the basic psychic organizers. After Sándor Ferenczi, who was the first to emphasize the idea of narcissistic splitting linked to the action of trauma (the "splitting/trauma" pairing), the most important contribution has come from Melanie Klein, whose work enlightens the idea of "splitting of the object" (in terms of "good/bad" objects). Many of her followers have worked with various aspects of pathological splitting, particularly in the clinical "borderline" or "non-neurotic" states (D. W. Winnicott, W. R. Bion, Donald Meltzer, Herbert Rosenfeld, Harold Searles, Joyce McDougall, André Green, etc.).

The idea behind this volume was to invite authors from different regions and orientations to promote a fruitful debate on the theme, thus enriching the seminal work of Sigmund Freud.

We would like to thank the Publications Committee of the IPA, represented by its Chair, Leticia Glocer Fiorini, for the suggestions and support always presented. Thanks are also due to Cesare Sacerdoti, former Director of Publications, and Pippa Hodges, publications assistant, for her dedication and competence.

Thierry Bokanowski & Sergio Lewkowicz

EDITORS AND CONTRIBUTORS

Gérard Bayle became a Paris Psychoanalytical Society member in 1979 and was a training analyst until 1989. He was Scientific Secretary of the Congrès des Psychanalystes de Langue Française (CPLF) for eight years, then President of his Society (2004–2007). This has involved him in the IPA recognition of the French psychoanalytic model. He practises private and institutional psychoanalysis with adults, children, and adolescents, and he trains students in classical techniques and in psychoanalytic psychodrama. Interested in the clinical and meta-psychological study of the defences, he has reported to the CPLF about the splitting of the ego, suggesting the conceptualization of a functional splitting. This has led him to a study of individual and institutional narcissistic perversions. He was granted the Maurice Bouvet Prize for Psycho-Analysis in 1991. His publications include *Formation au psychodrame analytique* [Training in psychoanalytic psychodrama] (with N. Amar & I. Salem); *Clivages* [Splittings]; *Épître aux insensés* [Epistle to the insane]; *Le trésor des phobies* [The treasure of the phobias]; and *Paul Claude Racamier*, which is a book about a famous French colleague.

Thierry Bokanowski is a training and supervising analyst of the Paris Psychoanalytical Society (SPP) and a member of the International

Psychoanalytical Association; a former secretary of the executive committee of the Paris Psychoanalytical Institute; former Editor of the *Revue Française de Psychanalyse*; and the current President of the Scientific Committee of the Paris Psychoanalytical Society. He has published several papers in various psychoanalytic journals, including the *International Journal of Psychoanalysis*. His books include *Sándor Ferenczi*, and *De la pratique analytique*, translated under the title *The Practice of Psychoanalysis*.

Stefano Bolognini is a training and supervising psychoanalyst of the Italian Psychoanalytic Society. He was the national scientific director of the Society, President of the Psychoanalytic Institute of Bologna, and IPA Board Representative for Europe. He was co-founder of the Serious Pathologies Committee of his Society, and he works as a supervisor in psychiatric public services and in day-hospitals for borderline and psychotic adolescents. He is president of the Italian Psychoanalytic Society (SPI) and co-chair of the IPA CAPSA Committee, as well as chair of the IPA's 100th Anniversary Committee. A member of the European Board of the *International Journal of Psychoanalysis*, he has published papers in the most important international journals. His book *Psychoanalytic Empathy* was published in Italian, French, English, German, Spanish, and Portuguese-Brazilian (a Greek edition is also forthcoming). Other translations are proposed for his recent book *Secret Passages: Theory and Practice of the Interpsychic Dimension* (2008). He also published *Like Wind, Like Wave* (2006), a collection of amusingly told personal anecdotes, each with its concluding pearl of psychoanalytic wisdom. He lives and works in Bologna, Italy.

Ira Brenner is a clinical Professor of Psychiatry at Jefferson Medical College. He is a training and supervising analyst at the Psychoanalytic Center of Philadelphia, where he is the Director of the Adult Psychotherapy Training Program. With over sixty publications, he has written extensively on the topic of psychic trauma, most notably in his books *The Last Witness: The Child Survivor of the Holocaust* (co-authored with Judith Kestenberg); *Dissociation of Trauma: Theory, Phenomenology, and Technique*; and *Psychic Trauma: Dynamics, Symptoms and Treatment*. He has also edited special issues of the *Journal of Applied Psychoanalytic Studies*, on Reverberations of the Holocaust (2002) and on Anti-Semitism in Muslim Countries (2007), with Nadia Ramzy. In addition, he has received a number of awards, including the Pierre

Janet Writing Award from the ISSD for his 2001 book *Dissociation of Trauma* and the Simon Gratz Award in 2000 from Jefferson Medical College as a distinguished alumnus, having graduated there with membership in the honorary Alpha Omega society. He is in private practice in the greater Philadelphia area and continues to share his knowledge nationally and internationally.

Louise Carignan is a member of the Canadian Psychoanalytic Society and a training and supervising analyst of the Canadian Institute of Psychoanalysis. She is currently Associate Editor of the *Canadian Journal of Psychoanalysis.* She was formerly Director of the QE-Ottawa Institute of Psychoanalysis and President of the Ottawa Psychoanalytic Society. She practises in Ottawa, Canada.

Penelope Garvey is a training analyst and supervisor of the British Psychoanalytical Society. She has private practice in Devon and also works as a consultant psychotherapist in Plymouth NHS. She teaches at the Institute of Psychoanalysis in London, in Devon, and in Europe.

Raul Hartke is a psychiatrist and a training and supervising analyst for the Porto Alegre Psychoanalytic Society, where he was a former Scientific Director, President, and Director of the Institute. He is Professor and Supervisor for Psychoanalytical Psychotherapy at the Psychiatry Department, Medical School of the Federal University of Rio Grande do Sul. He is also Associate Editor for Book Reviews in Portuguese of the *International Journal of Psychoanalysis.*

Luis Kancyper is a Full Member and Supervisor of the Argentine Psychoanalytic Association, where he is also a professor at the Institute of Psychoanalysis. He has published several books on different subjects, such as the confrontation between generations, the sibling complex, resentment and remorse, and the psychoanalytic field with adolescents. He has also focused on the study of literature and psychoanalysis.

Sergio Lewkowicz is currently the Scientific Director of the Porto Alegre Psychoanalytical Society; psychiatry and training and supervising analyst for the Porto Alegre Psychoanalytical Society; Publications Director of the Porto Alegre Psychoanalytical Society; a professor and supervisor for psychoanalytical psychotherapy in the Psychiatry Department, Medical School of the Federal University of Rio Grande do Sul; member of the IPA Publications Committee; member of the Programme Committee of the 43rd Congress of the IPA in New Orleans (2004); former President of the Society of Psychiatry of Rio Grande do Sul; and former Editor of the psychiatry journal of Rio Grande do Sul. He has published papers on psychoanalytic technique.

Julio Moreno was a Postdoctoral Fellow of the National Institutes of Health at UCLA during 1970–1974 and is currently a full member and training analyst of the Buenos Aires Psychoanalytical Association, and a child and adolescence analyst. He was Scientific Secretary of the APdeBA from 2003–2005 and is now a professor of the Institute of APdeBA, the current University Institute of Mental Health. He has published numerous papers and recently a book on psychoanalysis and human nature, *Ser Humano* [Human being].

Rubén Zukerfeld graduated in Medicine from the University of Buenos Aires. He is a full member of the Argentine Psychoanalytic Association (APA), and a founder member of the Argentine Psychoanalytic Society (SAP), where he was the Director of the Training Institute and is currently a training analyst. As a founder of the Psychosomatic Institute of Buenos Aires he has gained valuable psychoanalytic experience in the psychosomatic field. He is currently a professor in the Master's programme in Psychoneuroimmunoendocrinology at the Favaloro University (Buenos Aires) and also a professor in the Master's programme in Psychoanalysis at the University of Salvador (Buenos Aires). His interest in metapsychology anf interdisciplinary and systematic investigation is reflected in many publications as well as in two books written with his wife Raquel Zonis Zukerfeld: *Psicoanálisis, tercera tópica y vulnerabilidad somática* [Psychoanalysis, third topography, and somatic vulnerability] and *Procesos terciarios. De la vulnerabilidad a la resiliencia* [Tertiary process: From vulnerability to resilience]. He has won, among others, the FEPAL prize for the paper presented in Montevideo in 2002, "Tertiary Processes", and the Psychoanalytic Research Exceptional Contribution Reward given by the IPA for the paper presented in New Orleans in 2004, "Hope and Determinism in the Psychoanalytic Attitude: An Empirical Research on Some Theoretical Prejudices".

FOREWORD

Elias Mallet da Rocha Barros

In this foreword I wish to highlight the importance of the concept of splitting to contemporary psychoanalysis from the metapsychological as well as the clinical point of view.

An author is renowned not so much for the answers to problems he sets out to solve as the very quality and relevance of the issues he introduces. It is these that make it into history and that are at the essence of continuity. The author presents us with a problem that can no longer be ignored and that synthesizes the pressing matters of a particular time in a specific field of knowledge. They are issues that impose on and capture our interest, give rise to an open discussion, and are a font of ever-expanding knowledge.

It is in this sense that the concept of splitting, introduced by diverse authors, beginning with Freud and later modified by Ronald Fairbairn and above all Melanie Klein, Herbert Rosenfeld, and

---

Elias Mallet da Rocha Barros is Editor for Latin America of the *International Journal of Psychoanalysis.* He is Supervising and Training Analyst of the Brazilian Psychoanalytical Society of Sao Paulo; member of the British Psychoanalytical Society; and recipient of the Mary Sigourney Trust Prize.

W. R. Bion, reveals itself of great richness in generating a series of hypotheses and concepts that have come to characterize current psychoanalytic practice.

Today we no longer question whether or not there is a mental phenomenon called splitting, be it as a defence mechanism or part of a mind-structuring process. Once accepted as a key concept, currently we want to know how it partakes in mental structuring, what affects it produces, and how the split part of the self and the object can be restored.

In 1978, Donald Meltzer, in his introductory course on the thought of Bion given at the Tavistock Clinic, wrote,

> It is perhaps difficult for people unacquainted with the use of the concepts of splitting and projective identification, as well as for those who have become perhaps a little blasé about them, to realize the electrifying impact of Mrs Klein's 1946 paper "Notes on Some Schizoid Mechanisms", upon the analysts who were working closely with her. With the notable exception of Bion's later work it could be said that the history of the next thirty years of research could be written in terms of the phenomenology and implications of these two seminal concepts. [Meltzer, 1978, p. 20]

This perception anticipated what happens currently regarding this seminal idea, which continues to be the object of investigations and new reflections, as the present volume well attests.

To understand the tremendous importance of the concept and its meaning to the history of psychoanalytic theory and clinical practice, the diverse authors of this collection, whose names require no further elaboration as exponents of the orientations they here represent, invite us to travel through what Octávio Paz denominated as intertextuality. The history of the meaning of the term "splitting" from psychiatry prior to Freud, through Freud and then Klein and Fairbairn, culminating in Bion, is long and intricate. The very sense of the term and the manner in which the various authors conceived its function differ in accordance with the synchronic and diachronic readings of the diverse authors involved in the writing of this book.

The concept of mind splitting was already utilized in psychiatry and has been present in literary works since ancient times.

Although Freud began writing his article on *Spaltung*, or splitting/division of the mind, during the Christmas of 1937 and it was not published until 1940 (see Hartke, this volume), he had already referred to the theme in 1924.

In his article "Neurosis and Psychosis" (1924b [1923]), Freud states that "the ego can avoid *collapsing towards one of these three demands*, by deforming itself, by submitting to encroachments on its own unity, and even perhaps *by effecting a cleavage or division of itself*" (pp. 152–153, emphasis added).

The human mind has the power to isolate experiences that are painful to it or actively attempt to isolate itself from these. This has long been known. The novelty introduced by Freud on approaching the concept, later modified by Klein, Bion, and Meltzer, lies in the suggestion that two or more parts of the *self* can be split in the mental world and go on to living lives that are concomitant and isolated, functioning according to their own mental logic and differing among themselves.

In Freud the concept of splitting appears independent from the concept of projection, while in Klein both mechanisms are already inextricably linked. I agree with Laplanche and Pontalis (1967) that, in Freud, splitting is not a defence mechanism in itself, but an effect of defence processes. This splitting, they say, "is not properly speaking a defence of the ego, but rather a means of having two procedures of defence exist side by side, one directed towards reality (disavowal) and the other towards the instinct; this second procedure may lead to the formation of neurotic symptoms (e.g. phobic symptoms)" (p. 429).

For Melanie Klein the concept appears intermixed with the notion of states of non-integration, an idea she derives from Winnicott, a state prior to active splitting. In this context, splitting does not create the first mental structure, but begins to function concomitantly with it.

On associating it in 1946 with the concept of projective identification, Klein introduces an innovative idea of great consequences to clinical practice, in leading her to redefinitions broadening the concept of transference and launching the bases for countertransference that are the work tools of the analyst searching to understand the mental functionings of the patient. Klein also introduces the idea that a part split off from the personality, ejected outwards, can later be reincorporated.

Bion takes a step further, suggesting that not only parts of the self can be split, but also mental functions.

The more immediate consequence of mental splitting is the impoverishment of mental life. When a patient separates from a painful and unbearable emotion, he is also splitting from the part of the self capable of having that emotion. This impoverishment occurs in various manners. The person loses a sense of continuity of his mental life so that his capacity to hold himself responsible for his feelings and actions is diminished, and thus his capacity to interfere in his destiny is brutally affected. On splitting due to loss of links between emotional experiences, the capacity for symbolizing and the possibility of construction of mental representations is sensibly hindered.

I believe that in his chapter in this volume Kancyper touches on a problem that is central to the issue treated throughout this book regarding the concept of splitting, in view of its connotations to psychoanalytic practice and theory. He cites Roussillon (2006) to give relevance to the implications of splitting/split parts of the mental structure associated with the issue of historicization: "historicization, as a means of mastering psychic representation, as the ability to represent what one truly is, continues to be the royal road, the main road, to the understanding of the representative nature of what makes itself actual in the individual. Historicization is what opens the road to the essential transformational process that favours the subjective work of symbolization."

Thomas Ogden (1992) in his turn in defining the two positions (paranoid–schizoid and depressive) as "means of generating experience" presents a very rich reflection on the role that the individual has in being part of and in generating his own history, or not being able to do so, and the issue of the dialectical constitution of subjectivity. An a-historical means of generating experience deprives the individual of that which he calls I-ness—in other words, the capacity to interpret his own meanings through a "mediating instance between one's self and one's lived sensory experience" (p. 614).

The sense of historical discontinuity resulting from splitting leads to an emotional superficiality that also affects the possibility of keeping alive an intimate dialogue with one's self, or, as the Kleinians would put it, between internal objects. The impact of splittings of the self on the capacity to establish intimate relations with our selves or with others seems to me one of the most harmful effects of splits, as they interfere directly in the processes of construing meaning.

On establishing barriers between memories and/or mental functions (Bion refers to splitting not only of parts of the self but also of mental functions), the mechanism of splitting interferes with the core structure of human mental life by destroying or fragmenting the meaning of emotional experiences and consequently also impoverishing the capacity to produce symbols. In this sense, the clinical examples provided by Bokanowski, by Bolognini, and by Kancyper in this volume are elegantly clarifying. With the loss of a feeling of continuity in life, the individual also loses the possibility of adopting a certain distancing to re-signify experiences. And in this sense, Bokanowski points very appropriately to the fact that the overcoming of splitting is the only means to produce a re-signification. He quotes from Baranger, Baranger, and Mom (1987): "*Nachträglichkeit* is the attempt to constitute the trauma as such within a new historicization—that is, to make it comprehensible." Within this context, the insights lived during sessions of unconscious splits free the patient from a way of constructing a history of life profoundly limited by past emotional experiences that leads to repeating patterns automatically and living under a threatening atmosphere.

In this context, the integration of split parts has the same future-freeing function attributed by the historian Lucien Febvre (1946) to historical research when he says, "To make history, yes, in that history is able, and the only thing able, to allow us to live in a world of constant instability with reflexes other than solely those of fear." Today the re-integration of split parts of the self and the object are related not only to the re-structuring of a traumatic past but also, and above all, to the possibility of the individual's assuming himself as the subject of his history.

It is important to emphasize that repairing traumatic situations of the past is only possible with the integration of the split parts of the self and, as such, presupposes that the split parts have developed an intimacy among themselves as a prior condition to integration. This basically means that the affective networks of the patient's mind formerly split and disconnected have developed links between themselves and as such have begun to inhabit the same emotional universe.

I believe that among an important group of analysts there is now a consensus on the idea that countertransference originates in the processes of projective identification and thus has as basis a splitting. Through projective identification, the patient projects/splits aspects (or the whole) of the self into the analyst. The analyst (receptor of projective identifications) becomes for the moment those aspects denied/split by the patient in projecting. He transforms himself into the I/self whom the patient has conflicts in being and as such cannot be. Thus the analyst lives through/for the patient that which the patient is in conflict with or cannot bear living. The receptor of the projection (the analyst) becomes a participant in the patient's denial of his own self and so exists in his fantasy as a split subject. He is simultaneously the *self* and *not-self* of the patient. As such the projected part of the patient, which always refers to a split part of the self, is objectified in the subjectivity of the analyst. Ogden (1994a) states that the outcome of mutual denial is the creation of a third subject, "the subject of projective identification", who at the same time is and is not the projector nor the receptor. In this process, the receptor (analyst) denies his own self in yielding (creating a space) to the denied aspect of the subjectivity of the projector (patient).

The introduction by Freud of the concept of splitting, followed by the changes incorporated by those who gave continuity to it having a direct implication for the concept of countertransference, via the notion of projective identification, made possible the formulation of other clinical ideas and approaches that before perhaps were unthinkable. We could cite the concepts of "analytic third" proposed by Ogden in 1994 and "analytic-pair" suggested by Antonino Ferro as fruits of this seminal concept. And among these we could also mention, for example, the notions of container/contained and *revêrie.*

I believe we may end here by inviting the reader to read each one of the chapters with the utmost attention and bearing in mind that, thanks to the concept of splitting, today we can count on psychoanalytic theory and practice that is richer and, at the same time, more complex and challenging.

PART I

"Splitting of the Ego in the Process of Defence" (1940e [1938])

Sigmund Freud

SPLITTING OF THE EGO IN THE PROCESS OF DEFENCE

I FIND myself for a moment in the interesting position of not knowing whether what I have to say should be regarded as something long familiar and obvious or as something entirely new and puzzling. But I am inclined to think the latter.

I have at last been struck by the fact that the ego of a person whom we know as a patient in analysis must, dozens of years earlier, when it was young, have behaved in a remarkable manner in certain particular situations of pressure. We can assign in general and somewhat vague terms the conditions under which this comes about, by saying that it occurs under the influence of a psychical trauma. I prefer to select a single sharply defined special case, though it certainly does not cover all the possible modes of causation.

Let us suppose, then, that a child's ego is under the sway of a powerful instinctual demand which it is accustomed to satisfy and that it is suddenly frightened by an experience which teaches it that the continuance of this satisfaction will result in an almost intolerable real danger. It must now decide either to recognize the real danger, give way to it and renounce the instinctual satisfaction, or to disavow reality and make itself believe that there is no reason for fear, so that it may be able to retain the satisfaction. Thus there is a conflict between the demand by the instinct and the prohibition by reality. But in fact the child takes neither course, or rather he takes both simultaneously, which comes to the same thing. He replies to the conflict with two contrary reactions, both of which are valid and effective. On the one hand, with the help of certain mechanisms he rejects reality and refuses to accept any prohibition; on the other hand, in the same breath he recognizes the danger of reality, takes over the fear of that danger as a pathological symptom and tries subsequently to divest himself of the fear. It must be confessed that this is a very ingenious solution of the difficulty. Both of the parties to the dispute obtain their share: the instinct is allowed to retain its satisfaction and proper respect is shown to reality. But everything has to be paid for in one way or another, and this success is achieved at the price of a rift in the ego which never heals but which increases as time goes on. The two contrary reactions to the conflict persist as the centre-point of a splitting of the ego. The whole process seems so strange to us because we take for granted the synthetic nature of the processes of the ego.[1] But we are clearly at fault in this. The synthetic function of the ego, though it is of such extraordinary importance, is subject to particular conditions and is liable to a whole number of disturbances.

It will assist if I introduce an individual case history into this schematic disquisition. A little boy, while he was between three and four years of age, had become acquainted with the female genitals through being seduced by an older girl. After these relations had been broken off, he carried on the sexual stimulation set going in this way by zealously practising manual masturbation; but he was soon caught at it by his energetic nurse and was threatened with castration, the carrying out of which was, as usual, ascribed to his father. There were thus present in this case conditions calculated to produce a tremendous effect of fright. A threat of castration by itself need not produce a great impression. A child will refuse to believe in it, for he cannot easily imagine the possibility of losing such a highly prized part of his body. His [earlier] sight of the female genitals might have convinced our child of that possibility. But he drew no such conclusion from it, since his disinclination to doing so was too great and there was no motive present which could compel him to. On the contrary, whatever uneasiness he may have felt was calmed by the reflection that what was missing would yet make its appearance: she would grow one (a penis) later. Anyone who has observed enough small boys will be able to recollect having come across some such remark at the sight of a baby sister's genitals. But it is different if both factors are present together. In that case the threat revives the memory of the perception which had hitherto been regarded as harmless and finds in that memory a dreaded confirmation. The little boy now thinks he understands why the girl's genitals showed no sign of a penis and no longer ventures to doubt that his own

[1] [See, for instance, a passage in Lecture XXXI of the *New Introductory Lectures* (1933*a*), *Standard Ed.*, **22**, 76, and an Editor's footnote there, which gives a number of other references.]

genitals may meet with the same fate. Thenceforward he cannot help believing in the reality of the danger of castration.

The usual result of the fright of castration, the result that passes as the normal one, is that, either immediately or after some considerable struggle, the boy gives way to the threat and obeys the prohibition either wholly or at least in part (that is, by no longer touching his genitals with his hand). In other words, he gives up, in whole or in part, the satisfaction of the instinct. We are prepared to hear, however, that our present patient found another way out. He created a substitute for the penis which he missed in females—that is to say, a fetish. In so doing, it is true that he had disavowed reality, but he had saved his own penis. So long as he was not obliged to acknowledge that females have lost their penis, there was no need for him to believe the threat that had been made against him: he need have no fears for his own penis, so he could proceed with his masturbation undisturbed. This behaviour on the part of our patient strikes us forcibly as being a turning away from reality—a procedure which we should prefer to reserve for psychoses. And it is in fact not very different. Yet we will suspend our judgement, for upon closer inspection we shall discover a not unimportant distinction. The boy did not simply contradict his perceptions and hallucinate a penis where there was none to be seen; he effected no more than a displacement of value—he transferred the importance of the penis to another part of the body, a procedure in which he was assisted by the mechanism of regression (in a manner which need not here be explained). This displacement, it is true, related only to the female body; as regards his own penis nothing was changed.

This way of dealing with reality, which almost deserves to be described as artful, was decisive as regards the boy's practical behaviour. He continued with his masturbation as though it implied no danger to his penis; but at the same time, in complete contradiction to his apparent boldness or indifference, he developed a symptom which showed that he nevertheless did recognize the danger. He had been threatened with being castrated by his father, and immediately afterwards, simultaneously with the creation of his fetish, he developed an intense fear of his father punishing him, which it required the whole force of his masculinity to master and overcompensate. This fear of his father, too, was silent on the subject of castration: by the help of regression to an oral phase, it assumed the form of a fear of being eaten by his father. At this point it is impossible to forget a primitive fragment of Greek mythology which tells how Kronos, the old Father God, swallowed his children and sought to swallow his youngest son Zeus like the rest, and how Zeus was saved by the craft of his mother and later on castrated his father. But we must return to our case history and add that the boy produced yet another symptom, though it was a slight one, which he has retained to this day. This was an anxious susceptibility against either of his little toes being touched, as though, in all the to and fro between disavowal and acknowledgement, it was nevertheless castration that found the clearer expression. . . .

* * * * *

PART II

Discussion of "Splitting of the Ego in the Process of Defence"

1

On splitting of the ego: a history of the concept

Ira Brenner

Human thought leads us to wonder about the origin and nature of things. While such curiosity is not the exclusive domain of our species, our primate cousins appear to be more concerned with the more basic issues of finding food and a suitable mate and of surviving. We, too, concern ourselves with such instinctual demands, and with more sublime themes. Our wonderment about such matters as human nature, our existence, and the origin of the universe have occupied us for millennia and promise to vex us for many more. Such ineffable questions spawn not only scientific inquiry but also challenge our imagination, activate primary-process thinking, and provide a canvas onto which projective phenomena may be painted. As these mental processes converge, resulting in richly textured ideas, theories, and belief systems, it cannot help be noted that certain patterns keep appearing in our attempts to understand and organize our world. One of these patterns is that a thing can change by becoming divided, separated, or split into two or more parts. For example, the division of cells—mitosis—is a basic pattern of life. It is a spatial model, which seems to be more readily understood than a model based on the more abstract but more comprehensive space–time continuum, which is less readily apparent to our minds (Brenner, 2002).

This principle of division may be invoked in many situations ranging from the mundane to the most supreme. For example, sacred texts and ancient traditions addressing the "big questions" inevitably espouse a creation myth utilizing a variation of this notion. In the Western world, for example, where the Judeo-Christian influence has prevailed, the all-familiar first chapter of the Hebrew Bible, Genesis, describes how God said "Let there be light!" and thereby created day and night by splitting the primordial darkness. As creation continues, God then splits the water above and below the heavens as well as on the earth by creating land masses that divide up the seas. Comparative studies of creation, such as those done by Neumann (1954), a disciple of Jung (whose own "split" with Freud, incidentally, is one of the more well-known stories in the creation of the psychoanalytic movement), reveal the universality of this formulation: "In all peoples and in all religions, creation appears as the creation of light. Thus, the coming of consciousness manifesting itself as light in contrast to the darkness of the unconscious is the real 'object' of creation mythology" (Neumann, 1954, p. 6). He therefore sees "creation" as a metaphor for the topographic theory of the mind.

Despite Freud's being a "godless Jew" (Gay, 1987; Rizzuto, 1998), the impact of his own religious heritage has been the topic of considerable interest (Halpern, 1999; Ostow, 1989; Yerushalmi, 1991). It has even been speculated that the tradition of keeping things separate, such as those in the Jewish dietary laws, may have subtly influenced Freud's thinking about mental organization (Brenner, 2003–2004). He found the notion of a split in the psyche so compelling that in addition to splitting of consciousness and splitting of the mind (Freud, 1895d), he applied it in his formulations about neurosis (1940a [1938]), perversion (1923b), and psychosis (1940b [1938]). Although Janet predated Freud with his theory of disaggregation, or dissociation, being caused by a fracture of the psyche (Janet, 1889), his model posited a passive disintegration based on trauma and constitutional factors as opposed to Freud's dynamic model based on conflict, anxiety, and unconscious motivation. As Pruyser (1975) notes, "The lure of the split in the psyche . . ." has tempted many and has stood the test of time.

The evolution of Freud's ideas

In Freud's early writings, he and Breuer describe "splitting of consciousness" (Freud, 1895d, pp. 12, 67, 69, 123), in which there was a separation of mental contents from the dominant mass of ideas. It was a precursor to the "cornerstone" concept of repression. They also referred to "splitting of personality" (p. 45), where opposite behavioural states occurred. In addition, they wrote about "splitting of the mind" (pp. 225, 234), characterized by the simultaneous existence of conscious and unconscious ideation. This observation was particularly vexing because the patient could alternate between different states of mind, carrying on conversations, behaving in a volitional way, and having relationships one moment and then switching to another state and having amnesia for all of the above. Breuer described this phenomenon very well in the case of Anna O., whose "clouds", surly agitated moods, and hysterical symptoms would fluctuate as she amnestically shifted from her very disturbed self to her usual self. Utterly devastated by the physical deterioration and death of her beloved father, this very ill, grief-stricken young woman required both high doses of chloral hydrate and the "talking cure"—a term she herself coined. When it was determined that "the motive for splitting of consciousness . . . was that of defence" (p. 166), psychoanalysis was truly born. (However, it would take almost another century for serious discussion to occur about combining psychoanalysis with pharmacotherapy, which Anna O. also pioneered.)

In contrast to Janet's contention of constitutional weakness and an inability to maintain a synthesis of the mind, Freud recognized that dividedness of the mind could be understood "dynamically", from the conflict of opposing mental forces (Freud, 1910a [1909], pp. 25–26). However, his turning away from the study of altered states of consciousness, dissociation, and hysteria to repression, the structural model, and splitting of the ego was a decisive turn of events in the history of psychoanalysis, leaving much still to be learned from his earlier work.

A re-reading of his collaboration with Breuer suggests that he never fully embraced the former's notion of the hypnoid state, even back then. His own individual contributions to their volume—his case reports and his section on the psychotherapy of hysteria—seemed from the start to reflect their theoretical differences. Breuer emphasized "hypnoid" hysteria and "retention" hysteria, whereas Freud preferred "defence" hysteria, which he believed was at the root of the other two subtypes. Moreover, Freud did not feel as proficient in hypnosis as Breuer did and perhaps was a bit eager to replace hypnotism with his own method. In so doing, he seemed to overlook his own observation that spontaneous, autohypnotic states may occur (Freud, 1891d) that may, in fact, be quite refractory to free association unless the analyst is aware it is happening and can work with the patient while in the trance (Brenner, 1994). As a result, much of Breuer's work was never fully integrated into the mainstream or "dominant mass of ideas" of psychoanalytic thinking. However, the idea of a split in the psyche persisted and was reworked throughout Freud's lifetime. Splitting of the ego came to be seen as an alternative defence to repression and a form of psychological damage control to possibly stave off total disintegration, "by deforming itself . . . and even by affecting the cleavage or division of itself. In this way, the inconsistency, eccentricities and follies of men would appear in a similar light to their sexual perversion, through acceptance of which they spare themselves repressions" (Freud, 1924b [1923], pp. 152–153).

In the "last account of the ideas of which he was the creator" (Freud, 1940e [1938], p. 143), Freud's final written thoughts on splitting of the ego are summarized in Chapter VIII, "The psychical apparatus and the external world", of *An Outline of Psychoanalysis*:

> Two psychical attitudes have been formed instead of a single one—one, the normal one, which takes account of reality, and another which under the influence of the instincts detaches from reality. The two exist alongside of each other. The issue depends on their relative strength. If the second is or becomes stronger, the necessary preconditions for a psychosis is present. If the relation is reversed, then there is an apparent cure of the delusional disorder. Actually, it has only retreated into the unconscious—just as numerous observations lead us to believe that the delusions existed ready-made for a long time before its manifest irruption. [Freud, 1940a (1938), p. 202]

Alluding to a case of chronic paranoia in which the patient's dream was more based in reality than his daytime delusions, Freud (1922b) contended that splitting of the ego was operative in all cases of psychosis also. Federn elaborated upon and extended these ideas as they pertained to psychotic illness, describing ego states and introducing the concept of ego boundaries (Federn, 1952). Then, seeing the applicability of the notion of ego states, Watkins elaborated upon Federn's ideas and linked them back to the all-but-forgotten realm of dissociative psychopathology (Watkins & Watkins, 1997). While Freud was less sanguine about the efficacy of analysis in treating very disturbed patients, he nevertheless thought that they illustrated this phenomenon well. However, he felt that the condition of fetishism was even more illustrative and was "a particularly favourable subject for studying the question" (Freud, 1940a [1938], p. 203). In such cases, he contended that the dread of castration was so overwhelming that the young boy

> disavows his own sense-perception which showed him that the female genitals lack a penis and holds fast to the contrary. The disavowed perception does not, however, remain entirely without influence for, in spite of everything, he has not the courage to assert that he actually saw a penis. He takes hold of something else instead—a part of the body or some other object—and assigns it the role of the penis which he cannot do without. . . . This behaviour is therefore simultaneously expressing two contrary premises. On the one hand they are disavowing the fact of this perception—the fact that they saw no penis in the female genitals—and on the other hand they are recognizing the fact that females have no penises and are drawing the correct conclusion from it. The two attitudes persist side by side throughout their lives without influencing each other. Here is what may rightly be called a splitting of the ego. . . . In fetishism, therefore, the detachment of the ego from the reality of the external world has never succeeded completely. [Freud, 1940a (1938), pp. 202–203]

This phenomenon was also recognized by Freud to be operative in the dream state:

> The dreamer's ego may appear two or more times in the manifest dream, once as himself and again disguised behind the figures of other people. . . . In itself, this multiplicity is no more remarkable than the multiple appearances of the ego in the waking state. [Freud, 1923c (1922), pp. 120–121]

> [T]his splitting of the ego . . . neither so new nor so strange . . . is indeed a universal characteristic of neuroses . . . as regards some particular behaviour, two different attitudes, contrary to each other and independent of each other. In the case of neuroses, however, one of these attitudes belongs to the ego and the contrary one, which is repressed, belongs to the id. [Freud, 1940e (1938), p. 275]

Given the evolution of Freud's theorizing over time, he invoked the concept of splitting to describe a dividedness of consciousness, between the id and the ego, the ego and the superego, and within the ego itself. It fell upon his followers to apply this mechanism to virtually all of their own models of the mind, such as the normative split in the ego between observing and participating ego (Sterba, 1934), splitting in object relations theory (Klein, 1946), and the vertical split in self psychology (Kohut, 1971). Lacan also emphasized the dividedness of the ego (Lacan, 1953). However, there was a missing link that seemed to bridge Freud's frustrated wish to connect dream psychology with psychology (Lewin, 1954) as well as integrate hypnoid hysteria with "mainstream" analytic thinking (Brenner, 1999). Moving in this direction are the contributions of Fliess (1953), who described "hypnotic evasion"; Dickes (1965), who redefined the hypnoid state as a defensive alteration of alertness to ward off instinctual pressure; and Shengold (1989), who delineated the facilitating and vigilance-enhancing aspects of the "autohypnotic defense".

Clinical report

Perhaps the best way to illustrate the history of the concept of splitting of the ego and to elucidate this missing link is through a clinical report in which my appreciation of the nature of the division of a patient's mind evolved and deepened over two decades of analytic therapy.

There would be times during a session when "Mary" (Brenner, 2004) would suddenly take off her glasses. Since the magnification of her lenses accentuated the deadness of her eyes and the blankness of her expression, the contrast of seeing her eyes ablaze with rage after this abrupt gesture was even more dramatic. At these times, the patient's voice, syntax, body language, and overall demeanour changed. It was as though a mildly sinister prisoner who had been blindfolded and shackled had just broken out of his restraints, ripped off his eyeshades, and mockingly declared to his startled captors, "I'm free! Try to stop me!" Preferring the stealth value of being unknown, this aspect of the patient's mind functioned like an ominous terrorist bent on secretly sabotaging and disrupting the daily functions of a society. Almost as though taunting me, the patient's anger seemed to feed off being in my presence. Initially, I felt a sense of uneasiness and puzzlement as the patient just glared and sneered at me, speaking about Mary in the third person as though she were being held hostage.

Significantly, changes in her visual perception were prominent in her symptomatology. Sometimes she would lose her peripheral vision and feel as if she were wearing blinkers. Other times, things looked very blurred to her as though she were opening her eyes under water, while at other times her field of vision just went dark. While these disturbances were much more consistent with hysterical conversion symptoms, the more inexplicable change in her vision was apparently in the ocular refraction that enabled her in a certain state of mind to see as well, if not better, without her glasses. Indeed, were she to keep them on in this ego state, then her vision would have become even more blurred once again. Had I not seen this phenomenon in several other patients, where, for example, one woman used two different pairs of glasses with very different refractions prescribed by two different ophthalmologists, it would have made me question the veracity of her claim. In another such case, a woman who also wore glasses most of the time like Mary except when she, too, was in a certain frame of mind made the mistake of going for laser surgery to correct her nearsightedness. Despite my urging her to postpone the surgery at least until we could learn much more about when and why she did not need her lenses, her denial of the possibility of the presence of split-off ego states was so great that she went ahead with the procedure. I was concerned that the irreversible surgery to correct her nearsightedness would be disastrous for her when she lapsed into this mysterious other state resulting in grossly impaired vision that might not be ameliorated even with another set of glasses. Unfortunately, I was correct and she suffered with a very unsatisfactory result that absolutely baffled her ophthalmologist. With these clinical experiences in mind, I had to consider the possibility that the involuntary muscles that controlled the shape of Mary's eyeballs and the focal length of her lenses were being affected by her shifting mental states in an unusual manifestation of a psycho-physiological disturbance.

In addition, the patient had amnesia for the time she was in her glaring, angry state. Not only did she not remember what was said during these episodes, but she did not even remember that she had them. For many months, she was not even aware that she had lost any time. Rather, she would be astounded that the session had seemed to end so quickly and tried to mask her confusion about it lest she betray the secret about her seemingly separate selves, a secret that she was apparently trying to keep from herself most of all. Enlisting her curiosity was most difficult as she exuded a blasé attitude about it all, an attitude that was quite consistent with "*la belle indifference*" described in hysteria.

As described in Breuer's celebrated case of Anna O., the first symptom to be relieved by the "talking cure" was her inability to drink water. It was associated with her repulsion over seeing her governess's dog drink out of a cup, which was linked with her father's dying of complications of tuberculosis and his expectoration. Her disgust over seeing her pet dog drink out of a glass was so overwhelming to her that her mind resorted to a rather drastic and disruptive solution—a splitting of her consciousness. In their jointly authored, preliminary notes, which Breuer later reiterates and Freud refutes, it is observed that "the splitting of consciousness which is so striking in the well-known classical cases under the form of 'double consciousness' is present to a rudimentary degree in every hysteria . . ." (Freud, 1895d, p. 12). Jones was apparently impressed enough also to mention that Anna O. was a case of double personality (Jones, 1953), whereas the hysterical conversion symptoms were apparently of much more interest and perhaps fit more easily into Freud's formulation than the problem of double personality. Indeed, Freud confessed that "Strangely enough, I have never in my own experience met with a genuine hypnoid hysteria" (Freud, 1895d, p. 186).

Interestingly, it was striking to learn after a number of years of treatment with Mary that she, too, had a deep connection with dogs.[1] Her connection, however, was much more intimate than

Anna O.'s. Whereas the mere sight of seeing a dog lap up water with the use of its tongue triggered Anna O., Mary ultimately recalled that as a young teen she had actually utilized a dog's tongue to lap up her personal fluids for sexual pleasure. While babysitting for a family with a particularly affectionate canine, she literally taught the dog to lick her vagina until she reached orgasm. She pursued this secret, shame-laden, sexual practice for several years each time she babysat but then, somehow, put it out of her mind until we began to recognize the presence of her absences. Whereas Anna O. reportedly improved after the recovery of her memory, Mary continued to deteriorate as we both began to wonder how it was that such a young girl would have ever come up with the idea to enlist the dog as a sexual partner in the first place. Indeed, even early on, Freud was a bit sceptical about the cathartic method in and of itself being curative due to the complex mental organization of traumatic memories and pathogenic ideas "which is stratified in at least three different ways" (Freud, 1895d, p. 288). He described different zones with alterations of unconsciousness organized according to chronology, theme, and word connections around a nucleus of the original trauma.

For Mary, the retrieval of the memory of cunnilingus by a dog was, indeed, the tip of the proverbial iceberg, as disturbances in the family, which were alluded to early on in the treatment, took on a more ominous quality. Recovery of these memories, however, was piecemeal, painful, and over time. Mary was bent on obliterating her capacity to think and remember by drinking large amounts of alcohol quite frequently. She noted that after the "happy hour" before dinner her job was to prepare the drinks for her father. He became so drunk that he faded from the family picture, leaving Mary and her sisters to the mercy of their dictatorial and sadistic mother. Apparently identifying with the alcoholic father who withdrew and did not "know" what was going on, so, too, did Mary enhance her own psychological wish not to know with alcohol. What was known and remembered was sequestered in the angry, glaring, altered state of consciousness as well as in a number of other eventually identifiable states.

As Breuer and Freud originally described it, "There is a tendency to such a dissociation, and with it the emergence of abnormal states of consciousness (which we will shall bring together under the term 'hypnoid') [which] is the basic phenomenon of this neurosis" (Freud, 1895d, p. 12). At this point in his theorizing, however, Freud struggled with reconciling Breuer's idea of the pathogenic effects of traumatic events occurring during autohypnotic, self-hypnotic, or hypnoid states and/or traumatic events causing the hypnoid states themselves versus his own idea of repressed sexual instincts as the underlying aetiology of hysteria. In Mary's cases as well as Anna O.'s, there was growing clinical evidence of both hysterical visual symptoms and hypnoid states associated with amnesia. The role of early trauma had not yet been delineated with Mary, but the importance of unconscious sexual urges had emerged because the precipitating event bringing her to treatment was homosexual panic associated with the seductive overtures of an older woman, which overwhelmed the patient with guilt and suicidality.

The dramatic event that brought the presence of the seemingly separate selves into clear focus was when she cut herself with a razor blade that had been hidden in the binding of a book. Unbeknownst to Mary in her usual state of consciousness (i.e., her "dominant mass of ideas"), in a "*condition seconde*" (Freud, 1895d) she deliberately put the razor in an obscure place that could not be found unless one were knowingly looking there. Thus, the blade had stayed for days until an opportune moment of desperation presented itself and her alter ego could generate enough strength to cathect and "take over" consciousness in order to execute the deed. When discovered, the patient, in an inappropriately calm voice and demeanour, identified herself as Priscilla and described the incident in the third person, insisting that "she" did the best she could to limit the bloodshed and implied that there was a separate, destructive influence inside that was barely contained. That destructive influence, eventually known as Ralph, was the one who did not need the glasses and, in "his" mind, did not need any form of therapy either.

Over time, a number of different personifications came to light. For example, there would be times when the patient would be plagued by a mysterious auditory hallucination of a terrified young boy saying "God is trying to kill me!" Usually associated with agitation and confusion, Mary would become inwardly distracted and listen to this repetitive plea for help. This voice was associated with a young boy, Timmy, trapped inside, who believed that if the patient continued to speak, then "he" would get annihilated. Another force that stopped the patient's speech was an elderly woman, Flora, who was the personification of a censor and constricted the patient's throat ever more tightly until she gasped. These two "others", representing a symptom and an inhibition, effectively prevented Mary from continuing with her associations and, as we came to realize later, served as a deterrent from revealing any secrets about her relationship with her mother. In addition, there were several young girls whose cries of sadness, fear, and pain could be heard inside and then outside if they were to take over consciousness and express themselves directly to me. Then there was the "transparent guy" who functioned like a psychological prism directing energy to either Mary or Ralph. If the latter was fuelled by the "transparent guy", then he could become even angrier, stronger and take over again.

This dazzling array of other "personalities" and a host of many more whose appearances were fleeting and rare seemed to populate the patient's psyche and serve a variety of functions for her. On one level, they represented her intrapsychic conflict, which she experienced in the form of an interpersonal conflict between these different parties. As a multipurpose structure with their own biographies and cohesion, they could convey a sense of overall continuity of the self as a defence against the lack of self-constancy and object constancy, which was associated with separation and annihilation anxiety. They housed contradictory views, affects, fantasies, drives, and ego capabilities. For example, Mary was the only one who could drive, whereas both Ralph and Mary could paint equally well but usually rather different subjects. Ralph painted bloody, graphic, violent scenes that terrorized Mary, who eventually gave up painting out of fear that whatever project she might start would get hijacked by Ralph. Then, once her deep, unconscious troubles would become represented on the canvas and externalized, the image would then "work back on her" and constantly torment her. Having the effect of an unwelcome and poorly timed interpretation that can be overwhelming and increase resistance, Mary's artistic associations then became blocked; she stopped painting for more than a decade.

In his bid to "take over the body", Ralph suffered from a quasi-delusion that if he could merely kill off Mary then he would be victorious and free to do whatever he wanted. What he wanted was a sex change. "He" believed that he was a man trapped in a woman's body and, as such, the patient experienced a transsexual conflict in the form of Mary and Ralph fighting over the fate of the sexual anatomy of the body. If Ralph had his way, he would cut off the breasts either by himself or with the help of a surgeon if he had the money, close up the vagina and craft a penis. Arrangements were being looked into for male hormone injections to acquire facial hair and facilitate the gender transformation. The patient also joined an organization of transgendered people to get support while going through this process. The patient even notified the members of her community that henceforth people should call her by the male name "Phillip", the name of a latency-age boy she believed was residing inside who went deeply underground around puberty.

When breast buds developed and menarche started, "he" could not tolerate the reality of becoming a woman, which resulted in a split in the patient's ego, analogous to the previously described mechanism Freud attributed to fetishism. Yearning for a return to a less conflictual time, the patient hoped to redo her sexual development and become a man this time. However, the patient's sexuality was even more complicated in that it appeared as though different selves had different forms of sexuality. For example, Mary was in a committed lesbian relationship where she was the more passive sexual partner to an aggressive and demanding lover. Ralph, on the other hand, hated the partner and tried to strangle her on more than one occasion. He had strong sadomasochistic, erotic tendencies and would become very aroused with the transference fantasy of shattering the glass in one of my picture frames, grabbing a shard, rushing over to me, slitting my throat, cutting off my penis, and having an orgasm during the process. So, it appeared that perverse sexuality in the form of bisexual sadomasochism, transsexualism, and bestiality existed in separate ego states. Urges to stalk young children were also expressed but not actualized. In particular, the patient's profound desire to be a male was apparently the strongest and associated with so much distress, internalized aggression, and shame that much of her suicidality was organized around the struggle over the domination and sexual fate of the body. The patient dressed in men's clothing and often wore a rolled-up sock in her panties to create a penis-like bulge. In fact, she sometimes kept it there for many days at a time, not changing her underwear, resulting in urinary tract infections from poor hygiene. In addition, the length of the hair on every part of the body became a battleground on which this war was waged, often with life-and-death implications. Having taken a massive overdose and not telling anyone until several days later following her lapsing in and out of a coma and throwing up repeatedly resulting in aspiration pneumonia, her plight was taken very seriously. Furthermore, since she did not cry out for help but silently withdrew instead, a pattern seen during interruptions and breaks consistent with an adult version of an avoidant-type of attachment disturbance, she was especially worrisome. Massive regression could occur if the hair on the head got too long or if underarms and legs were shaved, and over time I was able to intervene as a mediator during these very intense "territorial disputes".

The memories of childhood trauma that emerged were sparked by seeing a painting of a woman braiding a young girl's hair while straddling her with the legs wide apart. Mary contacted me and said that she had something very urgent to tell me. She revealed that her mother had required her to be a sexual partner and a source of pleasure for her as far back as she could remember and even until the present time. This astounding revelation was fleshed out over time with the help of her personifications, the resumption of her painting, and the remembering of her dreams. Not infrequently, Mary would report a dream in which she was a detached spectator, witnessing an unknown child being hurt and molested in a certain way. Then, within days of the dream, she might involuntarily lapse into a "hypnoid" state and become a very young child who narrated or abreacted a traumatic experience almost identical to what was described in the dream. However, in the autohypnotic state, the patient would have no memory of the dream and vice versa. This reciprocal amnesia seemed to sever the connection between memory, dream, and reliving, maintaining a split in the ego for defensive purposes.

One major recurrent theme of her dreams was being underwater for so long that she could no longer breathe and imagined that she could fly and breathe underwater. In her dissociated child state subsequent to such a dream, she would alternate between describing being held underwater in the bathtub by her mother for so long that her mind cut off, to re-experiencing the gasping, burning throat and emotional blankness after being let up from the water. Intersubjectively, I experienced the horror for her that she was too deadened from the experience to feel consciously. The historical symptom of blurred vision, "as though being underwater", was also linked to this torture and was ameliorated after several of these abreactive episodes in treatment. During the reconstruction of her childhood, Mary recalled that her mother would undress and sit on her face, straddling her with her legs apart—as in the painting—teach her to lick her vagina until she was satisfied and then roll over off her in exhaustion. The young child knew nothing of sexual excitement, orgasm, or menstruation and was terrified but required to perform her duty on demand at any time under any conditions or else she would be severely punished. Being thrown into the bathtub and nearly drowned into submission was apparently a diabolically effective means of breaking the child's spirit, making her into an automaton (Ferenczi, 1933) and sexually enslaving her.[2] Cloaked in religiosity and the curse of God if she were to reveal this heinous form of baptism, she was repeatedly told that "God would kill her" if she ever told anyone. Hence, the hallucination of Timmy's "God's trying to kill me!" was apparently the dissociated child's cry in response to this aspect of her brainwashing and soul murder (Shengold, 1989).

In addition to understanding the traumatic origin of the blurred vision and the auditory hallucination, it also became clear that Mary knew how to teach the dog to perform cunnilingus because she, too, was trained like an animal to perform the same act. In addition, it appeared that the near drownings resulted in an altered state of consciousness, perhaps not unlike a near-death experience, which was encapsulated and contributed to the formation of a dissociated child self (Brenner, 2001). As Mary grew up and tried to live a "normal life", attending school, church, and playing with friends, she also, side by side and simultaneously, lived a secret life as her mother's sexual slave which required the deployment of all efforts available in her psyche to keep things separate. Splitting of consciousness and splitting of the ego reached psychotic proportions when she became convinced that her mother could read her mind, know her inner thoughts, and know her whereabouts at all times. Manifested in the transference, Mary was convinced at these times that my office was bugged with recording and surveillance devices that went directly to her mother, believing I was in a conspiracy with her to keep her daughter mentally ill and totally submissive. This tendency towards paranoia was rather intractable at times, as her permeable ego boundaries (Federn, 1952) and grossly disturbed body ego predisposed her to such periodic regressions with this additional manifestation of splitting of the ego. At these times, she simultaneously existed in one reality—that I was simply her analyst trying to help her—and in another reality—that I was a spy in league with her mother, where even the slightest movement of the chair in my office from one session to the next was a secret message that she had to decode. While she was trying to outwit her mother and be loyal to her by not revealing anything about herself, she was also trying to get help and understand the nature of the disturbance of her mind.

Obscured by the dramatic and disturbing nature of the psychopathology, the nature of "Ralph's" involvement with the mother remained an unsolved and crucial part of the puzzle of the patient's disturbance of identity. Over time, "Ralph" began to open up and assist in the following reconstruction: At some point after Mary's adolescence and the transformation that occurs during that turbulent time, the disavowal of the reality of her female gender identity required more ego-weakening dividedness of her psyche as her incestuous relationship with her mother continued. She remained "on call" 24 hours a day, 7 days a week, for the mother's pleasure. No matter what the patient was doing, she might be interrupted by her mother's calling her name in a certain melodic way as if to say, "Oh, Mary, do you know what time it is? It's time for me!" Mary obediently stopped whatever she was doing and followed her mother to the bedroom in an entranced, obedient state. While in that state, the mother taught her a new form of sexual pleasure, commonly known as fisting. She was instructed to insert her hand, one finger at a time, make a fist, and then forcefully pump the mother's vagina, which caused her much pain. It satisfied the mother's sexual masochism and stirred up the patient's own sexual sadism. Initially repulsed by this demand and unable to perform this duty, she became overwhelmed with anxiety, lapsed further into an autohypnotic trance, and switched to her major alternate consciousness, Ralph, who took over. This opportunity to inflict pain upon the mother to further identify with the aggressor and to "fist fuck the mother" further consolidated "Ralph's" sense of himself truly as a "motherfucker". "He" took every opportunity to live up to such a reputation, and this erotically fuelled cruelty staved off the patient's despair over being a menstruating female with breasts and without a penis.

Becoming mother's phallus literally, rather than remaining an unconscious fantasy or a symbolic derivative (Lacan, 1982), the fist was used as a penis and rage was "his" predominant affect. "He" experienced no guilt whatsoever, and it was not until many years later, after countless cycles of the patient's expressed sadomasochistic wish to revel in a blood orgy in the transference and my containing these fantasies within my own psyche, that Ralph began to acknowledge hidden positive feelings for me. Concurrently becoming able to tolerate ambivalence for me without dissociative splitting and switching, another sign of integration of the patient's psyche was Ralph's "feeling" Mary's guilt and horror over fisting the mother. Furthermore, when Mary was "out", she became able to recover the memories of this experience of her mother and to talk about them. This detente between two tortured selves was beautifully represented in a painting that depicted the merging of Mary's and Ralph's bodies, complete with breasts and a penis, in which both were embracing each other.

Summary and conclusion

To help understand the complexities of Mary's psyche, which bears resemblance to the "double conscience" described by Breuer and Freud during the inception of psychoanalysis, we may apply the theoretical elaboration and metapsychological advancements in the concept of splitting of the ego and then return to the archaic concept of hypnoid hysteria, in order to reconsider it in a brighter light. Under certain traumatic conditions in childhood, it may be impossible for one mind to reconcile the contradictions necessary for psychic and possibly physical survival, such as the need to maintain an attachment to a murderous, sexually violating mother. Under such circumstances, there may be a coalescing of self- and object representations into seemingly separate selves maintained in autohypnotic, hypnoid states. Analytic work with such patients with this lower-level dissociative character (Brenner, 1994) who fulfil the diagnostic criteria for dissociative identity disorder (APA, 2004) reveals the presence of organizing influences that seem to contribute to the creation of these personifications, which Fairbairn (1952a) considered to be a variant of the usual functioning structural units of the mind—that is, the id, the ego, and the superego. The organizing influences that analytic exploration has revealed to be underlying these selves include perverse sexuality, the autosymbolic phenomena seen in dreams, hypnoid and hypnogogic states (Silberer, 1909), near-death experiences, and the overall mentally divisive effects of aggression as seen in Mary's case. Intergenerational transmission of trauma has also been described in other such cases (Brenner, 2001). This unique and idiosyncratic assemblage of representations has survival value and, despite major disturbances in relationships, may result in areas of very high ego functioning, such as in the realms of creativity, language, and mathematics (Oxnam, 2005).

Whereas it is a generally accepted principle originally posited by Freud (1915e) that the unpleasurable or "bad" self- and object representations tend to be externalized and the "good" self- and object representations remain internalized, the analyst may see a pseudo-externalization and displacement to the inside, dissociated selves as an additional "ingredient" to these structures. In addition, the amnestic, autohypnotic barrier adds to the unique qualities that make them more encapsulated and distinctive than the contradictory selves separated by disavowal and the vertical split described by Kohut (1971).

Because of the presence of not only various ego functions but also drive derivatives from the id as well as superego prohibitions and aspirations, these personifications might also be considered "pathological intersystemic suborganizations". This concept, described by Schafer (1968), has been advocated by Lichtenberg and Slap (1973), who contend that "'pathological intersystemic suborganization' is a more precise designation for contradictory psychic groupings as exemplified by fetishism than is the term 'splitting of the ego'" (p. 784).

In their own splitting of Freud's usage of the term "splitting" into four categories—that is, a general developmental principle, an organization of psychic contents in infancy, as a defence, and as a way of maintaining contradictory psychic groups—Lichtenberg and Slap argue for a *restrictive* use of the term "splitting" to reduce the confusion of tongues (Ferenczi, 1933) that plagues our theorizing. Their recommendation is to limit the use of the term "splitting" to "the tendency in infantile life by which an organization of memory traces of the earliest expression is based on primordial quality of pleasurable good or painful bad" (Lichtenberg & Slap, 1973, p. 784). While this effort may reduce definitional ambiguity, in so doing we may even further obscure and threaten to relegate to the dustbin of history the still not fully appreciated significance of Breuer's and early Freud's "splitting of the mind". The compelling nature of its successor, "splitting of the ego", has had so many far-reaching implications that perhaps ironically it has suffered from its own success. The history of this concept, reviewed through a contemporary case report resembling Anna O.'s, may help put this term back into historical perspective and further more understanding of some of our greatest clinical challenges.

Notes

1. The role of dogs in other patients' case histories has been well documented (Escoll, 2005).

2. Ferenczi's own contribution to splitting and trauma are enormous, as exemplified by his observation that "If the shocks increase in number during the development of the child, the number and the various kinds of splits in the personality increase too, and soon it becomes extremely difficult to maintain contact without confusion with all the fragments, each of which behaves as a separate personality yet does not know of even the existence of the others" (1933, p. 165).

2

Splitting, processing loss, and borderline states

Gérard Bayle

Borderline states involve some degree of instability of the sense of identity both in the individual and in his or her objects. Intrapsychic conflict no longer remains within the confines of neurotic structures; it involves attacks and retreats between the intrapsychic and intersubjective modalities. The frontier between inside and outside is more or less blurred by projection and by projective identification, carried out or endured (Green, 1990).

Given the continuous fluctuation between neurotic and psychotic processes, the aetiology of borderline states involves very many factors. I shall take one of these as the starting point of this chapter: the failure of the work of mourning or, more specifically, that of processing loss. I have been studying this subject for over twenty years now (Bayle, 1988).

Emergency barriers and the impact of loss

When the object is no longer there, the drive-related impulses that were linked to it fall as it were into a void. If that absence is a lasting one, what results is a massive drive-related outflow that may prove fatal. The loss of libido generates so much distress and anxiety that it can lead to helplessness [*Hilflosigkeit*].

Protecting oneself then becomes a matter of urgency in order not to disappear or die with the lost object. All kinds of defence mechanisms are called upon in order to alleviate the intensity of that pain and anxiety and to try to minimize the loss of libido. These defensive tasks are many in number, and the cost is high. To put it briefly, they involve denial of absence and idealization of what remains of the internal object.

The period when pain is denied corresponds to the sensory isolation of the point where that pain erupted. All degrees are possible between denial that remains stable without recourse to any expedient and one that requires behavioural, temperamental, and perverse forcing to make it solid enough. When intrapsychic space is overwhelmed, recourse is had to intersubjective relationships that are simultaneously feared. When these are too close, they encroach upon the sense of self; when they are too much at arm's length, they leave the patient in the midst of nowhere.

This is where a circle of friends and family can help socially to maintain the denial, particularly when religious beliefs come into the picture. Although the object has disappeared physically, some degree of cathexis is still present, and that sustains a psychic object. This is the result of what we could call "processing loss", which precedes the mourning process itself. Working through loss prevents an endless outpouring of the libido that could lead to death or to disability.

The vicissitudes of emergency splitting

The aim of processing loss is to create a split-off part of the ego that will keep alive the belief in psychic survival, acting to some extent as a plug placed at the very spot where the loss is felt, where the haemorrhage occurred. That splitting must, as a matter of urgency, be maintained by means of significant outlays of libido. What, then, will become of it?

In the first place, if it disappears too quickly, another denial will have to be set up; this brings the person back to where he or she started, in a manner reminiscent of trauma in two stages. It follows that these attempts at denying loss must be respected; contrary to what happens all too often in some behaviour therapies, one should avoid trying to force through interpretations—otherwise the result could be a depressive or melancholic breakdown, or a manic explosion, given the fragility of defensive processes at the frontier between id and ego and the fact that the weakened ego cannot make use of secondary-process functioning.

Secondly, the pain may be released in small quantities. This is when significant personal restructuring can take place, facilitated by cathecting the self. When the individual can again begin to dream, this is a good indication of the fact that repression and formal regression are once more active. In that sense, dreaming marks the *beginnings* of the work of mourning once processing of loss has been carried out, not the *end* of the mourning process. It may then become possible to carry out the long and painful work of mourning that Freud described so vividly in "Mourning and Melancholia" (1917e [1915]). Through a series of retroactive understandings, and by fragmentation, the ego will be able to deal with the impact of the loss, which otherwise would have been too overwhelming. Each time a memory of the object emerges, it will be over-cathected to a painful yet tolerable extent, then gradually de-cathected, giving way to unconscious identification by means of introjection.

A third possibility is that no painful affect linked to mourning is allowed to emerge. In such a case, no work of mourning is possible; serious disorders will be the outcome. Maintaining such a split-off, denied, and isolated structure will entail both immediate and long-term consequences; these will impact also on future generations because of the de-subjectifying and de-symbolizing effects that are typical of borderline states.

The metapsychology of splitting

The two drive-related currents

I have described the temporary outcome of processing loss in terms of what I call "functional splitting" (Bayle, 1988), as well as the structures that ensure that it will be maintained, its "locks" (Racamier, 1992). I shall make use of Freud's description of the metapsychology of repression as he theorized it in particular in his metapsychological papers of 1915 and in *Inhibitions, Symptoms and Anxiety* (Freud, 1926d [1925]). Basing his description on Freud's diagram of the psychic apparatus that we find in *New Introductory Lectures on Psycho-Analysis* (Freud, 1933a [1932]), Michel Neyraut (1995) suggests that we should distinguish between the two currents that are followed by drive-related outflows. The slower of the two is that of repression. Here, drive-related impulses draw thing-presentations towards word-presentations—this makes it possible to initiate the psychoanalytic "talking cure". The swift-moving current short-circuits the slower one. It evacuates drive-related impulses towards the external world; as it does so, it feeds into whatever is needed for creating hallucinations, somatic disorders, and actings-out of all kinds, including perverse ones. It is all grist to the mill for giving shape to these drive-related manifestations typical of borderline states. Symbolization plays no part in that current.

Narcissistic countercathexes

When a cruel sense of loss is experienced, what is left of the psychic object has to be isolated from the rest of the ego. This neo-structure must be kept free of any secondary-process logic that would bring back the idea of loss and thus invalidate the defensive manoeuvre that the denial was intended to bring about.

That isolation will be set up by means of a barrier made of countercathexes that stand in the way of any penetration of elements linked to the reality of the loss, just as, at the frontier between ego and id, they block any penetration of forbidden wishes. Their function is to fight against any anxiety about being abandoned by the internal object that is henceforth part of the splitting of the ego. I have called these highly specific countercathexes—the task of which is to create a buffer zone in the ego so as to isolate a part that, although it has become "mad", plays a life-saving role—*narcissistic countercathexes* (Bayle, 1996). Their energy comes from the ego, and they keep the split-off part isolated from the rest.

That part is thus denied, kept alive, and isolated thanks to the cathecting energy of the ego. Given the emergency, the situation is safe, but there are consequences for the rest of psychic economy.

Pregenital regressive reinforcements

The ego does not have unlimited reserves of energy. The barrier set up by the countercathexes of repression will gradually become weaker or at least impossible to reinforce. The pressure of repressed wishes will be less easy to contain; they will slip through more easily and bring about in the ego a state of ever-increasing excitation. Pain gives way to anxiety. As is well known, there is no loss without at one point or another a concomitant excitation that may take on regressive aspects, thus indicating the return of repressed infantile elements. This may account for the strengthening of hysterical, phobic, obsessional, hallucinatory or perverse disorders, or of sublimation in the immediate aftermath of the loss of the object. The result ought to have been a deferred-action (*après-coup*[1]) repression, but what in fact occurs is the acceptance of a derivative of the unconscious, the aim of which is to sustain neurotic symptomatology (Freud, 1915d, 1915e).

To this are added drive-related regressions that are sometimes channelled into social and religious rituals (the meal that mourners share after a funeral comes to mind), as well as into anal ones. These reactivate pregenital fixations. They tinge narcissistic libido as it increases in strength with narcissistic countercathexes. The need for libido can then be satisfied by regressive autoerotic acts that oscillate between phases of co-excitation and depressive despondency (bulimia, anorexia).

Character-based reinforcements

The weakening of the ego diminishes the effectiveness of the repressive process. Gradually, the libidinal energy of the id sweeps more directly and more rapidly into the ego. The intensity of that upsurge may create manic outbursts or paranoid reactions; it may also cathect the day's residues or word-presentations and lead to hallucinatory manifestations. However, if the ego is still able to direct that energy towards the group of narcissistic countercathexes, then these will be strengthened. As I mentioned above, these take on the pregenital features of oral and anal regressions. With the raw libidinal energy coming directly from the id, the barrier set up by splitting receives an enormous strengthening of its power, so that it becomes even more compact, massive, heavy, and immovable.

In each case, the result is a functional amputation of the ego (Freud, 1940e [1938]); the active part of the ego that maintains the splitting is over-cathected, thus making certain character traits or behaviour patterns stand out. Given the hostile feelings directed towards the object before its disappearance, in addition to the unbinding of the drives that is part of denial, there may well be a never-ending succession of suffering and torment—in my view, one of the oldest representations of this is Hell. This is particularly true of mourning processes that begin after the long, painful, and slow death of an object that was hated, or if the object had been subjected to dreadful horrors. On the other side of the splitting, the conscious and preconscious ego goes on managing everyday life; it is the *locus* of a residual fatigue linked to maintaining narcissistic countercathexes. The character patterns that isolate and contain the neo-structure are particularly severe: the object that has disappeared is never again mentioned.

Carried to the extreme, that attack ends up by focusing on thought processes, weakening them more and more, to the point where character neuroses and instrumentalist thinking open the way to somatic illnesses.

Identifications linked to functional splitting

A major quantitative change as regards the ego's defence processes takes place with a change of generation. Until that point, repression was in the service of a functional splitting that enabled denial to be maintained. This kind of splitting can be passed on through modifications that take place within it in many different modalities. When these are mixed together, a particularly toxic mind-structure may arise—this is the structural form of splitting, as described by Freud in his study of the psychoses and the perversions.

Clinical manifestations of how splitting is passed on

Oedipal transmission

As the Oedipus complex becomes less intense, incestuous and murderous wishes are given up. That renunciation leads to identification by means of introjection. However, attempts to preserve oedipal wishes often take the form of hysterical identification with a character trait of one or other of the parents.

I am thinking here of a woman, who had been taking lithium over a 20-year period for manic-depressive psychosis. Her mother had suffered from that disorder and had taken the same medication when she was prescribed it some forty years earlier for postpartum depression. The hypothesis of genetic transmission had contributed to the fact that the psychiatrist was taking the same medication as her mother. She did indeed have mood swings, but, after a few discussions with her, I had the impression that these occurred in situations that would otherwise have given rise to neurotic and fantasy manifestations typical of the psychic bisexuality that was hidden behind her mood swings. With the agreement of her psychiatrist, the medication was stopped temporarily—in fact, she never had to take it again, and her mood swings vanished.

Oedipal craftiness enabled her simultaneously—thanks to an unpleasant symptom—to have in fantasy both homosexual possession of her mother and heterosexual possession of her father, by offering herself to him dressed up in her mother's most conspicuous character traits. In such situations, all that exists is a false form of splitting through an incorporative identification of a narcissistic feature of one parent; there is, however, no true splitting.

Transmission through foreclosure

Many have studied the impact on children of a failure to process mourning in one of their parents. Most of these studies have taken as their starting point clinical situations in which incest or processes of narcissistic perversion were uppermost.

For Lacan (1954), this has to do with foreclosure. In such

situations, the transmission of a symbolic abolition creates an irreparable laceration in the symbolic fabric carried by language. His famous statement according to which "the unconscious is structured like a language" led him to hypothesize that something is lacking in the symbolic structure and that this gradually gives rise to a defective and psychotic mode of functioning, which is compensated for by hallucinatory activity. The parents failed to pass on a fundamental signifier, the name-of-the-father.

However, those controversial theoretical hypotheses have come up against other French thinkers who also base their hypotheses on their clinical experience—Jean-Luc Donnet and André Green (1969) on the one hand, and Paul-Claude Racamier (1992) on the other. In many respects, their ideas are close to those of Harold Searles (1965).

Some people who have within themselves a functional splitting impose on their immediate circle the creation of a situation that itself generates splitting. That brought to my mind, as I was thinking about Melanie Klein's theories, the idea: "Split thy neighbour as thyself"—but in order to do so, an incestuous psychic complicity is necessary.

If that complicity is acquired either by seduction or by the oedipal desire for a child, for example, it becomes possible to use the other person's energy to fill in any gaps and contain one's own drive-related impulses. This is the clinical domain of narcissistic perversion, with the structural splitting that it induces.

Splitting of the self: "Flora"

Flora's parents lost their entire family in a Nazi concentration camp. They never talked about it, and they defended themselves against thinking about it by hyperactive social, scientific, and political commitments. Her mother had brief but violent fits of rage, and her father adopted certain inflexible behaviour patterns. Flora knows how her grandparents died.

She alternated between bulimia and anorexia, the object of which could be either food or sex. The worry she thereby created in her parents gave them, as it were, another plug for containing their own unprocessed mourning. She lent support to their functional splitting. They spent a huge amount of time thinking about her.

She and her sister were "well brought up", as they say. An excellent student, Flora was always top of her class, although she had no idea what to do with herself outside of her schoolwork; to all appearances, she was highly successful. Marriage brought her material wealth and professional success. Her sister, however, four years younger than Flora, committed suicide after a long period of opposition that caused something of a scandal in the family. Ever since her suicide, the parents worshipped their dead daughter. Flora looked after them, then everything began to go wrong for her: anorexia nervosa, bulimia, nymphomania. After she gave birth to a child, she became depressed. She came to see me on leaving the psychiatric unit; she was again pregnant and was afraid that she might have a relapse.

Initially, our discussions were face-to-face, then she had three sessions per week lying on the couch. It was very difficult for her to come to her sessions. She would spend most of the time talking about the trauma that surrounded her sister's death and followed on from it. Narratives were like pockets being opened and letting their contents pour out—contents that she thought were devoid of any emotional potential. At first her affects worried her, but she gradually came to accept them. Many traumatic dreams followed her sessions. When her second child was born, she did not, in fact, relapse into depression, but we were both extremely distressed by two tragic situations that occurred while I was away on a two-week holiday. One day, as she was walking beside a pond in the country, holding her new-born baby in her arms, she fainted. The baby fell face down into the water, and, when Flora regained consciousness, the infant's face was blue and he was unconscious. A neighbour revived the child and took him to hospital—he made a complete recovery. One week later, when she was alone with her children, Flora locked herself inside her flat, stopped up all orifices in the kitchen, turned on the gas in the oven, and briefly put her head inside. Then she pulled herself together and let air into the room. Those two terribly dangerous events were followed, like exhumed memories, by traumatic dreams.

I said to her that she was making me feel very afflicted and distressed with all that violence, just as, whenever her parents hit her, she herself must have felt that they were like Nazis and no longer, for that period of time, her parents, removing themselves from the sense of identity as a family that she shared with them. I added that my going away on holiday had recreated in her the feeling of psychic death that she had experienced before and awakened in her a sense of hatred that she tried to turn back against herself in order to put an end to the pain.

More traumatic dreams followed. In each of them there was at one point an image that evoked a concentration camp. In the course of this period of dreams, Flora returned to the subject of her sister's death, but with upsurges of love and hate. This enabled her to get in touch with more intimate feelings and sadness.

My hypothesis would be that Flora was born into a world in which depressive affects were simply not expressed. No intellectual knowledge was refused her, but she was not to have sad feelings. The ability to feel moved by the death of her sister shows that the possibility of access to the depressive position implied oedipal guilt feelings that, once latent, were now being revealed. She carried within herself a similar kind of splitting, but in a twofold modality. Hysterical identification could not explain everything; there was also her adherence to her parents' negative values and her clinging to their defensive processes, especially to those of her mother.

It is not particularly clear why her sister committed suicide. I imagine that, like Flora, that young woman also had a narcissistic deficiency that was protected and sealed off by her parents' efforts to maintain a common denial of the deaths that had taken place. With the onset of puberty in their daughter, the parents probably had to distance themselves from that function of maintaining a common denial; in other words, they withdrew from their role as a stopgap for the narcissistic deficiency in their daughter. The decisive factor was probably the fact that the father began to distance himself from all of this, the justification being the oedipal need to stand back somewhat—a father ought not to have any physical intimacy with his daughter. That distancing, desirable in the case of a well-developed ego, proved catastrophic for the part that was in deprivation. Nothing could seal it off in any stable manner. Drugs, delinquency, prostitution, narcissistic passions—nothing was of any use; the Moloch of deprivation had to be nourished by pouring into it whole areas of highly developed resources until, one day, that inexorable decline was halted by her suicide.

Flora's oedipal development was not quite so dangerous because she did not have too much difficulty in keeping her teachers as prosthetic objects; also, her marriage, very classical and successful in both content and form, served as a rampart against the degrading effect of the avid gaping hole that was her narcissism. In order to be fully herself as a mother, a woman, an integrated human being, Flora had to face up to that gaping hole that she actualized and sealed off through her anorexia, her fits of bulimia, and her voracious appetite for culture and then for sex. Once her children were born and by their very nature used as stopgaps, she had to lose them and lose herself in order to find them again and to find herself again, while at the same time setting up an enacted and fantasy scenario that was rich in affects, the very affects against which her family were protecting themselves. Those affects were experienced both by Flora and by me in the transference situation.

In so doing, Flora found it possible to give symbolic value to the relationship that she had had with her sister when they were both infants. Each had been for the other an indisputable narcissistic complement—indeed, that was never disputed. Consequently, neither had been for the other a separate, whole object. Through losing herself and losing her children, through finding herself and finding them again, Flora gave them and herself the status of a subject. In a retroactive sense, she could do the same with her sister. In the past, her sister's death had implied that part of her own self had been amputated, in a narcissistic regression that included their parents. By treating her sister as a subject, Flora could begin the work of mourning her death. She then began a similar mourning process with respect to other relationships that over time she had lost, relationships that until then she had pushed aside. The process of treating them as subjects in their own right then mourning their loss began to run through the whole of her mental life, past and present. Nevertheless, from time to time she still had systematically to enter into casual love affairs that went beyond the pleasure principle.

The vicissitudes of splitting

Those who carry within themselves that kind of splitting seldom recover from the narcissistic wound linked to the loss that they have experienced: they use behaviour as a stopgap. In addition, since they are forever trying to fill up the gaps, they draw heavily on the barriers of repression, so that they are often prone to drive-related states of regressive excitation, anal and oral. They have to deal with these as best they can with the help of their defensive behaviour patterns and obsessional mechanisms; a certain degree of unbinding takes place between the life and death drives, to the advantage of the latter. Such people sometimes group together in order to fight more effectively against the dangers that threaten them—the opening of a narcissistic wound and regressive sexual trauma. Denial is thus common to and shared by all of them.

What, then, becomes of the children of those who, finding it impossible to accomplish the work of mourning, isolate a living-dead object and banish from their vocabulary and their behaviour anything that might evoke the split-off part of themselves? What is handed down to these children? What do the parents refrain from passing on? Clinical practice shows us that, alongside conscious, preconscious, and unconscious transmissions, silence is imposed upon them. The children must not ask certain questions; they have to adopt countercathexes similar to those of their parents. The important element here is that, contrary to what happened with the parents, these countercathexes will not come into conflict with any kind of content. There are, of course, crypts, but these are empty, at least at first.

Later, they will fill them up; what is passed on is the isolation, the fortress of narcissistic countercathexes.

The barriers are passed on without any indication being given of what they are meant to stand in the way of. That would seem to have something meaningless about it, having no significance as it were, and hence a deficiency as regards the symbolic organization of the ego. What is not passed on is not something unconscious that has been struck out by repression, nor is it something that has to be kept secret—it is something that is purely and simply missing, in an absolute sense. This will turn out to be a narcissistic deficiency. It will not be seen as such while the person's immediate circle of family and friends plug the gap by means of false answers to any questions that might be asked. Typical schemata of preordained destinies, the mental equivalent of ready-made, pre-arranged thoughts, hypercathexes of knowledge and learning (Prudent, 1988) will all come along to fill up deceptively that gaping hole of the narcissistic void, paving the way for a conventional attitude towards life, creating people for whom only appearances count, with no preconscious symbolic depth to them. One example of this would be *Mars*, by Fritz Zorn (1982), or Marguerite Duras's *The Ravishing of Lol Stein* (1964), where we read:

> Lol's home was a model of neatness. This obsessive orderliness, both in space and in time, was more or less of the kind she desired, not quite but almost. . . . It would have been impossible, everyone around Lol agreed, to come any closer to perfection. . . . The decoration and furnishing of the bedrooms and living room were the faithful facsimile of model rooms displayed in store windows. . . . Lol was imitating someone, but who? the others, all the others, as many people as possible. [Duras, 1964, p. 24]

We could therefore say that in every human being there is a sector of mental life that, although it is not the dynamic unconscious, eludes any control by the ego. This is the realm of narcissistic deficiency, which, in order to function, depends on adhering to an object cathected narcissistically. That object has a specific status; peacefully present and fulfilling its role as a stopgap, it is a narcissistic part-object. When, however, it is absent, it takes on the characteristic features of an absolute object without which nothing can be held together. When that object is absent, it becomes a god. Its loss cannot be mourned. To have access to it, it must first be made into a human being, at which point it is lost as a god.

That is always the case with losses that are impossible to mourn; they correspond to primitive states of mind. I am thinking here particularly of children who early in life lose an object the function of which was precisely that of protecting them as regards their primary narcissistic deficiencies. If that loss is one day to be mourned, a substitute object will have to replace the one that has been lost, then that substitute will also have to be lost and rediscovered with a change of status—that is, it will go from being a godlike object to one that is human, one whose loss can conceivably be mourned. A similar situation to that of children occurs when patients lose their analyst. If the analyst happened at that moment to be the mainstay of the analytic process at a time when narcissistic wounds and deficiencies were being laid bare, the abruptly interrupted consubstantial experience will have all the hallmarks of a loss that is impossible to mourn for want of a separate object.

> A young man played the part of an object narcissistically cathected by his father; then his father committed suicide. The young man began psychotherapy, which developed into an analysis. After three years' work, the analyst died. Shortly after that, the young man made an appointment with me. We brought together the scattered fragments of his life. One day he stopped coming, although he knew that I did not agree to this. Two months went by. I then wrote to him saying that I had decided that I would not keep his sessions available for him any longer. Another three months went by, then he reappeared; by then, everything had changed. He was at that point able to tell me of his fear that I might need him just as absolutely as he was afraid that he might need me, a vital need.
>
> He could then settle down more comfortably in the analytic relationship, with four sessions per week. He managed to talk about everything that he had never mentioned before concerning his childhood and the structuring of an infantile neurosis that had not hitherto been analysed. A stopgap part-object for his father, he was unable to think of himself in any other way with respect to me—until he became able to deal with a loss that was agreed upon and integrated, in the way that I had informed him of in the letter that I sent him.

This clinical example shows how the functional setting-up of a narcissistic deficiency in a parent can generate a structural narcissistic deficiency in the child. Each has a part of him/herself welded, as it were, to a hole in the other person, like two wounds stuck together that seal each other off. In analysis, such patients are on the lookout for their analyst's deficiencies so as to coordinate their own with these.

A therapeutic approach to failed mourning processes

I have described some of the possible outcomes when mourning processes are unsuccessful and how their impact may extend over three generations. It is important, therefore, to forestall such situations, to treat them when people who are in mourning seem not be making any headway with that process and to try to modify the damaging consequences such failures may have on their descendants.

Preventing functional splitting

As I have pointed out, these patterns are inevitably present when loss occurs, and they are necessary for the individual's psychic survival. Chronic suffering comes about when they are kept up for too long. We must therefore treat them with respect and take care not to intervene simply as a matter of course. If the individual's past history predisposes him or her to it, the work of mourning will end up being done. It all depends on how that person's mental functioning operated in the past, on his or her repressive ability (Le Guen et al., 1986), and on access to the depressive position (Klein, 1935, 1940) or to what Racamier (1992) calls primal mourning. Any therapeutic approach will therefore depend more on the person's past history than on the current mourning situation. If the traumatic impact is so intense that deadly repetitions take place very early on (e.g., nothing at all being said about the situation, compulsive activities that act as diversions), it may be helpful, in an emergency, to pay close attention to detailed narrative accounts and paradoxical countertransference responses.

The aim here is to facilitate some degree of porosity within the functional splitting. Clinically speaking, this will take the form of significant emotional responses in both analyst and patient. A vast number of stopgaps may be called upon in situations of narcissistic deficiency. Their role is and always will be that of a defensive behaviour pattern that is fetishized; when this becomes too overwhelming, madness may be the outcome.

Fetishization may lead to perversion in patients who need other people to seal off their narcissistic deficiencies. They set up a narcissistic perversion in such a way that those who become their stopgaps—Racamier (1992) calls them "predestined" stooges or porters—need their perverts in order to exist, so that their life may have some meaningful aspect to it. If they have no such perverts, they either die or recreate them themselves in a vampiric way.

This, too, is a fundamental aspect of the analyst's countertransference: the analyst feels him/herself to be in the grip of a demand for perversity that often will take the analytic setting as its target. This is then an extremely important indication of the kind of relationship that these patients set up. They are the prostheses of their perverts, and at the same time they need those perverts as crutches. If ever the parasitic nature of that relationship is exposed, they either interrupt their analysis or have a breakdown.

The reason is that, in such a pattern, there are only things and actions that prop up words; there are no words to represent things. When there are no more things, no more words, a gulf opens up and with it comes a desperate call for more prostheses. This was the situation in Duras's novel. Lol Stein "has no memory, not even an imaginary one, she has not the faintest notion of this unknown. . . . By its absence, this word ruins all the others, it contaminates them . . ." (1964, p.38).

Sadness could arise not only where the behaviour patterns used to act as a barrier but also where the unbinding of the drives that generated hatred created a kind of self-maintenance of the catastrophic situation. A word of explanation is necessary here. It is not a big step from personal protection via character-based defences to that offered by narcissistic perversion. If the rejection of everything that involves depressive affects cannot be accomplished by means of a functional barrier or by character-based defences, it may be achieved by offloading onto someone else the whole task of dealing with it.

Treating functional splitting

When functional splitting has been going on for some time, it tends to maintain the situation of poor-quality mental life in contrast to the better quality that existed before mourning had to be dealt with. That drop in quality is not always obvious since, as we have seen, in order to maintain functional splitting, fetishized activities are required. On a social level, these are often highly regarded. What is of poor quality, however, is the individual's fantasy and dream life, love life, capacity for humour, and the ability to remain healthy. Such patients consult when something goes wrong in one or other of these aspects of life. Whatever the recommended treatment—psychoanalysis or psychotherapy, psychodrama or relaxation—there will come a time when the analytic process comes up against a stumbling-block, either as to its continuation or even perhaps before the actual process has been properly initiated with the patient. At that point the psychotherapeutic approach should aim, here too, at encouraging detailed and well-constructed narratives; a certain time-interval between these is required, depending on the ability of the patient's ego to deal with recurrent themes of a traumatic nature.

A therapeutic approach to structural splitting

As I have pointed out, in these cases there is an innate narcissistic deficiency. Even before birth, those individuals who will go on to suffer from such a deficiency have been programmed by their forebears, so that they cannot have access, no matter how limited, to the functionally split-off domain of those who came before them, those whose life had been marked by mourning processes impossible to carry through spontaneously. Through identification, these patients have taken upon themselves the processes of defence that their forebears set up—but without taking on board the content against which those defences were required. An analogy would be that of maintaining guards in a place where there is no longer any reason for them to be on duty. An illustration of this can be found in Dino Buzzati's *The Tartar Steppe* (1940).

As long as their narcissistic deficiency can be filled up by their environment, everything seems to be fine. But when things change, particularly at adolescence or in motherhood, the emptiness of that deficiency may be filled up with some very strange contents indeed.

From structural splitting to transitionality: the foreshore

How can someone break free of the terrible economics of narcissistic deficiencies that use all available means to avoid becoming the locus of the emptiness that is madness? How are we to make contact with someone who is already cut in half? Experience, nonetheless, teaches us that it is possible to do so, and that a positive outcome may be reached as long as we are able to resign ourselves to the loss of narcissistic illusions as regards both the patient and ourselves. I would like to propose, as a metapsychological representation of this kind of situation, to oppose and to associate two images: that of splitting, as precipitous as a cliff that separates the sea from the land, a dangerous place that has no space; and that of transitionality, gentle and expansive like a beach. Winnicott (1971, p. 95) himself had that image in mind when he quoted Tagore: "On the seashore of endless worlds, children play." I would argue that we have to agree to live for a certain period of time in unstable equilibrium—frozen to the spot—on the edge of the cliff. We have to accept the place occupied by (but not the role of) the pervert or the stopgap, and to be, depending on the circumstances, the fetishistic object or the actual fetishist. We can live like that for a time, with the ebb and flow of the tide, for it is not such an immobile world as one may like to believe. Little by little—but, sometimes, quite quickly—we can settle down more comfortably on the gently sloping beach and play there with the patient thanks to the very special flora and fauna that have made their home in that area that, in the language of seafarers, is called the foreshore.

The foreshore is neither the sea nor the land; it is that part of the shore that is uncovered at low tide and filled with water at high tide. There is life there, life that is neither that of the sea nor that of the land mass. The world in which we live with our patients is neither that of their delusion nor that of reality. It is transitional, and it enables each of us, as a first step, to catch our breath after the horrific vertigo of the cliff, then, later, to play on it. At a still later stage, it will help the patient—when things turn out well and thanks to progress in symbolization—to enter alone into other domains, keenly aware all the time that it is no use expecting miracles and that some degree of anxiety and failure will always be present. In this sense, structural splitting can be thought of in terms of a special case of transitionality, and vice versa. The image of the foreshore leads us to that conclusion, as do the results of certain psychoanalytic treatments.

Conclusion

In starting with the pathology of mourning, I realize that the hypotheses that I have developed in this chapter have brought me very close to attributing the whole of psychopathology either to loss and mourning as such or to their consequences. I have, nevertheless, left to one side neurotic pathology, which comes from a failure in the process of mourning one's oedipal desires; I have preferred to focus on the developments that lead from the pathological consequences for oneself in one's own mourning processes to those that are attributable to others through those same mourning processes. That movement, which goes from a state of repression with character-based defences and functional splitting to one in which denial and a narcissistic deficiency created by structural splitting are predominant, opens up new fields in psychoanalysis that are at present being made ready for future harvesting. New therapeutic approaches will grow out of this; in the era of their pioneers, these cannot but produce some sudden shivers.

Note

Translated by David Alcorn.

1. The usual English translation of *Nachträglichkeit*, "deferred action", is often considered to be unsatisfactory. The French term "*après-coup*" appears to be closer to what Freud meant.

3

Separating and splitting up

Penelope Garvey

In the final phase of her analysis, Mrs A., who had over the many years of her analysis managed to recover split-off aspects of herself, become more defined as a person, and was able to stand up for herself without feeling humiliated by being seen to have feelings and wants, became increasingly anxious about how she was going to survive the loss of the analysis and feared a return to a state of feeling nothing. She had the following dream:

> *The car was parked in the yard outside her parent's house. The car caught fire and, afraid that the fire would spread to the house, she called in the air force to bomb it.*

Mrs A. bombed the car—which I thought stood for her caring, containing ego—in order to protect me and herself from knowing about versions of me in her mind that could take over and destroy the good feelings that she had about me and her analysis. The bombing broke up and fragmented her ego, propelled out her feelings, and left her feeling nothing. Much has been written about this kind of fragmentary splitting, its developmental origins, and its tendency to reappear in situations of stress. The bombing, as we shall see, occurred not only in her dream. Phantasies do affect reality, and Mrs A. returned to a state that I knew well from the past. Melanie Klein describes something similar:

> He turned his destructive impulses from his object *towards his ego*, with the result that parts of his ego temporarily went out of existence. In unconscious phantasy this amounted to annihilation of part of his personality. The particular mechanism of turning the destructive impulse against one part of his personality, and the ensuing dispersal of emotions, kept his anxiety in a latent state. [Klein, 1946, p. 19]

The concept of splitting is pivotal in Klein's developmental theory and is centre stage in her conceptualization of the two positions: depressive position (1935) and paranoid–schizoid position (1946). I will make some links to Freud's thoughts on splitting, but it is Klein's ideas and those of her followers that are the focus of this chapter.[1]

Overview of Kleinian theories of splitting

Right from the start, Klein draws attention to the protective splitting of the object (1921), the splitting up of the superego (1929), and the splitting of the id[2] (1932), and she repeatedly explores the evidence for an earlier and more violent type of defence than repression. It is in her 1946 paper "Notes on Some Schizoid Mechanisms" that she writes about the splitting of the ego and importantly observes that if the object is split, the ego is correspondingly split. Klein thought her ideas about splitting to be enormously important, and in the Melanie Klein Archive she calls this 1946 paper, "my splitting paper" (Spillius, personal communication). Prior to this, in her early work, splitting, projection, expulsion, deflection, exploration, and sadism are hard to disentangle. and it is not always easy to differentiate normal from abnormal processes or to distinguish between developmentally useful activity and anti-developmental activity. These distinctions become clearer once Klein connects together the strands of her thinking about splitting into her theory of the paranoid–schizoid position, but they nonetheless remain problematic and the term is used quite loosely to cover different activities with differing aims.

Normal binary splitting and fragmentation

Klein conceives of the immature infant as experiencing itself and others in terms of physical parts—breast, penis, and so on (part-objects). In 1946 she describes binary or primary splitting—the separation of the good and loving parts of the self and object from the bad and hating parts—as the first act of the ego and as absolutely essential for mental health. The early unintegrated ego, traumatized by birth and threatened by the anxiety of annihilation from within, projects and also deflects this anxiety or death instinct outwards into the mother. The internal persecutor is now in phantasy omnipotently located in the mother, who is in consequence experienced as dangerous. The remaining death instinct is bound by libido; some is turned into aggression and directed (deflected) towards the now "bad breast" mother, and some remains within and may threaten the ego. The "bad" mother is introjected and is experienced as a damaged and split-up retaliatory presence within, a presence that correspondingly splits the ego. The "bad" internal objects are in turn projected out, and a cycle of re-introjection and re-projection ensues.

Simultaneously with this "bad" relationship, life instinct or libido is in phantasy projected out and attaches to the "good" object. This first "good" object is introjected and is protected and kept as far apart from the "bad" self and "bad" object as possible; in fact, their existence is denied. The good object is idealized and imagined as all powerful and in this way provides a sense of security. The ego identifies with the good object and, with sufficient life instinct and sufficient good experience, a benign cycle of projection and introjection gets going and the ego increases in strength and is able to tolerate and integrate the "bad" self and the "bad" object. Klein's sets this out with clarity in her later paper "Envy and Gratitude".

> To return to the splitting process, which I take to be a precondition for the young infant's relative stability; during the first few months he predominantly keeps the good object apart from the bad one and thus, in a fundamental way, preserves it—which also means that the security of the ego is enhanced. At the same time this primal division only succeeds if there is an adequate capacity for love and a relatively strong ego. My

> hypothesis is, therefore, that the capacity for love gives impetus both to integrating tendencies and to successful primal splitting between the loved and hated object. This sounds paradoxical. But since, as I said, integration is based on a strongly rooted good object that forms the core of the ego, a certain amount of splitting is essential for integration; for it preserves the good object and later on enables the ego to synthesize the two aspects of it. [Klein, 1957, pp. 191–192]

Projective identification

The 1946 paper also contains Klein's first mention of the process of projective identification. The concept of projective identification describes the phantasies concerning the location of the split-off parts of the self and their relationship to external and internal objects. It illuminates the transference, and it informs technique. Bion (1959, 1962) extends the idea of projective identification, and he differentiates normal (communicative) projective identification from abnormal (evacuative) projective identification. In normal projective identification, feelings are contained by being split off and projected into the mother or analyst, who, all being well, will be emotionally affected but not too disturbed and will communicate back her understanding. The communication can be understood as a kind of exploration, in which the analyst's countertransference is the essential tool, to quote Bion in "Attacks on Linking"; "Projective identification makes it possible for him [the patient] to investigate his own feelings in a personality powerful enough to contain them" (Bion, 1959, p. 106). Communicative projective identification is the basis of thinking, whereas evacuative projective identification leaves the individual depleted.

Integration and splitting in the depressive position

In normal development, via the continuous processes of projection and introjection, an exchange takes place in which the ego strengthens. It becomes possible for the individual to separate phantasy from reality and self from object and, in doing so, to take back split-off aspects of the self that have been projected out.

Others become more realistically perceived and experienced, and internal objects become less extreme.

For the infant, the recognition that the loved mother is also the hated mother causes great feelings of pain and guilt: pain at the recognition of separateness, at the loss of an ideal self in relationship with an all-powerful mother; jealousy at the recognition of a mother who has other relationships; guilt and concern about a mother who is vulnerable and has been hurt. All of these and other "depressive" feelings are hard to bear; damage may be felt to be great and repair difficult or impossible. The pain and the renewal of splitting in this period is well documented; guilt can become persecuting and may cause a retreat into splitting, in which good or bad experiences are wiped out and omnipotently denied. Damage may be magically repaired.

Klein's initial 1946 thought is of the positions as "intermingled and interacting", with some fluctuations between integration and splitting during development, but later (1957) she thinks that permanent integration is never possible. A hard dividing line cannot be drawn, and it is commonly accepted that there is to and fro between paranoid–schizoid and depressive position activity, a point emphasized by Bion (1970) and Britton (2001), who stress the importance of disintegrative activity for development.

Pathological splitting and fragmentation and pathological organizations

Klein considers the paranoid–schizoid position to be the fixation point for the psychoses. If splitting is too "extreme", with parts of the self rigidly separated from each other, the individual may feel persecuted or empty, may be unable to think or feel, and may fluctuate between different attitudes, and integration is likely to be difficult or impossible. Frustration, greed, and envy all lead to an increase in splitting into small pieces, and in her later work, following Rosenfeld (1952), Klein (1957) emphasizes the destructiveness of envy. Both the avoidance and the expression of envy involve attacks on the envied object, with the aim of destroying its goodness and obliterating difference. This is achieved in various ways, one of which is the splitting off and evacuation of bad aspects of the self into the envied object. The result is confusion between self and object and between good and bad, impaired primal splitting, and a damaged or destroyed good object, felt to be in pieces. Bion (1957), writing at the same time, describes the mutilating attacks made by the envious individual, not only on the object but also on his own ego functioning.

Rosenfeld (1950) writes about the terrifying nature of confusion in patients who are unable to discriminate between good and bad. In 1952 he describes patients who cannot stand the terror and guilt caused by the feeling of containing dead or destroyed internal objects that operate inside them as what he calls an "ego-splitting superego". Klein and others describe similarly destructive superego activity: Klein (1957) writes of the "envious superego", which she sees as being "based on the earliest internalized persecutory object, the retaliating devouring and poisonous breast"; Bion (1959) outlines an "ego-destructive superego", which refuses to take in projections and attacks linking; and O'Shaughnessy (1999) describes the "abnormal superego" and notes the connection between all of these and Freud's idea of defused death instinct.

A number of writers focus on the stability of some patients with schizoid defences, in whom the splitting and projective processes are organized and protect against, or are a response to, fragmentary processes. These patients can be difficult to treat: the dependent self is split off, controlled by a powerful internal object and kept away from contact with the analyst (Joseph, 1989; Meltzer, 1968; O'Shaughnessy, 1981; Rosenfeld, 1971; Segal, 1972). Steiner (1993) brings in the term "pathological organization" for this system of defences, which occur particularly at moments of transition towards integration. Great attention is given to the way in which the object relationship is played out in the transference and to the perverse pleasure that some patients experience in avoiding direct emotional contact. Smith (2006) suggests that these kinds of enactment in the transference are examples of Freud's idea of disavowal.

Rosenfeld (1971) divides his patients into two groups, and Britton (2003) makes a similar distinction according to the degree to which the patient's turning to an idealized internal object is self-protective rather than motivated by hostility to the external object.

Levels and internal structures

Klein imagines that the infant contains many "good" and "bad" versions of internal objects, which have been introjected at different times during different phases of development. She seems to equate the phases with levels—possibly of consciousness—which she considers relate more or less closely to reality. The first introjects, which are taken into both the ego and the superego, are the objects into which the life and death instincts have been projected, and they are therefore felt to be extreme. The superego—which in Klein's theory arises at the start of life—contains these extreme unrealistic objects that play a part in what Klein calls the early severe superego.

Klein suggests that while integration may take place at one level, splitting may continue at another less conscious level. Levels may be more or less porous, and internal objects at one level may or may not influence those on the next level. Unresolved splits lead to rigid rather than porous barriers between what is conscious and what unconscious. As I discuss later, in 1958 Klein removes the extreme primary objects from the superego, places them in what she calls the "deep unconscious", and excludes them from the activity of exchange with internal objects on other levels.

Also pursuing a line of thought about a division in the personality, Bion (1957), the year before, draws attention to a neurotic part of the personality within the psychotic and states that in the severe neurotic there is a psychotic part that splits into minute pieces the capacity to be aware of internal and external reality. In 1940 Freud had described a disavowal of the perceptions of reality in the neurotic:

> the ego often enough finds itself in the position of fending off some demand from the external world which it feels distressing and . . . this is effected by means of a disavowal of the perceptions which bring to knowledge this demand from reality. Disavowals of this kind occur very often and not only with fetishists; and whenever we are in a position to study them they turn out to be half-measures, incomplete attempts at detachment from reality. The disavowal is always supplemented by an acknowledgment; two contrary and independent attitudes always arise and result in the situation of there being a splitting of the ego. Once

> more the issue depends on which of the two can seize hold of the greater intensity.
>
> The facts of this splitting of the ego, which we have just described, are neither so new nor so strange as they may at first appear. It is indeed a universal characteristic of neuroses that there are present in the subject's mental life, as regards some particular behaviour, two different attitudes, contrary to each other and independent of each other. [1940a (1938), pp. 203–204]

Bion describes how this leaves the patient feeling "imprisoned in the state of mind he has achieved", and, like Freud (1940e [1938]), Bion (1957) refers to "an ever-widening divergence between . . . these parts of the personality".

Clinical material

I want now to return to Mrs A., whose dreams illustrate some of the splitting mechanisms that I have described.[3] When she first came to see me Mrs A. cried, but she had no idea what could be upsetting her. Her speech was broken up, and it was very difficult for me to piece together the meaning of her incomplete sentences and words; I had the impression of someone who was being strangled while trying to speak. I was reminded of Bion's description of "destructive attacks on the link between the patient and the environment or between different aspects of the patient's personality" (Bion, 1959, p. 106). I came to think of Mrs A. as someone with an ego-destructive superego that did not allow her to have any weakness or imperfection.

Mrs A. seemed to settle a bit into the analysis, but I took a half-term break in her second term and, with little time to prepare for this break, her feelings disappeared from the sessions and I was left with little to go on other than a sense of failure, guilt, and unease about myself. I was also left uncertain about whether she had been more emotionally engaged before this break or whether it was something that I imagined. Had I killed off all live connection? It was not until two or so years later that she confirmed that the break had been extremely traumatic and that it was then that she had completely cut off from directly expressing her feelings. A dream at that time gives an idea about her version of the analysis.

> *Mrs A. had to live in my house while she was having analysis. But I went out and left her, and she wanted a drink. She found and drank from a tap, out of which came a visceral liquid. The liquid paralysed her and was going to kill her. She then found herself being looked after by a Russian au pair in the basement.*

The Russian au pair in her dream made her think of a TV programme about Eastern European midwives in which, when the baby was born, it was wrapped up and put on a shelf on a trolley and then taken to the mother at strict times, all babies being taken in turn. It was clear to both of us that Mrs A. experienced analysis as a completely impersonal, cold system of feeding to which she felt she had to submit. She had to find a way to manage being left by me, and this was to drink something that paralysed her. Segal writes:

> all pain comes from living. . . . Birth confronts us with the experience of needs. In relation to that experience there can be two reactions, and both, I think, are invariably present in all of us, though in varying proportions. One, to seek satisfaction for the needs: that is life-promoting and leads to object seeking, love, and eventually object concern. The other is the drive to annihilate the need, to annihilate the perceiving experiencing self, as well as anything that is perceived. [Segal, 1993, p. 55]

I think the break was traumatic, I think Mrs A. was able to tap into my viscera, but I think also that the visceral liquid that kept her going was perhaps a viscous (sticky) liquid that contained some righteous grievance, and this allowed her to viciously cut herself off from her own upset feelings and to punish me—a situation in which we were to remain stuck for some time. She felt superior, not only to me in the basement but also to the infant her. I was the au pair below, who did the work of making the link with my unresponsive patient in identification with a cut-off mother. It was also the other way round: she was the au pair who made the considerable effort to get her to her sessions with her unresponsive mother-analyst who did things by a timetable. The sessions were denuded of feeling, stripped by my abandonment of her and by her response.

From this experience and from her dreams, I understood that Mrs A. felt threatened by the possibility of reaching out and finding nobody there, and I thought, that in part this is what she created in the transference, I was to feel that I was nobody and that she was without feelings. I was up against a pathological organization. My gut feeling was that the prime motivation was defensive rather than destructive, but I could not be certain, and both were clearly present.

Mrs A. avoided contact with her feelings by splitting up and fragmenting her emotional self and scattering it around in other people, people who I suspect fitted the projections well. This activity perpetuated and increased her feeling of emptiness. She was very active on behalf of others, who she felt had little capacity to control or to care for themselves and who needed her to look after them; she felt under great pressure to race all over the place in response to their needs. For quite a long period I was included in this group of people demanding her attention, and she was far more aware of her activity in relation to me than of her passivity in helping me to understand her. She found the sessions relentlessly meaningless, boring, and without value, and I was treated like an unreasonably demanding child who just would not understand that she had been given more than enough.

Mrs A.'s concern for herself was largely split-off and, in the transference, was located in me. I felt that she needed me to work hard on her behalf picking up pieces of what she said, collecting parts of her from where they were projected into me and other people, and linking her up with what she might be feeling and why. It was possible for me to make contact with her when the emotional meaning made sense to her. Over time I became valued as someone who could sort things out, and slowly she allowed herself to have feelings. She still far preferred to suffer virtuously than be selfish, greedy, or aggressive, but she was able to recover, to some extent, these aspects of herself, although she could not use them for self-protection and I had to watch her suffering.

Two or three years before the end of the analysis, I became increasingly convinced that Mrs A. could do more on her own behalf and that she could make more sense of things in the sessions than she wanted me to know. I thought that she got some satisfaction out of watching me do the work. I thought that what was going on was similar to the development described by Edna O'Shaughnessy (1981), in which certain patients, who need the security of being with a responsive object, will, once secure, get pleasure in being in control. When, in relation to chaotic material that she brought, I put some of this to her, her immediate reaction was defensive, but in the following session she was more coherent and thoughtful than the day before. She said that, although she had "not been locked out of her car or had a splitting headache recently", she was very afraid of how she would manage without me and then went on to say "a funny thing happened in the holidays, the council told us that we had to sort out our rubbish and said that the collectors would only take away what was sorted out". I replied that I thought she felt that I had said, "you cannot leave me to do all the work of making sense of what you say, you have to sort out what you can yourself".

She agreed and went on to tell me a dream

> *We were going for the weekend to stay with William, who has bought a house in Devon. I didn't know the way, and then Marina, his wife, came down the drive and so I followed her. There were other people and they also followed her, and we went into the house. There was a door, which Marina changed into a window to let in light, and then William came in and he had a lot of children with him. He had brought them back from his travels; you know he goes on these expeditions. We were talking about it and I did not know the difference between the Arctic and the Antarctic, and we were talking to the children. Then he fed them and they were very hungry and they changed into animals and the food was running out and so he got some more, a leg of pork or ham. It was on a spit and he was anxious that it would not be cooked fast enough. The children had not been like animals before.*

She had an association to a man on TV licking milk out of a saucer, eating like a cat; she had found this very disturbing. It had made her feel very uncomfortable to see him doing something so humiliating.

There are aspects of this dream that I did not understand, but I think that it is possible to see that the analysis, like the window in the dream, had shed some light on what happens between us when I bring parts of Mrs A. in from the cold and feed her with my attention and understanding. She becomes hungry for my attention but a "viewer" her looks down on herself with disgust at exposing this animal side of herself. I said to Mrs A. that she feels that being hungry turns her into an animal and taking food from me—in fact, having good feelings towards me—makes her feel very uncomfortable, as though she is doing something quite disgusting and degrading. I went on to say that she is much more comfortable with a version of me as the rubbish collector. She replied: "I don't think it has changed. I still feel it is humiliating to be hungry."

I want to go back now to the last phase of the analysis and the session with which I began this account, the one in which Mrs A told me the dream of calling in the air force to bomb the car. In this session she spoke at length about organizations and individuals with whom she was involved and who were in need of her help, and she told me that there were others, "extremists", with whom she was planning to work and with whom she would, she said vaguely, "share her thinking". I had lost the patient who was anxious about leaving, the one who was soon to be parked outside the analysis and in danger of damaging me with her extreme feelings; instead, I now had a patient, familiar from the past, with a bombed and dispersed ego, someone very much in demand and who, feeling it important to treat people equally, could only give everyone limited attention. I thought that, with the impending ending, she was avoiding close involvement with me and with others, in order not to face the limits of her and my powers. The next day she brought a dream:

> *She was in a lift, carrying the children's clean washing and wanting, but being unable, to get out at the first floor. She was carried by the lift on to the fourth floor, and there, after some difficulty, she was able to squeeze out into a flat where she found two gay men and a pool full of frogspawn. The frogspawn began to spread everywhere in a way that made her very distressed and anxious.*

I felt rather desperate at the return of the old Mrs A., and I thought that the dream described our situation, she in a high state and both of us surrounded by fragments of a vulnerable her, with which she had no emotional contact and which seemed to be increasing at an alarming rate. I said that I thought that she had been carried up into a high state in which she had lost contact with herself and with a capacity to be more grounded and realistic. She was hurt and angry and complained that I had brought her down in a very unkind manner. She repeated this to me the following day and told me sharply that this way of being spoken to was an aspect of her analysis that she was not going to miss. My intervention had lacked subtlety, and I was aware that there were a number of things in the dream that were only now beginning to make sense to me. I said that I thought she had in her mind a version of me as very narcissistic, someone who valued myself highly and who imagined that I had helped her by "sharing my thinking", and who was now going to swan off, leaving her vulnerable and undefended, without any awareness of the limits of the analysis that I had given her and the difficulties that she was left with and which she would now have to manage on her own. The atmosphere improved.

Later I had other thoughts, and these were confirmed by material in subsequent sessions. I think that I was the trapping lift that Mrs A wanted to accuse of having trapped and involved her in a long and intensive four-times-a-week analysis when all she had wanted was something more distant, once a week, and much shorter. Had she been able to get out earlier, at the first floor, all would have been well. She could have left, as she had said to me more than once, when she still idealized my powers. Instead she now found herself having to face the limitations of the analysis, and, as she had said at one point in the middle of her analysis, "who wants the depressive position? I can't see why anyone would want it."

After these sessions, Mrs A became more grounded and returned to feeling sad and fearful about the ending. Her anger came more to the fore with a version of me, as I have mentioned, as narcissistically preoccupied with myself. She also remembered the fragment of a dream in which there was blood under the carpet. It became clear that she had been trying to keep the "blood on the carpet" "under the carpet" and was frightened by two equally disturbing versions of the ending of the analysis: in one, I was the murderer; in the other, she was the murderer. She also knew that she wanted to end and that her analysis could not go on and on for ever.

Discussion

To what extent has Mrs A been changed by analysis, has her tendency to fragment reduced, and have the early idealized and terrifying internal objects been modified?

Threading through her papers Klein repeatedly goes over similar questions about the degree to which psychoanalysis is able to alter the primary internal objects. In 1927 she writes, "I am led to believe from the analysis of children that their super-ego is a highly resistant product, at heart unalterable" (Klein, 1927, p. 155). In 1929 she states that the early severe superego can modify, but in 1933 she thinks that even so "analysis can never entirely do away with the sadistic nucleus of the superego" (Klein, 1933, p. 256). In 1952 she refers to the "progressive assimilation of the superego by the ego" (Klein, 1952, p. 74), and, in notes on this same paper, she elaborates that "persecutory and depressive anxieties are diminished, as one might say, at the root" (p. 91) only by a thorough analysis of the negative as well as the positive transference. The modifying effect on the superego of working in the transference is fully spelt out by Strachey (1934).

Klein's last word on this issue is in 1958 when she comes up with a solution that allows for both modification and unalterability. She concludes that aspects of the extreme early introjects are split off into the deep unconscious where they remain unmodified, but other aspects of the same extreme objects are located elsewhere—in the ego and the superego—and, by interaction with each other and with the external world, have the opportunity to become modified. In a healthy individual these figures erupt into consciousness only when under extreme stress, but for others, less developmentally strong, whether due to constitutional weakness or insufficient good experience, these figures may be much more disruptive. Klein makes the point that the extreme early introjects are predominantly made up of defused life and death instincts, whereas the objects that are located in the ego and superego are formed from a fusion of the two instincts:

> These extremely dangerous objects give rise, in early infancy, to conflict and anxiety within the ego; but under the stress of acute anxiety they, and other terrifying figures, are split off in

> a manner different from that by which the superego is formed, and are relegated to the deeper layers of the unconscious. The difference in these two ways of splitting—and this may perhaps throw light on the many as yet obscure ways in which splitting processes take place—is that in the splitting-off of frightening figures defusion seems to be in the ascendant; whereas superego formation is carried out with a predominance of fusion of the two instincts. Therefore the superego is normally established in close relation with the ego and shares different aspects of the same good objects. This makes it possible for the ego to integrate and accept the superego to a greater or less extent. In contrast, the extremely bad figures are not accepted by the ego in this way and are constantly rejected by it. [Klein, 1958, p. 241]

Klein's final theory accommodated both the extreme, unmodifiable, terrifying figures and also the severe but modifiable figures of the superego.

Conclusion

Mrs A.'s case could be extended and explored in a number of directions, but I have narrowed my account to limit my focus to the topic of splitting. In the dream from early in the analysis, Mrs A. is inside her object, but in a devalued place, the basement. She presents a picture of herself desolated and abandoned and in the hands of a neglectful object who leaves her to find the tap herself. Quite a change can be seen by the second dream, with its picture of an emotionally responsive object who brings her in from the cold, feeds her, and is anxious about her getting enough and who is part of a couple. I am felt to be not only someone who takes away rubbish, but also someone who makes emotional connections and provides her with understanding and, significantly, with the means to look at herself, think about herself, and make her own emotional connections.

As the end of her analysis draws near, Mrs A. is more emotionally alive, but the impending separation, with its realization of loss, provokes an eruption from the deep unconscious of a terrifying internal object that does not accept the pain or shame of loss and that threatens to destroy her good containing object, the parental home/me, probably with the accusation that separation is equivalent to murder. Concerned for her object, Mrs A. calls in the bombers. This causes her to fragment, evacuates the pain of loss, and she returns to an identification with her "ideal" but actually hateful and hated unrealistic object—nothing really there. All this could be thought about by both of us, and Mrs A. recovered her balance.

Notes

I am grateful to Jane Milton and Edna O'Shaughnessy for their comments on an earlier draft of this paper.

1. Grotstein (1981) excellently reviews the development of the concept.
2. This later becomes the splitting of the ego.
3. The patient's history, although relevant, is omitted for reasons of confidentiality.

4

Real wolves and fake wolves: alternating between repression and splitting in complex clinical cases

Stefano Bolognini

On the heels of a century of psychoanalysis, we are faced in our field with an extremely complex theoretical dimension, enriched by a myriad of scientific contributions, which are coming from various directions and which take care of, at least in part, illuminating ever-widening areas of the individual's psychic life and of the analytic couple's functioning at work in analysis.

Most analysts set themselves to the long and demanding task of getting to know, augmenting, evaluating, and selecting a kit of conceptual tools that can be gathered together from the literature, seminar studies, and congresses. The goal of getting equipped this way is to integrate new theoretical breakthroughs that prove themselves to be useful for understanding a continually mutating clinical reality and, at the same time, prove to be consistent and sufficiently in tune with one's own analytic identity, founded earlier on.

This approach is profoundly different, then, from ridding oneself of that which one has learned, substituting it in block form with that which seems new.

General comments of this nature are pertinent, in these times, for that which relates to neurosis—a subject that was studied a great deal in the past, as much as it is neglected today, perhaps due to the progressively, indisputably decreasing recurrence of "pure" clinical cases, which were once so common.

And yet, it is precisely the complexity of current clinical cases that suggests that we keep close at hand the clinical-theoretical kit that is applicable to neurosis. We know all too well how often contemporary psychoanalysis finds itself (with good reason) alternately "tracking", in practice, between defensive organizations of a neurotic type and more primitive ones, surrounding itself by a maze of adjustments and pathological solutions of "mixed breed", above and beyond the simplifying formulas so dear to the various 3rd, 4th *DSMs*, and so on.

As do many colleagues, I also hold that, in the area of clinical neurotic cases of the type with defences built on repression, displacement, fixation, false connection, and relative conflictual and structural drives, competence is no less necessary today than it was in the past if one is to practise our profession.

Pathologies mutate, and a crisis is recognizable—in family, cultural, and social contexts—of superego representations that were once the traditional generators (along with characteristic configurations of the defensive ego) of conflict and repression: on multiple fronts there are reports of diffuse deprivation of internal and external representations of the paternal series, just as there is a progressive decline of religion and politically "strong" ideologies, and so forth; *vice versa,* it seems as if the same sociocultural context values narcissistic, perverse, regression-causing forms of pseudo-solutions of the Oedipus complex.

Nevertheless, neurotic "passages" appear to be inevitable in most analyses, and the difference compared with the past seems to be mostly in the frequency and intensity with which they characterize complex pathological configuration.

In the same way, psychoanalysts' theory and diagnostic tool kit is in constant change—so much so that rereading clinical cases of "hysteria" from the pioneering era more and more often suggest a diagnostic reformulation in the direction of "borderline states" or even psychosis.

Without entering into whether these assessments are correct, in this chapter I address, on the other hand, the connections and the existing articulations between neurotic defences and complex clinical cases that correspond only in part to the traditional concept of neurosis, but which do not differ from it enough to merit a clean-cut collocation outside of neurosis itself—a "mixed" category that corresponds, I believe, to an all but small number of the cases that we handle in our offices on a daily basis.

My chapter consists of the presentation of and commentary on clinical material regarding two diagnostically well-described cases with which I hope to show how neurotic mechanisms can come to be constructed, respectively:

1. in the first case, the dynamic pretext to a partial disturbance in sexual identity;
2. in the second case, a condition "of passage" in a subject who tends towards being borderline, who switches among neurotic, pre-psychotic, and perverse defences.

The aim of this brief chapter is not that of developing a precise theoretical point of view on specific aspects of neurosis, but, rather, that of highlighting the utility of an underlying attention to *neurotic aspects that are present in complex forms of pathology*, which I hold to be heavily represented in the current clinical caseload of contemporary psychoanalysis.

I will outline, therefore, two clinical cases that are highly characterized by, and which differentiate themselves strongly on, their seriousness and the difficulties they present in treatment.

They hold in common, however, an intertwining of neurotic-style defences and symptoms with others of a different degree of pathology.

I maintain that in both cases a one-sided, simple diagnosis, which of its own would not be "wrong" in the absolute (respectively, that is, of "disturbance of sexual identity" in one case, and of "borderline states" in the other), could bring with it a "cover-up"—or even a "by-pass"—of the neurotic component, with some difficulties in understanding the patient's psychic functioning and in the choice of complex technical modalities that could be opportunely adopted during treatment.

Case 1: "Roberta"
"Beware of the wolf: from baby goat, to pseudo-wolf, to wolf girl"

Roberta is a 30-year-old woman, with pleasant-enough features, but who carries herself in a masculine way nonetheless; now and then she switches from a grey skirt (the "old maid" kind) to trousers, but she regularly has sensible shoes and wears "serious" colours, and her hairstyle "for women"—"dictated" by the hairdresser—seems to be put on over her face as if it were a hat, not spontaneous and not in keeping with the rest of her.

In our first meeting I find myself with the curious sensation of having to do with a woman who may be feminine but who cultivates masculine ways, rather than with an all-around masculine woman.

She requests analysis after having been seen by a couple of neurologists for a relatively recent condition (three or four months) of generalized anxiety—absolutely new to a decisive person like her. She finds herself frightened and "disoriented" by this symptom. In this same period she has the sensation of being tired and losing energy.

Both specialists, after having done the appropriate clinical tests, diagnosed a neurotic disturbance and recommended she consult a psychoanalyst.

Roberta is a dentist, who inherited her office from her father, who had inherited it from her grandfather, who had inherited it from her great-grandfather.

She lost both of her parents, one soon after the other—six and five years previously—with great suffering.

From the very earliest accounts in our sessions, here and there emerges the fact that as a girl she was inseparable from her father, who treated her and considered her, however, to all effects, as a son. She had an older brother by five years, but he had shown himself to be weak and problematic early on, and the father had ended up considering him a lost cause.

Their father was enthusiastic, however, when she—in short trousers and with a crew cut—would "beat up" the children in the neighbourhood; when she would make an arrogant goal on the parochial football field; when he would take her hunting with him, having bought her a small rifle—small but authentic, which shot for real.

Femininity was the prerogative of Roberta's mother—a beautiful, elegant lady who was very taken up with herself, revered daily in the downtown boutiques, and brilliant as the *grand dame* of society evenings.

Roberta acknowledges not having any sort of care for her own aesthetic appearance, and she confides in me that she has never been able to choose a dress for herself in a shop.

The patient, in any case, despite her fragmentary references to it, does not appear to be completely aware of having lived this paradoxical oedipal arrangement: *she was the favourite (male) son of her father.*

Added progressively to the evident identification she had with her father as a defence to the drives in his regard, and to the difficult sustainability with regards to a mother who was so beautiful and fascinating, was a reinforcement of her own phallic aspects that the father (satisfied by his wife's femininity and disappointed by the first-born son) had furnished in a massive way for the girl, distorting in part her own gender identity.

This "graft" of the paternal expectations should have had success, because the patient showed notable narcissistic investment in her own way of being, which appeared to be legitimated and exploited from within.

With all this, Roberta had not given up her feminine identity entirely and, since adolescence, had had some male admirers; however, they were mostly immature softies who were happy to rely on a strong, pragmatic woman like her, needy of a "structuring" phallus that would sustain them and would organize their existence in a strong, reliable way.

During the first months of analysis Roberta repeated in transference the tendency to experience me and treat me like her father, in the sense that she had managed to get me accustomed to her as—and to esteem her for being above all—an avant-garde and "career-oriented" dentist, cultivating correspondingly a strong idealization in my regards. This paternal transference tended to make her stereotypically repeat a consensus model through hyper-invested professional militancy: the superego was satisfied (and seduced) by impersonating an Ideal of the superego.

I, in turn, could perceive a complementary strong implicit pressure that I should impersonate (reproducing in myself the internal axis by induction) this father who was so enthusiastic about his "first-born Roberta's" performance, and that I should make up with her a couple that was more "monolithic" than analytic, not to be crossed by drives or by contrasts.

It took nearly three years of analysis at four sessions per week to start to modify this internal situation and to give it some dynamicism.

Roberta never gave up entirely being my "patient/son–first-born–favourite–like-me", but as she become more and more aware of this transferral tendency, she was ever more able to recognize, understand, re-size, and transform it.

In the meantime, through complex analytic vicissitudes that I will not report here for brevity's sake, authentically feminine aspects began to bloom in her: she would wear skirts more and more often, she started to be able to "see herself" in pretty outfits, and so on. I know that this type of analytic evaluation is neither rare nor original, that every colleague has seen developments of this type, with the progressive, conflictual appearance of dreams and fantasies in which the patient experiences the birth of desire and starts to represent herself as a woman, and so forth.

I offer this evolving picture in order to provide the basic context for recounting a specific session in the third year of analysis. In that session one can observe, among other things, the technical problem of interpretation as non-destructured selective deconstruction, to which I will pay specific attention.

The appearance, in the preceding sessions, of the desire to have a child (Roberta had married an ex-university colleague) had generated in the patient a problem of the following kind: would accepting being pregnant mean giving up once and for all being a male? And would it have, at the same time, meant giving up being the most brilliant specialist who had come out of the university dentistry clinic in the last ten years?

Session

[Today Roberta comes swaggering into the office, rather obviously imitating an athlete she idealizes greatly (a famous basketball player), and with a very determined look in her eye, like someone who has a task she must bring to term; today she is wearing trousers, while in the last sessions she had been dressed in a rather feminine way, with a skirt. Lying down on the couch she seems to stretch out, but also to "deflate" herself a bit; the impression is of a sort of indeterminable distance, mixed with fatigue. Then she regains her shape and starts to speak.]

P.: "Here we are. (Pause) Yesterday evening, big think with Giorgio [the husband] about what car to get. The car has to be replaced, the one now, the old "coupé", just can't cut it any more, it's not very practical and then it loses parts, it's not worth it to invest money in repairs, even if I am sorry about it some . . . Giorgio is pushing that we get a Volvo estate car . . . yes, it is a beauty . . . but it's enormous! Too big!! Where can I put it? . . . it'll block things up . . ."

[The atmosphere at the beginning sounds brilliant, detached, "sporty": "*Here we are* . . .", "*big think* . . .". Roberta comes across as playful, but soon enough her restlessness comes out. I think that the patient is talking about herself and the need/opportunity/perhaps inevitability of a change of her own: "*The car has to be replaced* . . .", "*can't cut it any more, it's not very practical and then it loses parts*". The husband "*pushes*" (a multifunctional, and sexual expression) to have a car-container, with a belly, but Roberta is scared, she doesn't know "*where to put it*" (where to collocate it in her internal representation of self) . . . "*block things up*" (also in the sense that it will take up space, internally and externally, away from other activities and characteristics of hers: now she is a super speedy coupé/dentist; if she becomes a mummy/estate car she'll lose the sporty/phallic aspect, etc.). It is an interesting start to a session, but I feel that it is better not to offer interpretations and to let the associative flow develop, which continues with sufficient fluidity despite the conflictual content.]

P.: "It would fit in the garage; the problem, for me, is driving it . . . I've always preferred small cars, which can find a spot anywhere."

A.: "Which can find a spot anywhere? . . ."

P.: "The less you block things up, the more you can find a spot . . . (*a few minutes' pause; clear, perceptible sensation of opening and internal connection*) . . . When I was little I loved a story about a wolf and seven baby goats: the one where the wolf enters the house and eats up all the baby goats but one, the littlest one, who manages to save itself by hiding in the pendulum clock . . ."

[I think that the problem of a feminine Roberta (Volvo/vulva), pregnant (estate car), is not a simple static problem ("*in the garage*") of the self, but relates to the adjustment of ego functions ("*driving it*") to the new, eventual feminine maternal identity that is "so bulky", which could after all be refused ("*not find a spot*") in her mind today, like in the mind of her father once upon a time. I am quite struck by the idea of cars/little creatures that "*find a spot anywhere*", and I am about to ask her something about the fairytale of the wolf and the seven goats, particularly about that "littlest" goat who manages to "fit anywhere", even in the pendulum clock, when Roberta starts talking again.]

P.: ". . . and then you know that when I was three months old my father saved my life by rushing me to the hospital, by car, fixing me up in a box because he was alone and my mother was out of the house? I had a respiratory crisis due to acute bronchiolitis; they told me about it, naturally, I don't remember a thing of it."

At this point the patient "moves on to other things" (her words), and goes on for twenty rather boring minutes, all of it focused on her being the right arm of Prof. X, head of the department and recognized head of the school, and about certain controversies of his with colleagues.

Roberta is certainly a very good specialist in her field and genuinely passionate about the subject matter, but the boring aspect of her speech is that of her political-institutional militancy as the "trusted man" of the professor in the institute's scuffles. Roberta presents herself as a soldier united on all fronts with her boss, as if she were a part of him, with the tone of someone who agrees *a priori*, and with a separation that is too clean-cut between the "dishonest losers" (the others) and "the serious ones" (the boss and his entourage); the boss, on his side, uses this transference, assigning difficult tasks to her and assuring himself of confirming support in any institutional conflict.

At other times, on the other hand, Roberta "*is*" integrally he and talks just like him, in a state of total identification.

A.: "It seems that the thought of being able to be pregnant has brought up various problems for you: in part with yourself, because you are used to being light and fast like a coupé, and you have a hard time imagining yourself as a container, "family sized", like an estate car; in part with Prof. X, who expects complete dedication from you, at the institute, and whom you fear "betraying" with your husband and a child of yours."

P.: (*with difficulty*): "Well, . . . in a certain sense . . . he did do a great deal for me: he got me into the clinic; if it hadn't been for him . . . professionally, I owe everything to him."

A.: "Like your father, who—getting you to the [paediatric] clinic with great alacrity—saved your life. And in fact I think that you did not really 'move on to other things' when you went from talking about being brought to the hospital at the age of three months to talking about Prof. X: two fathers to whom you 'owe everything'."

P.: "As a matter of fact, they have only done me good . . ."

[There is definitely perceptible a sense of guilt at the idea of "going beyond" the father equivalents.]

A.: "In the facts, it is possible that it is that way. But there is an element which doesn't fit in this ideal picture, and it is the story of the wolf and the seven baby goats. There, there is "a grown-up" who is actually bad, who wants to eat the "little ones": and the littlest one saves itself because it manages to hide. I'd like you to notice that it manages to keep itself from being found by hiding in a very particular object: inside a long, slim, straight object and . . . "technological": the tower of the pendulum clock. It could have hidden inside or under something else, instead it went right there . . ."

P.: "It's true. I never thought about it."

And there, in the clock, ends our session, in fact: the 45th minute finds the patient pensive and perplexed, with an air of suspense.

Commentary

As you might imagine, this session opened up new prospects for the patient's treatment.

In the following sessions this material was analysed further, and it is still a work in progress. I report here in synthetic form the configurations that are emerging, and these will allow me to highlight the neurotic aspects found in a mixed psychopathological scenario, not serious in an absolute way, but which relate to the area of identity disturbance as well.

Roberta has avoided the Oedipus complex in part, with all her fantastic vicissitudes and drives, identifying herself with the paternal phallus (= hiding in the pendulum clock), and impersonating the phallic ideal of her childhood father (on the gymnastics/sports plane), of the current professional father (on the technical/institutional plane), of the internal father in her oneiric, timeless universe. And she would be inclined to do the same thing over again with me, in the neurosis of transference, with a convincing normotic adaptation in the "pendulum clock/militant analytical attitude".

This reproduces *ad infinitum* a problem of inauthenticity and of false self. (I think of the false self as a product of a projected identification with an incorporated or internalized—but not introjected—object).

The analytic work ahead of us seems long and complex.

On the one hand, we will have to find again, in analysis, the little baby goat hiding in the pendulum clock and allow it to come out despite the fear, and in so doing have it go back to its original self and face the relationship with the object: Roberta must re-encounter her own self, which is afraid and which was repressed/hidden in the clock.

This fear is the repressed "treasure" to be recovered.

The scene where the father brings the three-month-old infant to the hospital, with a fear of death (the bronchiolitis) "while Mother was out of the house", and the immediately following association—adjacent, in fact—with the fairytale about the wolf and the seven baby goats, create a permanent oneiric picture, at base, which asks to be revisited in analysis: it is as if the father/crib saves the daughter from a death that is tightly connected to the mother's absence and that, directly following and with the contiguous associations, an absent mother cannot save a daughter from a father/wolf who is too present, intrusive, and devouring.

This oneiric picture seems to condense *in a single, timeless scenario* the two distinct phases of a dramatic event: (1) the primary-object relationship infused with fear of death, with a splitting of the "present" object (the saviour father, to whom she "owes everything" in the sense of gratefulness for her survival) on the one hand and the "absent" object (the narcissistic mother) on the other hand; (2) the oedipal configuration with a father "to whom she owes everything" (this time in the sense, different and specific, of not succeeding in getting away from it) and a mother who "is out of the house" and who does not protect with her own presence.

If wolf, baby goat, and pendulum clock redefine themselves (and if the mother/mamma goat/analysis can in some way reappear at the door of the house/mind, with its containment functions first for the fear of death, and then for the para-excitation regarding the incestuous dimension), the outcome of the event might be able to be different.

One could object, as I suggested, that this clinical material has more to do with a disturbance of sexual identity than with neurosis in the strict sense: in the end, Roberta could seem, from the outside, like a woman who is experiencing a specific difficulty in self-representation and self-realization in her feminine/maternal aspects, and who tends to present a masculine self.

I believe that these formulas hyper-simplify a more complex reality and that the neurotic component of the patient is fundamental in this clinical case, even if it is joined to the use of defence mechanisms that have traditionally been considered to be of a more primitive level, like identification.

In particular, I think that the first experiences of death, and the following arousing oedipal vicissitudes, have, yes, found a "radical" solution in identifying with the father, in splitting the father-object, and in the choice of functional aspects of herself for an idealized "father–son" configuration; but the split and identification mechanism must have been taken on in the context of a basic attempt to repress her desire, fear, and guilt, which had been "by-passed" only in part to favour the other defence modalities.

The symptoms that brought Roberta to a neurologist are, in fact, the signal light of a strong effort to repress her feminine self; those symptoms were anxiety and fatigue, with a sense of loss of energy.

This brings us to a key point in this chapter. There is a characteristic *energy expenditure in repression*: the counterbalances needed to keep repressed conflict-generating content bring with them a high economic cost, of which tiredness is the symptom.

Patients who can make robust splits of internal parts of the self end up being simplified and impoverished in the self, as well as "lighter" (I say that they "travel without hand luggage"), relatively symptom-free, and perhaps inclined towards a maniacal drift; the neurotics, on the other hand, caught up in costly repression, are often "weighed down", tired, suffering.

Economically speaking, *the former lose "share of capital"* ("capital" meaning the internal world's patrimony, as a basic endowment of the self), releasing themselves from it and in a certain sense giving it up, given that in this way they avoid conflict.

The latter—the neurotics—do not lose capital, but they must meet very high costs in order to keep the repression working and to keep in the unconscious "safe box" the conflictual elements that would upset the arrangement of the "living room" of the self: exhausted by the energy costs, they have, as it were, dark circles under their eyes, exhaustion, and/or, in any case, neurotic symptoms.

As far as Roberta's other symptom, the "signal anxiety" (*Angstsignal*: Freud, 1926d [1925]), is concerned, we should remember how it works as an alarm system aimed at avoiding the trans-humanist experience of death/psychic disintegration: at the borders of the id, repressed contents exert pressure, in a conflictual way, so that they could modify the whole internal organization of the person, and precisely the risk of generalized crisis of self-image and personality organization is experienced subjectively as fear of death.

One could naturally object that the wolf evoked by Roberta, with its devouring manner, represents in a targeted way the patient's oral aggression and at the same time, along with it, the primary maternal object involved in a very archaic projection game, following a dyadic, pre-oedipal reading.

Without doing away with this component entirely, I feel that

I do not have to validate it very much: Roberta, beyond the specific "masculine/feminine" problem, has basic functioning that is sufficiently harmonious, authentically moderate, and respectful of reality.

She does not show typically oral aspects in a significantly accentuated way, such as urgency, summarizing one's possibilities with the "all or nothing" model, the tending towards panic buying, being caustic, or being confused; nor does she show reactive formations directed towards negating the existence of such traits.

She is generally a well-functioning person, esteemed and enjoyed by the people who interact with her.

Roberta's masculine identification is not primary.

There is an interesting complexity in my countertransference experience as well: if at first I often feel forced to do the unified couple bit with her, experiencing her as the "perfect son", subject to an attempt on her part to collocate me in the idealized paternal cliché, later, and in the ins and outs of the session, I notice that I am getting a glimpse of the young girl who is hiding in her, and who is scared.

To help Roberta get back in touch with her fear, I have to *deconstruct her stereotype of the father* too, which has been idealized and split, and I have to reintegrate it with the wolf-component. This is already happening in analysis, through the interpretative work on transference, which mobilizes desires and fears, directed at times to the analyst, her husband, and other figures in her memory or of the outside world; an interesting thing is the inevitable extension of this work to an understanding of Roberta's relationship with Prof. X, an area in which the patient starts to see things in a completely new way.

Prof. X is, by the way, truly a worthy professor, and all that he has taught (and will teach) Roberta is truly precious: that, if possible, must be saved.

The introjected partial identifications (Grinberg, 1976) are those that make one grow.

The total identifications (the little goat in the clock, Roberta-the-father-and professor's-"phallus") must be deconstructed—that is, taken down, taken apart by separating the elements that make them up and refurbishing them with different meanings and connections (Bolognini, 2002).

More specifically: will Roberta be able to become a mother and at the same time continue to be a good dentist, heir to specific paternal elements, well integrated into a feminine self? I don't know, but I dare to imagine a possible path there.

I believe we will, in the near future, have to *deconstruct Roberta's militancy without getting rid of competency*, taking apart the monolithic identifying phallus and separating the authentic (introjected) from the defensive (incorporative and projective).

In Prof. X's regards also, in any case, Roberta must go through an experience of recognizing her basic fears (the fear of "being nothing" in the institute and in her professional identity) and her desires, connected to the fantasy of being the professor's favourite student.

This way, perhaps, Roberta can with full due become a little bit of a "wolf girl".

Case 2: "Umberto": from hangdog to real hyena, and back as a puppy

My second case history takes us into an area where neurosis, psychosis, and perversion alternate in a seamless flow, shifting through different levels of functioning, in what is generally termed the "borderline". I wish at the same time to stress the neurotic component that forms part of the complex picture and whose dynamic and economic importance should also be considered. We will see that empathy, though by no means an intentional working tool, may arise in a complex interpsychic clinical situation; it as an unscheduled yet significant event, also in terms of psychoanalytic theory.

Umberto, a high school teacher in his fifties, is now well into his fifth year of analysis. Having started treatment because of generalized anxiety, he soon lifted the lid on a seething mass of perverse fantasies of seduction and violence concerning his pupils, usually the youngest and most defenceless girls.

Today is Tuesday, and there are only two sessions to go before the Christmas break. After 45 minutes of virtual silence in yesterday's session, the patient has a crazed air about him. I know the state he is in; it is typical of the period immediately before an interruption, and I will describe it shortly. Lately, however, Umberto has given the impression of being awkward, indecisive, shy, inconclusive, and inhibited. Hidden behind his thick lenses, he trips on the mat, makes verbal slips and omissions, and denies or quite obviously holds back his emotions, especially his aggression, resulting in a variety of obsessive symptoms.

Umberto often goes from this neurotic state to one of mental annulment, gazing into nothingness and appearing to communicate that "inside me there is nothing". When he does this, I think he is feigning ignorance, playing the "dead fish", cancelling his capacity for thought. He presents himself as a decerebrate or a pre-psychotic subject, with an inextricable mixture of hysterical exhibition of his supposed mental nullity and effective attachment to his thoughts. As I mentioned earlier, just before and just after this type of separation, a further change takes place: from out of the "brainless dreamer" peeps a perverse child who expounds horrifying sadistic intentions with a pretend angelic air.

We can therefore imagine the following sequence:

1. at the start of the session, there is Umberto the inhibited teacher, who is under stress, bears the symptoms, and sometimes reports his dreams;
2. after a while, he is replaced by a middle-aged man who is lost, demented, and incapable of thought;
3. out of this human larva springs a diabolical child, a-conflictual, fast and decisive in ideation, who plans to sequester, humiliate, and dominate a female slave (his mother, his female pupils, the analyst in the session, the object in his dreams), to vindicate his being abandoned in the past and omnipotently avoid the risk of future abandonment.

The first situation (Umberto the inhibited teacher) corresponds to a neurotic level of functioning, with massive repression, a considerable amount of energy required to maintain the repression, and the inevitable symptomatic consequences.

In the second situation (the demented middle-aged man), we may observe the equivalent of a psychotic mini-breakdown from which there emerges situation number three, the perverse "diabolical child", a solution based on splitting and role-reversal: a big, bad Umberto (the child is really an infantile disguise to remove responsibility) dominates and has his sadistic way with the powerless woman, but also with his own affective and dependent self, split and projected into her.

In the session I report here, Umberto, with a singular communicative capacity, appears to be on the threshold of situation number three.

He addresses me as if I were a superego to trick and tease provocatively.

The patient seems to be suggesting that it is not only his desire to seduce these pupils but he "really would like to do it, really act, and I'm telling you this and looking at you out of the corner of my eye to see whether you're going to say anything".

Umberto is excited these days by the voice of a weak and submissive 18-year-old girl, who has actually been a rape victim. He fantasizes inviting her to his house on a pretext to do with school work, giving her a drugged drink, tying her up, and abusing her.

As he talks, his teeth seem to turn into wolf-like fangs.

I experience discomfort as I listen to his fantasies and imagine the scene he describes. Umberto delegates to me completely the function of feeling grief for the suffering girl, thus enabling him to "travel light, without baggage" (as regards symptoms, dreams, and energy expenditure).

I want to underline again this main point: repression requires energy expenditure. The counter-loads needed to keep repressed the content that produce conflicts require a high economic cost, whose symptom is fatigue.

On the other hand, patients who can decisively split inner parts of themselves simplify and impoverish the self but are able to travel light (with, as we said before, "no baggage"); they are relatively symptom-free, though perhaps inclined to be maniacal. Neurotics, by contrast, are engaged in costly repression and are therefore weighed down, fatigued, and suffering.

In terms of psychic economy, the former lose part of their "capital" (i.e., the patrimony of their inner world, the basic equipment of the self), sacrificing part of it to avoid conflicts. The latter keep their capital but incur heavy expenses to cover the cost of repression and store in the cellar of the unconscious the conflictual elements that would disturb the "daytime zone" of the self. With such high costs, they have—so to speak—bags under their eyes and suffer from listlessness and/or neurotic symptoms.

I feel that Umberto functions by alternating between these modes. On the one hand, he seems to really believe in this solution—which is at the same time both sadistic and maniacal—to his anxieties about separation (he fantasizes about separating and imprisoning the object/girl) and inadequacy (he thinks of dominating her and holding her in his power). On the other hand, I know and feel that he does not function completely like this and that I must bear in mind that I am dealing with a complex interlocutor, in whom vertically split levels (Grotstein, 1981) exist side by side with various degrees of organization and cathexis, like real "characters" with their own intrinsic cohesion, who alternate on the scene.

According to my conception of empathy (Bolognini, 1997, 2002), I manage to make contact with him only when I can perceive and represent to myself sufficiently well the multiplicity and complexity of his internal structure.

This patient lives in a condition that fluctuates between neurotic, psychotic, and perverse modalities of psychic functioning. He is moderately and partially conflictual; he is not a "pure" pervert (if you will allow the expression). He has para-psychotic functional breakdowns but recovers very well and manages to take on attitudes that are genuinely mature, coherent, and well integrated as regards his thoughts and emotions, in moments of relative internal and relational well-being, even at an ethical level.

When I speak to him, I have to be careful to address his various functional levels, those that are manifest as well as those that are potential, because I am now used to discovering that *all these levels are listening, even when they do not seem to be.*

As on previous occasions, I encourage him to report his fantasies, which are in fact disturbing to listen to but which show me the extent of the original suffering of his self. Being split, he himself is not in contact with this suffering but identifies with the aggressor, projecting his sensitive self into the girl.

However, the "Umberto who identifies with the aggressor" is clearly consolidated and structured as an independent element, narcissistically cathected and coherent within the self, regardless of its defensive origins.

I reached this level of understanding only after a long period of time and a great deal of work with the patient.

At the beginning, I felt only horror and indignation, having lost contact with his healthy parts in the same way as he had (defensive transference from the patient to the analyst, as Anna Freud wrote in 1936), sharing the splitting (Bolognini, 1998, 2002). Now, after years of personal acquaintance and psychic contact, I can tolerate the sadist in him in order to foster that inner contact.

Analysis can now penetrate deeper because the patient spontaneously associates the memory of a highly significant film: *The Hairdresser's Husband*, by Patrice Leconte. It is the patient's wish to set up and maintain a fusional symbiosis with a maternal equivalent, just like in the film. When the sessions are interrupted by a longer break such as the holidays, Umberto first becomes confused and withdraws psychotically; then, without realizing it, he "breaks up", splits, and becomes maniacal, turning psychically into a monster.

In the film, the heroine played by Anna Galiena commits suicide to escape the gilded cage of symbiosis. This seems to represent both the desire and the refutation of this through the work of reality. The patient's associations with the film indicate that considerable representational work is under way, and I feel I can say this to the patient: "*I know I am talking to two Umbertos. One is sorrowfully aware of his separation anxieties (from the mother, in the past and now from the analyst) and inadequacy. The other Umberto deludes himself and contents himself with a sadistic solution, which makes him feel extremely powerful. I respect the former, but I have to say that the latter deludes himself in vain because the continuous union he desires is impossible, even if he sequesters the girl student. Above all, I believe that it cannot have escaped your attention that this idea takes shape around the same time as the break in sessions, and therefore our separation.*"

There is silence, a pause for thought, a feeling that the message has reached its destination in the patient's inner world, and an impression of work in progress. Slowly and with effort, the patient comes to himself.

The sadist does not completely disappear; it does not "die", but understanding the mechanism strips it of its narcissistic prestige and it no longer dominates. Through clenched teeth, Umberto is placed in contact with his own suffering.

We have been along this path before, and the promising thing about it is that each time the return trip takes less (the time for re-integration). In this case, pointing out the splitting to the patient did not entail strengthening the splitting. The problem is more that of addressing the patient's ego when the message is capable of being received.

The specific association with that particular film showed me that Umberto's mind was beginning to represent something of the way it worked and therefore could begin to contain a sorrowful element, since the film, while showing an idyllic fusionality, ended in tragedy.

I particularly want to stress how it was possible for Umberto to gain access gradually through analysis to the representation and working through of his ways of functioning in a more unified manner.

There is a hyena inside him, and Umberto the neurotic inhibited teacher should not be spared the recognition of this fact. This hyena has a forerunner in "little Umberto" annihilated by abandonment and infirmity, and this original aspect is to be recognized and recovered in the course of our work.

It is worth noting that, in such cases, we should not limit ourselves to the concept of ambivalence to save the unified nature of the subject. The subject is not unitary in time or structure, not even in the partially resigned (i.e., in a Kleinian sense, depressively accepting a painful reality) and relative meaning we analysts give to the concept.

Repression keeps him periodically in the dark as to the volcano seething within him. In the phases in which neurotic modes predominate, the repression of his anxieties and his disruptive and resentful aggression turn him into something like a pet dog, kept on a chain not so much by a persecutory superego ("what would they do to me if they found me out?") or a reparative–depressive attitude ("how much suffering I've caused!"), as by an ideal social superego ("how terrible I would feel if they tumbled to me!").

The successive transitory psychotic disorganization reduces him, *en passant*, to the condition of a sub-confusional larva, anaesthetized and with all responsibility removed.

When repression ceases, the splitting and projection into the other of his own fragile and needy self allow the emergence of "the hyena", full of vindictive hate, determined sadistically to restore the narcissism and omnipotence by dominating the object. Undoubtedly, the hyena is the result of a series of splittings of a psychotic nature. The patient's subsequent hiding of them and his attempt to deny their nature by dressing them up with bows and ribbons like a poodle are all neurotic devices.

The analytic work aims to place the patient in contact again with his own suffering (by gradually deactivating perverse defences), with his memory (by deactivating neurotic defences), and with his thoughts (by deactivating psychotic defences). Repression, splitting, and projection are organized to alternate and operate effectively within the patient. The analyst must point out to the patient that the alternation of these elements is by no means random. In order to do this, *the analyst must be to some extent "inside" the experience.*

Moreover, I am also rather struck by a certain "naturalness" in my analytic work with Umberto. Our mental "cohabitation" brings about a growing experiential knowledge, which enables me to take account of the variety of different defences, especially when I decide on a way of intervening. Interventions should be specifically targeted and without simplifications. Once the rapid and episodic larval phase has passed, the patient seems to take the form not so much of a hyena as a puppy. I represent all this to myself conceptually, but I know and feel it through our shared experience.

To recapitulate

1. Repression produces serious and perceptible symptomatic consequences (anxiety, stress, phobias, obsessions, etc.) as well as the presence of a tendency to produce dreams that represent the conflicting elements. The patrimony of the self is not detached and projected away.

Roberta, who in analysis is exposed to the neurosis of transference at work, pulls out again in *my* regard the same defensive splits she used for her father.

But she cannot escape from perceiving, with anxiety, internal developments and fantasies that are related to her feminine side's repressed desire. She lives with the fatigue and economic expense of the conflict (which she cannot consistently substitute with masculine identification any more), and she produces dreams like the one cited.

In my lingo, she "travels with her stuff" (symptomologic, oneiric, economic) "in her handbag", in a regime of ever-more precarious repression in the dynamic unconscious, and the self's patrimony is not projected far into the cosmos nor is it even detached.

Umberto, in the first phase, is the inhibited teacher who is under stress, bears the symptoms, and sometimes reports his dreams.

2. When serious vertical splitting comes into play (amounting to dissociation, in the psychoanalytic not the phenomenological sense), it "compartmentalises the experience" (Gabbard, 1994).

The mental functions and contents tend to arrange themselves in a series of parallel "conscious-es", like Umberto the hyena, fast to idealize and diabolically a-conflictual. In this split state, the subject has given up the "burden" of part of the self, rather in the manner of a lizard losing its tail so that it can run to safety more quickly.

A patient in this compartmentalized and impoverished state tends to show no symptoms and feels no stress or fatigue because he avoids expenditure of energy on conflict and projectively delegates onto the other the responsibility for feeling the inner parts of the self and, if possible, their representation.

Patients in such a condition often appear simplified and tend to dream less. As Bion (1959) theorized, they use projective identification rather than repression—which the unconscious would create—and the pieces of the self and the objects find themselves situated, in a hallucinatory way, in the outside world, rather than represented in dreams.

The analyst's countertransference experience, therefore, feels the alternation and predominance of the use of repression and/or splitting by the patient, and this may or may not develop into empathy.

Thus, Umberto, the inhibited teacher, with his stress, his slips, and his neurotic symptoms, aroused in me a sense of inevitable suspension and anticipation, faced with a subjectivity that was repressed, unexpressed, and at least partially disguised and false.

Later, this patient led me to experience violent feelings of sorrow, anxiety, pity, anger, and indignation, evacuated onto me during the phases in which, as a "diabolical child", he split from his own affects, from his sensitive self, which he projected into me, as his superego.

But at other times, when this person was reintegrated, I naturally had an instinctive feeling of sharing and respect towards his suffering. My listening to the sources of that suffering was accompanied by a spontaneous interest that grew up within me and did not merely follow the dictates of analytic technique.

I would not have been able to understand and treat this patient, even to the limited extent I did, if I had rushed to "empathize" with a pre-selected level of his mental life or with a privileged inner configuration, or if I had not mentally cohabited with him for a lengthy period, sharing many experiences but also keeping a sense of separateness and internal structure, and if I had not received during training the complex instruments for perceiving, recognizing, and representing to myself, for example, the alternation of neurotic, psychotic, and relatively healthy levels in their particular way of being and functioning.

At this point, I feel I can state that psychoanalytic empathy is—at the very least—a great deal more complex than the abstractions formulated by many thinkers would have us believe.

Conclusion

If the pioneers of psychoanalysis feared the interference of the analyst's emotions with the proper development of the therapeutic process in a systematic way (a realistic assumption, since they were treading on the unsure and unknown ground of a new skill), after a century of scientific learning and reflection we are able to operate more freely and with less defensive recourse to emotional isolation or split emotivity. *This is due precisely to the fact that we are more aware of the complexities of an analytic relationship and of our internal make up.*

This may also appear to be a paradox to laymen. And yet caution, more understanding, and respect for its complexity can lead to a more confident degree of comprehension, in which emotions are both a means to explore and an essential part of the general picture.

Essentially, we must not disregard emotions, nor credit them as having an all-embracing magical function.

5

The splitting of the ego and virtual reality

Julio Moreno

1

It is advisable to discuss first the concepts of *splitting of the ego* and *virtual reality* separately, for besides having been coined in dissimilar contexts, they refer to different phenomena. I will then ponder their relationship.

The "splitting of the ego" is a notion that appears late in Freud's theory. He himself admits in his 1938 posthumous text that this late incorporation into his theory may have been a mistake. "The whole process [of splitting and disavowal] seems so strange to us because we *take for granted* the synthetic nature of the processes of the ego. But *we are clearly at fault* in this. The synthetic function of the ego, though it is of such extraordinary importance, is subject to particular conditions and is liable to a whole number of disturbances" (Freud, 1940e [1938], p. 276; emphasis added).

As I understand it, "being at fault" may refer here to the fact that in the inceptions of his theory, Freud defended somewhat fervently the idea of the oneness of the ego against those who spoke of its multiplicity. At the turn of the nineteenth century, studies in psychopathology (e.g., those by Janet, Binet, and Breuer himself) were permeated by terms such as "split personality", "double consciousness", and "separate psychical groups". According to Janet, for instance, the splitting of the psyche into different associative groups is conceived of as a secondary regrouping of a psychic world that has disintegrated due to a primary associative weakness (Laplanche & Pontalis, 1967).

Against this "associative weakness", Freud wagered an ego endowed with an associative strength that rendered it undivided and the bearer of remarkable synthetic ability. Consequently, in the face of possible inconsistencies originating in disturbing irruptions of the drive world or of the external world, Freud envisioned an ego that appeared consistent thanks to its "defences". This idea became a sort of pillar of his early theoretical developments.

"Reality", as conceived of by the ego, was produced through a consistent and solid cluster of representations—the ego's representational set. If conflict emerged, it was caused by the intrusion, due to the return of the repressed, of an unconscious element or of a portion of the unrepresented "external reality" that the ego had simply expelled, as it occurred in psychosis.

The world of the ego was thus, in a way, "closed" to the external world. This does not mean that it was not affected by what occurred "outside", or by the emergence of the drives. Rather, if "the thing" disturbed the associative logic that articulated ego representations, these quickly closed ranks so that no radical difference might disorganize the homogeneous representational set.

These ideas were influenced by the fact that, as I already mentioned, Freud's conception of hysteria was born in opposition to those theories that saw the splitting of the ego as the cause of this illness. By contesting such a view, Freud was developing—somewhat imperceptibly—a theory of an ego that was basically consistent, possessed of synthetic ability, and devoid of contradictions. If these eventually emerged (due either to the perception of "something" disturbing in the environment or to the return of the repressed), *conflict* developed. The two warring factions were *articulated* by a defence—something very different from splitting. In the face of conflict, the ego could generate a symptom that would render this conflict manifest and somehow suture its disturbing effect.

2

Freudian theory (at least in the first topic) grew stronger by considering one and only one splitting—the one taking place between consciousness and the unconscious due to primal repression.

"Belatedly", as he himself says, Freud acknowledged that the ego is able to avoid the impact of an unpleasant or horrifying perception by generating a remarkable situation—by *splitting* into two parts that neither influence each other nor create mixed formations. He developed these ideas based on three notions—fetishism, disavowal, and the splitting of the ego. For instance, in fetishism (1927e) the defensive process does not lead to the formation of a compromise between present attitudes. Rather, opposite views are simultaneously upheld without the development of a dialectic relation between them. That is why fetishists do not perceive fetishism as a symptom or an abnormality. The sense and purpose of the fetish Freud describes in this essay is always one and the same: substituting for the woman's penis that children once believed existed. Fetishists refuse to abandon their belief because recognizing the lack entails the possibility of castration. Children thus maintain the belief that women have phalluses, but at the same time—and this is what is novel and strange—they have abandoned it.

Freudian terminology already included a word for making a representation or affect disappear from consciousness—"repression" [*Verdrängung*]. Now, however, Freud wants to differentiate it from "disavowal" [*Verleugnung*]. After the disavowal of a perception, its traces do not disappear entirely. They persist, and a great effort is necessary to keep them dissociated.

Since his work on fetishism, Freud seems to have become open to the idea that the splitting of the ego is another possible recourse to face a horrifying event. It seems that the cause of horror ceases to be *necessarily* the maternal lack of a penis, especially after 1927. For instance, he mentions the case of two children who had lost their father at 2 and 10 years of age. Despite having "scotomized" their loss, neither became psychotic. One trend of their mind, Freud says, did not acknowledge the father's death, while the other one did, and both were present "side by side" in the ego. We are left with the impression that had it not appeared so near the end of his oeuvre, Freud would have followed this line of thought, thus rendering his theory more complex.

Freud's tendency to incorporate splitting to the psychopathological complex of his theory becomes more evident in his essay *An Outline of Psycho-Analysis* (1940a [1938]). He states there that even "in some corner of their [the psychotics'] mind (as they put it) there was a normal person hidden, who, like a detached spectator, watched the hubbub of illness go past him" (p. 202). In all these cases, he states, two *psychic attitudes* have been constituted. The normal one takes reality into account; the other one, under the influence of the drives, separates the ego from reality in a *psychic split.*

This series of occurrences of the concept of splitting culminates in Freud's posthumous work, "Splitting of the Ego in the Process of Defence" (1940e [1938]). Let us imagine, says Freud, that a child is under the influence of a powerful drive demand that he is used to satisfy, and he is suddenly frightened by a severe and real threat that will be realized if he continues to find satisfaction in the same way. The child thus faces the alternative of either acknowledging this danger and abandoning satisfaction, or disavowing reality and convincing himself that there is no reason to fear this danger. In this way, he will be able to continue to satisfy himself. The child, however, can choose either to take neither of these paths or to take both simultaneously. On the one hand, he rejects reality and does not accept prohibition; on the other, he acknowledges the threat, treats it as a pathological symptom, and tries to rid himself of his fear. Yet this behaviour has a price—a crack in the ego that will never heal and will tend to reopen over time.

Freud is already speaking here of two independent logics; two simultaneous paths that, like those of Borges' *The Garden of Forking Paths* (1941), do not interfere or interact with each other. To follow this novel logic, it is true, we should abandon at least in part the central idea of the dialectics of conflict, based on confrontations that lead to the constitution of intermediary formations, so typical of associative processes and so dear to psychoanalysis.

3

We should examine the concept of virtual reality (VR) within a new conception of the world—so-called postmodernity, or, as

Bauman (2000) and Lewkowicz (2004) have designated it, *liquid modernity*. The latter label seems to me particularly fortunate because it equates the difference between two types of modernity with the difference between two states of matter—liquid and solid.

Medieval *premodernity* believed that the given world already possessed everything it ought to have, and therefore nothing must change. Conversely, the typical and recurrent feature of *modernity* has been the dissolution of the established order. Being modern means not being able to stop, being always in search of a new design that is critical of the existing one. In this sense, the West has been modern for the past five centuries. Yet in the last forty years things have dramatically transformed—the pace of change has accelerated, and both this acceleration and its consequences keep escalating in an astonishing way.

During solid modernity—when psychoanalysis was created—we might have believed that established knowledge would allow us to banish the disturbing presence of the contingency of fluidity, connectivity, and inconsistency. This view, however, has become increasingly hard to uphold. Institutions simply do not guarantee it. The prevalence of phenomena tied to VR and liquidity renders *logos* and the fanatical rationality that supported the reign of solidity (and the creation of psychoanalysis) difficult to sustain.

Social changes are always tied to changes in the means of communication that accompany them. We have thus witnessed the rapid expansion of instant messaging (e.g., "chat"), a computer application that through an Internet connection enables written and simultaneous communication between an increasing number of users. In this way, the notion of the essential disjunction between one—as a solipsistic island—and the world is disappearing. By means of *Web 2.0*, intercommunication is propagating through novel and accessible "social networks".

It is not surprising, perhaps, that Freud's first theory, which posited a homogeneous ego, would have been conceived during the height of solid modernity, when compared to our experience today, events were quite predictable. This was a solid ego with no heterogeneous sides. It faced confirmable realities that were relatively unchanging and consistent.

Let me compare now the relationship between the consistent and unified early Freudian ego and the ego that suffers the impact of VR, on the one hand, and, on the other, the similar relationship between classical movies and present-day post-film and clips—a contrast between two modes of processing information originated on a screen. Until recently, filmic images followed one another to manage the duration of the movie. Films demanded that its sequences be recognized and respected. Each sequence must last long enough to close a meaning that was not immediately exhausted, but could always be recovered later and understood in its totality throughout the film. Classical film was slow. Its narrative matter developed in an extended chronological time. Consequently, movies (like the ego we have been discussing) constituted a closed and hegemonic totality within which articulated sequences formed "the plot".

As Beatriz Sarlo (2000) points out, things are very different in post-film and clips. Chronological time has ceased to be a key element. The clip is not interested in the duration of the sequences but in their accumulation. As though obeying a command by the discourse of immediacy, these must be extremely short. We are dealing here with a high-impact discourse, founded on the speed with which an image replaces a previous one that it must supersede. Image 1 must be erased by Image 2, which will vanish when 3 appears, and so on and so forth.

The art of clips and of advertising shorts demands that the previous images weaken, superimpose, and be compressed to leave room for the following ones. In other words, this is an example of the obsoleteness required by a liquid medium to give rise to what must inevitably come.[1]

4

We know today that modern aspirations for the total mastery of our world and of our animality were but an illusion. Nonetheless, the technological transformation that gave rise to the utopia of the mastery of the real object has succeeded in generating *realities* with no materiality, where the observed object is pure artefact. These are simulacra capable of blurring the differences between subject and object and of altering the space we inhabit. They are known by the contradictory name of *virtual reality* and escape the classic separation between science and fiction, objectivity and subjectivity, truth and illusion. VR is beyond such categorizations because its images *are* what they represent.

Ultimate reason, the minimal unity of the essential heterogeneity between reality and the real, is the radical disjunction between representation and what is represented. If this space collapsed and enabled us to capture the real—or if virtuality drew the perfect contour of demand—we would melt in a motionless incandescence. By contrast, if this space expanded to the extent that the real did not affect us and we remained immune to inconsistencies, we would be like robots with a flat history.

Humans, instead, are marked by the imperfection with which we grasp the world around us. Each of our steps leaves a trace that irreversibly directs our future.

"Reality" is determined by the consistency between perception and representation—that is, by the ego's expectations regarding "how things ought to be". To date we are not equipped to come into contact with the world without the mediation of the sign, of representation, and of expectations. The instantaneous, what the sign does not mediate, the radically and brutally novel is not just inaccessible to us; it could unhinge us. In any case, VR aims to have us rid ourselves of the associative journey and to attain the prevalence of what I have called elsewhere a connectivity dominated by a logic different from associative logic—the logic of the instant (Moreno, 2002).

I wish to stress here the lability of this essential hiatus that joins and separates representation from the represented. Through this half-open window between reality and the real, chaos may intrude to some extent in our ordered, predictable, and illusory conception of the world. If this intrusion is minimal, it may enable us to make contact with radical novelty. Perhaps it is no coincidence that precisely this gap houses the technological simulacrum capable of virtually generating realities, namely, VR. The name *virtual reality*, which came to life in 1989, bears a wide range of meanings and evokes topics linked to simulation, hyper-reality, the effects of information technology and postmodernism (such as the presence of multiple realities), and those of collective thinking, brought to the fore by Web 2.0.

As we have seen, the sealing of the space between representation and the represented effected by VR does not happen through the symbolic capture of the real, as it did in the modern dream. Rather, it occurs through a *simulacrum* that consists in the creation of a "reality" that is neither real nor unreal: virtual reality. Its images do not represent; they *are*. What I would like to emphasize here is that *one* virtual reality does not exclude a simultaneous connection with others. In the same way, one TV channel or one Internet "site" does not interfere with the simultaneous presence and connection of the hundreds, thousands, or millions that swarm around everywhere and nowhere. VR has this potential of presenting and offering itself for surfing and for the assured subjectification of everyone, without interfering with other "realities". One may thus be, in a way, many. The ego faces a manifold reality, and multiplicity prevails.[2] That is one of the reasons why VR usually arouses concern. Its success might imply the disappearance of frustration and the collapse of the space between representation and the represented—the driving forces of mental development as we know it.

An urgent question must be asked regarding the effects of VR on our culture: Is it an impasse of human growth, a lethal attack on creativity, a sort of desubjectification? Or are we facing the appearance of a new form of creativity, subjectivity, and growth? Are we experiencing a return to our simian past, as Jean Baudrillard (1995) seems to think? Or is it that our mind is expanding, as Andy Clark (2000) suggests when he claims that "human cognition . . . flows both within and beyond the head" (p. 4)? Does the new information technology aim to alter our reality and our contact with our natural environment and destroy the cultural tenets that history has bequeathed us since the Greeks? Or are we facing *a different* reality to which we did not even have access in the past because we lacked the right technological tools?

We should neither rush, nor fall into, an unscrupulous technophilia or a negating technophobia. Perhaps we are not in a position to assess the costs and benefits of these transformations. As they say, changes associated to the current technological revolution are just starting, and in the first stages of a process it is not easy to differentiate between a transforming event and an imminent catastrophe. Perhaps the 2050 world will not find the production of subjective meaning as useful as it is for present-day psychoanalysis or art. Perhaps by that time humanity will have abandoned the modern ideal of "being one". Ways of being, subjectivity, and the ego may be linked more closely to *multiplicity*. Perhaps soon all human endeavours will be affected in the same way as the production fields more influenced by technology, which avoid what has become known as the *human factor*. Solid modernity praised and valued the human factor, but all the efforts of current technology are aimed to eliminate it.

What is more, two fundamental features of the Web 2.0—a new trend in network applications that appeared around 2004—speak clearly of the dramatic contrast between modern productions (even those of the most imitated modern heroes) and the creations of present-day computer reality. First, the growth, effectiveness, and improvement of the latter's products are increasingly and homogeneously dependent on the number of participants summoned by the novel *social networks* (as happens, for instance, in wikis, blogs, and so on). Second, a sort of requirement inherent to computer productions since their creation is their *obsoleteness*.

We may be witnessing the end of an era, which naturally renders apocalyptic the view of the subjects who grew up in it. Times of crisis such as ours may be followed by catastrophes, it is true. Yet radical novelties may ensue whose emergence, as we know, always disturbs the established order. Be that as it may, our efforts should be directed to attempt to anticipate the reality we are living as best we can. Even though it may seem to be hostile, this reality may be beneficial in the long run. We should be enlightened here by Wittgenstein's words: "The world is what happens, and the worst would be to consider that what is happening is a mistake" (1953).

In 2004, Prensky established an appealing division between media users—namely, *digital natives* (born into this technology) and *digital immigrants* (those who, without being natives, have approached it). I would add a third category: the *digital illiterate*. The three groups coexist today in superimposed worlds. For natives, power lies in sharing knowledge, and they do not care about understanding, associating, or synthesizing the various ways of being with reality. Immigrants, by contrast, still believe that power lies in knowledge, and that associative syntheses are necessary; while illiterates remain stunned by what is taking place.

5

The media claim that in these times individuals are responsible for being what they are. No longer are there "given" pigeonholes to inhabit or occupy. It seems, therefore, that it is each person's task to "be" what he or she is. Instability prevails, as well as a feeling of omnipotentiality that forces men and women to be in constant motion, with no promise of completion. In a way, identity (including gender identity) is conceived as the individual's creation. It is the outcome of playing the character one is or—what seems to be the same thing—the character one intends to be. In the virtual world of the web site *Second Life*, for example, this is the main thing.

From the time they are born, children must prepare themselves to face an always uncertain, liquid, novel, and changing future with means that already promise to be obsolete.[3] In this context, an ego with multiple sides, which we might even call a "split ego", may be not only a way to disavow painful realities, but also a way to survive in the context of a liquid environment.

There is also news regarding the normal–abnormal dichotomy that used to dominate the question of sexuality, identity, and subjectivity (in the sense of "way of being"). The norm has neither been abolished nor become unnecessary—heterosexuals, formerly "normal", may continue to be so and consider themselves normal if they so wish. It is just that other loci have been created, other pigeonholes, so that there are many norms—many "normal" forms.[4] Each new locus bears a norm that coexists with the rest. Yet the phrase "many norms" itself entails a contradiction. Moreover, there is nothing to prevent us from *simultaneously* abiding by different norms.

Just as in modern children the tendency to *symptoms* and *neurosis* prevailed, so in present-day children (and probably also in adults) an incipient but powerful tendency to *splitting* appears. Such splitting may occur between the manifold realities that the media and society provide and/or in the face of difficult situations or horrifying presentations, as Freud had explained.

Yet in addition, individuality—the solitary and progressive figure of the hero of modernity's biographical productions—vanishes today in a blend of anonymous authors and readers who operate collectively in the time of the instant. This can be appreciated in blogs, photologs, wikis, YouTube, MySpace, Facebook, or—outside the worldwide web—in the popular and expanded invasion of graffiti.

Moreover, faced with setbacks and conflict, present-day children and adults increasingly resort to splitting instead of repression, and to acting rather than representing. In the same way, in film and television there is a preference for flashes of instantaneous and alternating presentations where the second one deletes the traces of the first, instead of linear and linked narratives where what follows complements or completes the meaning of what came before.[5]

A new idea that is spreading is that of *collective intelligence,* which appears in full force in the so-called *Planet Web 2.0* (Cobo Romaní & Pardo Kuklinski, 2007) in the guise of *fast-food media.* This notion has developed in a remarkable way, and it is mentioned in eloquent and diverse concepts and publications. Some examples are *intercreativity,* suggested by Berners-Lee (1999, 2005); *collective intelligence,* by Lévy (1997); *smart mobs,* by Rheingold (2002); or the *wisdom of crowds,* by Surowiecki (2004). It would be a mistake to believe that this trend is due only to the emergence of a new technology. Cobo Romaní and Pardo Kuklinski (2007) claim that Web 2.0 is, above all, *an attitude* that favours social networks. Solid and homogeneous structures—such as the pre-splitting Freudian ego—with no cracks or sides may become an obstacle to face the world we inhabit.

All this leaves us with more expectations and questions than certainties. It remains to be seen, of course—and this is one of the questions that intrigue me and that I would like to see answered—what is the connection between these modalities imposed by the discourse that regulates our interactions, and contemporary psychopathology. If this connection exists, how do this discourse and psychopathology modify each other?

Does the splitting of the ego suggested by Freud in 1927 as a form of defence against horrifying presentations of "reality" interact with the manifold sides imposed today by VR discourse, or is it rendered somehow more complex by them?

Even if we maintained the differentiation among neurosis, perversion, and psychosis with which we have worked so far, perhaps we should try to understand how they are influenced by phenomena linked to multiple realities, instantaneousness, and VR. Personally (I emphasize "personally" here so as to put it in perspective),

I think that we should revise classic psychoanalytic postulations (starting maybe with Freud's) on the basis of these new "realities". Even though they may be somewhat Manichean or sensationalist, they certainly "bite" deeply into the reality we chance to live, because they necessarily have an effect on the ego.

Notes

1. Beatriz Sarlo (2000) states that "spectators can gradually erase images with their eyelids as though with windshield wipers, because they know that the icon remains, ensuring the illusion of the continuity that has been infinitely fragmented by the syntax of the clip".

2. VR thus forces us to face a crucial question: Might the representation of an object subsume the effects of its presentation? This question is consequent with the following ones: *Is there anything of the object (in the sense of "entity") and of its effects on us that cannot be subsumed in the information it contains? Or, Is "existence" equivalent to "information"? Or, Can the atom be reduced to the bit?*

3. Obsoleteness is part of novel presentations. We are dealing here with "for now" instead of "forever".

4. As to sexual identity, one can be a normal heterosexual, gay person, transsexual, transvestite, bisexual, metrosexual, and so on.

5. This discursive mode alters our "ability to pay attention" to the monotonous, linear, and chronological narratives that organized classical pedagogy and may be linked to the prevalence of so-called attention deficit disorders (ADD and ADHD).

6

The "splitting/trauma" pairing: Ferenczi and the concept of trauma

Thierry Bokanowski

> If, in the analytic situation, the patient feels hurt, disappointed or left in the lurch, he sometimes begins to play by himself like a lonely child. One definitely gets the impression that to be left deserted results in a split of personality. Part of the person adopts the role of father or mother in relation to the rest, thereby undoing, as it were, the fact of being left deserted. In this play . . . we get glimpses into the processes of what I have called the "narcissistic split of the self" in the mental sphere itself.
>
> Ferenczi (1931), pp. 475–476

Sándor Ferenczi [1873–1933] contributed many ideas that have had a remarkable impact on the construction of the psychoanalytic *corpus*, none more so than those he put forward concerning his exploration of the metapsychology of trauma and went on to develop gradually between 1927 and 1933. These were not only ahead of their time; they remain, to this day, remarkably modern in outlook. The hypotheses he suggested—mainly concerning a re-formulation of the concept of traumatic seduction that had been a feature of Freud's work from the very outset—made it possible to specify both the clinical nature of trauma and its structural effects on the mind when splitting (and in particular what he calls in the above extract the "narcissistic splitting of the self") becomes the principal means of defence.

Ferenczi's suggestions, which amounted to a watershed in psychoanalytic thinking, meant that he was one of the first practitioners to try to account for the theoretical and practical issues that psychoanalysts who treat "complex" cases such as, for example, borderline or non-neurotic patients come up against in their daily work.

As we know, the answers, both technical and metapsychological, that Ferenczi proposed stirred up a painful conflict—indeed, given some of his theoretical and practical conceptions, a significant difference of opinion—between him and Freud (Bokanowski, 1996). As their relationship unfolded between 1909 and 1933, Ferenczi, of course, had been, in turn, Freud's promising pupil, his most faithful follower, his friend, and then his confidant.

It should, all the same, be pointed out that the ideas that Ferenczi put forward seem to have had a significant impact on those that Freud was later to express in his *Moses and Monotheism* (1939a [1937–39]). In the chapter of that book entitled "The Analogy", Freud re-states his conceptions as regards trauma and goes on to develop many of them in ways that were first suggested by Ferenczi.

Therefore, in order to assess the importance of Ferenczi's contribution—and to determine the impact it has had on certain approaches in modern psychoanalytic practice—it is necessary to summarize the history of how the concept of traumatism developed in Freud's work up to the point where Ferenczi put his own ideas forward.

A short summary of Freud's views

Psychoanalysis grew out of the seduction theory, which, in its initial stages, equated seduction with a sexual traumatism brought about by an external object. For Freud, from the very beginnings of the psychoanalytic *corpus* (between 1890 and 1897), the aetiology of his patients' neuroses involved past traumatic experiences. In his view, traumatism was what above all characterized the patient's personal experience: that external event, identifiable and dateable, becomes subjectively fundamental because of the distressing affects that it stirs up. Its dating can be pushed further back in time as the work of exploration (anamnesis) and analytic intervention (interpretation) digs deeper. From that point on, the concept of traumatism and the idea of the traumatic event were to be a hallmark of Freud's work: they became one of the distinguishing features that ran all the way through his theorizing—in his *Moses*, as I have said, he devoted a chapter to putting forward an overall view of the question.

Nonetheless, the conception of traumatism that Freud developed in the early stages of his work, in *Studies on Hysteria* (Freud, 1895d), is significantly different from that of his *Moses*—in its nature, quality, and general approach to mental functioning. In the initial phase, trauma was essentially thought to be sexual and was therefore closely bound up with the seduction theory (with its relationship to reality and/or fantasy); after what we nowadays call the "turning-point of the 1920s" (i.e., from *Beyond the Pleasure Principle* on: Freud, 1920g), traumatism in Freud's structural theory of the mind became the emblematic (metaphorical) concept of the economic aporias of the psychic apparatus: a traumatism is a "breaking-through of the protective shield against stimuli" (Freud, 1920g, pp. 27ff.).

Hilflosigkeit—the infant's helplessness—is thus the paradigm for situations in which anxiety becomes overwhelming, in circumstances where signal anxiety is insufficient to enable the ego to protect itself from a massive breach of this kind, whether it be of internal or external origin. At that point, *traumatic* and *trauma* are notions that go hand in hand with traumatism in its more general sense (Bokanowski, 2005).

A little later, starting with *Inhibitions, Symptoms and Anxiety* (Freud, 1926d [1925]), Freud's new theory of anxiety emphasized the link between traumatism and loss of the object. It is plain to see that, in the space of a few decades, a considerable number of developments (mainly from the economic point of view) concerning the metapsychology of the concept of traumatism were introduced by Freud himself, developments that greatly extended that particular theoretical domain.

The concept of trauma in Ferenczi's work: the "splitting/trauma" pairing

It was while this major reshaping of the concept of traumatism was being undertaken that Ferenczi, from 1927 on, began adding his own ideas—developments that would later lay the groundwork for certain ways of thinking about psychoanalysis.

Following the "turning-point of the 1920s", Ferenczi, like Freud, came to acknowledge the daemonic character of the *compulsion to repeat*: a stumbling-block both for the theory and practice of psychoanalysis, many analyses became bogged down or even failed completely because of it, one famous example being that of the "Wolf Man" (Freud, 1918b [1914]).

Faced with the clinical consequences of that process, and unable to avoid the transference implications that led to all sorts of therapeutic deadlock (stagnation, gridlock, negative therapeutic reaction, interminable analyses, etc), psychoanalysts inevitably had to ask themselves a number of questions: What can we do to resolve these issues? What concrete steps can we take to counter that process, if at all possible? Is there some way of avoiding it?

In an attempt to go beyond these questions, Ferenczi introduced some technical innovations that, in modifying the setting,[1] actually put it "on trial" (Cahn, 1983). He proposed to interpret the pernicious effects of the compulsion to repeat—at the root of rebellious and passionate transference situations—as pure repetition, in other words as amounting to a reproduction of the childhood trauma.

For Ferenczi, the metapsychological complexity of traumatic situations was not simply a matter of traumatisms linked to the sexual or fantasy-related "seduction" of a child; it was the outcome of a trauma that had occurred early in infancy, and in some cases before the acquisition of speech. The origin of a trauma would thus seem to be linked to certain manifestations of libidinal destiny, the excessive and violent actions of which were experienced by the person concerned as equivalent to those of premature sexual excitation.

Ferenczi then went on to broaden the theory of seduction as envisaged at that point by Freud, and in so doing he took a major step forward: he considered traumatic aetiology to be the outcome of a *psychic rape* of the infant, due to the denial or invalidation of the child's affects or thoughts by the adult involved or to the fact that the adult's language was that of passion while the child's was one of tenderness (*confusion of tongues*). This resulted in the creation of a narcissistic trauma that gave rise to splitting ("self-splitting" is the term Ferenczi, 1949, uses) in the narcissistic part of the self: a "narcissistic splitting of the self" with the ego being completely paralysed, and mental life itself being asphyxiated—the death throes of the mind. These are states of extreme pain and despair.

This meant that, for Ferenczi, trauma was a consequence of the absence (or of repeated absences) of adequate responses by the object to situations of distress. This kind of absence mutilated the ego for good and prolonged psychic suffering because of the internalization of a defective primary object—hence the feelings of primary distress that are reactivated all through life whenever circumstances lend themselves to such a revival.

In addition to the fact that the infant's narcissism and developmental potential are severely damaged, violent recourse to defence mechanisms such as projection and splitting may become so ingrained that the whole organization of drive-related economy will be seriously disrupted, as will the capacity for symbol formation.

In putting forward these ideas, Ferenczi was attempting to highlight the fact that the very nature of traumatism had to be looked at and understood in a completely different manner insofar as it called into question the quality of the object's response in distressful situations. The analyst's response in the course of an analysis also had to be reconsidered, given that the analytic situation itself may reinforce the manner in which the original trauma occurred.[2]

Ferenczi highlighted the risks that, in the course of an analysis, are entailed by certain unconscious counter-attitudes on the part of the analyst (especially in cases of "technical rigidity" or when the analyst behaves like a teacher driven by a passion to educate). He drew a parallel between the child traumatized by a confusion of tongues and the patient whose past traumatisms are re-awakened and perhaps even exacerbated by the analyst's "neutrality" (which for Ferenczi was actually "professional hypocrisy": 1932, p. 8). In Ferenczi's opinion, bringing back to consciousness during the analysis traumatic events from the past to the point of repeating them, then standing back in a benevolent way to observe what transpires—the attitude he felt was recommended by the "classical" technique—was structurally equivalent to those processes that had initially set up and maintained the original trauma. Such patients, like the excited child they once were, are at a loss, overwhelmed by excess (to some extent external, but mainly internal); with no possibility of discharge or working-through, they abandon themselves to the ineluctability of fate, at the same time withdrawing from themselves by means of "self-splitting". The specific and particular nature of this form of splitting—narcissistic splitting of the self—leads to the evacuation/expulsion/extra-jection of part of the ego, with the following results:

- the part of the ego left empty is replaced by identification with the aggressor, thus sustaining affects similar to "terrorism of suffering";
- the expelled or extra-jected part then becomes omniscient and omnipotent, losing all of its emotional potentiality. This may give rise to the "wise-baby" state of mind (a child who is intellectually highly precocious but emotionally immature) (Ferenczi, 1931).

For Ferenczi, then, trauma is a narcissistic kind of traumatism. It may cloak itself in sexuality (fantasies of seduction, castration, etc), but it refers essentially to an experience with the object in terms not only of what actually occurred but also of what did not take place, thereby giving rise to "incomprehensible and intolerable woe" (Ferenczi, 1931, p. 478). That painful experience, with its negative potential, reinforces splitting, which in turn brutally transforms object relations, henceforth impossible, into narcissistic ones (Ferenczi, 1949).

Narcissistic splitting of the self entails a certain number of consequences.

1. It interferes with binding of the instinctual drives, creates defects in the establishment of narcissism, and leads to major deficiencies in representation (thus damaging the ego).
2. It generates "mental paralysis" (everything comes to a standstill) while maintaining pain and despair—this is related to the internalization of a defective and unreliable primary object.

3. It brings about a feeling of primary distress that, depending on the circumstances, may engender passionate transference feelings, transference depression, negative therapeutic reactions, and so forth—thus bearing witness to the fact that destructiveness is the dominant force in mental life.

Those proposals, no matter how innovative they may have been, meant that conflict with Freud became inevitable. In Freud's view, they opened up a theoretical gulf, the demarcation line being the understanding of childhood traumatism. To argue that the compulsion to repeat was a repetition of the traumatic situation, with the object being held responsible for this, meant, according to Freud, that Ferenczi underestimated the resources of the mind and its capacity to transform trauma and the mental pain associated with it; in other words, Freud saw in the therapeutic and technical conclusions that Ferenczi drew from these clinical discoveries a step backwards (in particular to his pre-1897 *neurotica*[3]) and, consequently, a significant deviation from psychoanalytic theory.

Freud as "reader" of Ferenczi's papers

Ferenczi died in 1933. Freud, who had not written about trauma since 1926 (in *Inhibitions, Symptoms and Anxiety*), returned to the topic on at least three occasions, in papers we have come to regard as his legacy: in 1937, in "Analysis Terminable and Interminable" (in which he studied the effects of traumatism in terms of its participation in and impact on the production of neurotic disturbances); in 1938, in his *Outline of Psycho-Analysis* (in which he examined the effects of the threat of castration as "the greatest trauma" in a child's life—1940a (1938), p. 155—while at the same time having a structuring dimension for future development); and in 1939, in *Moses and Monotheism,* he discussed traumatism in terms of its role in the genesis of the neuroses and, for the first time, put forward his own conception of traumatism and its links with narcissistic issues. In that paper, Freud pointed out that traumatic experiences that originally established and organized mental functioning[4] may bring about "early injuries to the ego" and create "narcissistic modifications" (1939a [1937–39], p. 74) leading to splitting of the ego.

We would therefore be justified in thinking that Freud became not only a latent but also a manifest "reader" of Ferenczi's work. This may have been related to the painful and conflict-ridden mourning process Freud had had to go through after the death, some years previously, of his former follower, patient, friend, and confidant—after having initially rejected the technical consequences of hypotheses that, at the time, had seemed too rash and even subversive. Could this have been an example of what Ferenczi himself called "introjection" of the lost object? Ferenczi, as we have seen, was the first to put forward clinical and theoretical hypotheses about the effects of early trauma that give rise to splitting and narcissistic injury—the very idea that Freud appears to adopt in *Moses and Monotheism* when he writes of the narcissistic modifications consequent upon the effects of early traumatisms.

This hypothesis would seem to be confirmed when, a little further on in that paper, Freud discusses for the first time two kinds of effect that traumatism may bring about—positive and negative (1939a [1937–39], p. 75). The positive effect has a structuring dimension that in turn facilitates repetition, remembering, and working-through; the negative effect creates an enclave in the mind (a "State within a State", as Freud puts it, on p. 76), in which there is no room for repetition, remembering, or working-through ("the negative reactions follow the opposite aim: that nothing of the forgotten traumas shall be remembered and nothing repeated"), so that the destructive quality of the trauma is uppermost here. This is, after all, little more than what Ferenczi had discussed in the very last papers he wrote, particularly in his *Clinical Diary* of January–October 1932.

Ferenczi's "clinical thinking"

Building on the highly original and creative manner in which he listened attentively to his patients, Ferenczi went on to develop a clinical form of thinking[5] that was completely innovative, focusing on how to treat by psychoanalysis complex and heterogeneous states described as "difficult". In these multiple and ill-defined states, we find modifications of the ego, defective symbol-formation, and thought disorders consequent upon the vicissitudes of primary love and hate, which call into question the relationship between primal scene patterns and the classical oedipal dimensions.

This clinical thinking lies at the heart of Ferenczi's *Diary* (1932) and the "Notes and Fragments" (1949) that follow on from it. In these remarkable papers, purely private in character, Ferenczi noted his impressions on a daily basis with the intention of being completely honest and open-minded; he described his often painful experience as a clinician confronted with the difficulties and deadlock that are part and parcel of ongoing analytic treatment. Since therapy was at the forefront of his mind, he tried to identify as accurately as possible the countertransference and technical responses to situations of deadlock that occurred during the treatment of these borderline patients. In his view, the process-related aporias were a secondary effect, economically and structurally speaking, of trauma—in other words, splitting, which may go as far as fragmenting the ego because of the pain involved and lead to the death throes of mental life.

Ferenczi was thus a true pioneer in the study of these borderline cases; his clinical thinking strikes us even today as being astonishingly modern, because it laid the foundations for major developments by practitioners whose own innovative ideas left their mark on contemporary psychoanalysis. I am referring here particularly to Melanie Klein (Ferenczi was her first analyst) and to D. W. Winnicott.[6]

Splitting, fragmentation, and pain

At the very beginning of his *Clinical Diary*, in an entry dated 12 January 1932 concerning a woman patient whose initials are given as R.N., Ferenczi discusses splitting processes and attempts to outline their metapsychological characteristics as regards the geography of trauma.[7]

In her childhood and pre-adolescence, Ferenczi's patient had been the victim of sexual assault on three occasions (seduction and rape). The effect of these trauma on her mind was "the complete atomization of psychic life" and the "shattering" of her personality, described by Ferenczi as "shattered to its very atoms" (Ferenczi, 1932, p. 10). For Ferenczi, one result of fragmentation caused by repeated splitting is the establishment of "a sort of artificial psyche for this body forcibly brought back to life" (p. 10). On the basis of the clinical material that emerged in the course of the analysis, Ferenczi drew up a descriptive list of the consequences of the splitting processes to which the patient had had recourse until adolescence, whenever she found herself in a traumatic situation:

- the fixation, within the adult person, of a "seduced" child. Whenever the patient felt excited and overwhelmed by her drive impulses, she would countercathect them and protect herself by going into a quasi-hysterical "somnambulistic trance". It was "only with great difficulty . . . [that] the analyst [could] make contact with this part: *the pure, repressed affect*" (1932, p. 9), which, as Ferenczi writes, "behaves like a child who has fainted, completely unaware of itself, who can perhaps only groan, who must be shaken awake mentally and sometimes also physically" (p. 9).
- repeated fragmentations create a "soulless part of the personality", a "body progressively divested of its soul" (p. 9), because the mind has lost all vitality, and the self's feelings, experiences, and sentiments have been invalidated;
- such fragmentation may verge on the atomization or even pulverization of mental life.[8]

In an attempt to devise a global structural description for these clinical data, Ferenczi recapitulates the effects of these various forms of splitting as follows:

> From now on the "individuum", superficially regarded, consists of the following parts: (a) uppermost, a capable, active human being with a precisely—perhaps a little too precisely—regulated mechanism; (b) behind this, a being that does not wish to have anything more to do with life; (c) behind this murdered ego, the ashes of earlier mental sufferings, which are rekindled every night by the fire of suffering; (d) this suffering itself as a separate mass of affect, without content and unconscious, the remains of the actual person. [1932, p. 10]

These observations make it clear that, for Ferenczi, splitting and fragmentation short-circuit repression and generate such intense pain that the self is almost in agony ("murdered ego"; "the fire of suffering"; "rekindled every night"). As a result Ferenczi saw infantile amnesia as a phenomenon that follows on from splitting, linked to the shock wave generated by the trauma. The excluded part of the memory seems to live on in secret: split-off from all possibility of representation in a neurotic fashion, and with no way of being translated into words, it becomes manifest physically (hysterical trances). This is a very clear illustration of how Ferenczi's patient could function in two modes: psychotic (the "trances" said to be hysterical) and non-psychotic ("uppermost, a capable, active human being").

The task of the analysis

Some time later, on 24 January 1932, the same patient prompted Ferenczi to think about the content of splitting processes:

> What is the content of the split-off ego? . . . The content of the split-off ego is always as follows: natural development and spontaneity, protest against violence and injustice, contemptuous, perhaps sarcastic and ironic obedience displayed in the face of domination, but inward knowledge that the violence has in fact achieved nothing; it has altered only something objective, the decision-making process, but not the ego as such. Contentment with oneself for this accomplishment, a feeling of being bigger and cleverer than the brutal force; . . . [1932, p. 19]

Ferenczi is here describing a process of "self-healing" via the development of narcissistic splitting; this enables the establishment of a kind of narcissism that, though apparently protective, may become "megalomaniac" or even "terribly intelligent". Ferenczi later went on to develop this topic in his metaphor of the "wise baby".

After describing "paralysis of thought processes" (1932, p. 25) as a side-effect of trauma, Ferenczi goes on to discuss the idea that denial may reinforce repression. In another important note written later and entitled "Fragmentation", dated 21 February 1932, he discusses the work of the analyst when dealing with traumatogenic phenomena and splitting:

> Psychic advantages: the unpleasure that arises when certain connections are made is avoided by the giving up of these connections. The splitting into two personalities, which do not want to know about each other, and which are grouped around dif-

> ferent impulses, avoids subjective conflict. . . . The task of the analysis is to remove this split. [pp. 38–39]

Again in that extract, Ferenczi highlights how the twin functioning of psychotic and non-psychotic aspects of the self acts as a protection against anxiety, mental distress, and agony. In his view, the analyst's role (the "task of the analysis") is to "revive" the split-off, "dead" part that, even though it may be hibernating, may all the same find itself in the grip of an "agony of anxiety". He adds that the way to lift splitting is via the analyst's capacity to "reflect on" the traumatic event.

In other words, to use a more contemporary psychoanalytic vocabulary, the work of the analyst consists in offering the patient thoughts and representations that, by means of word-presentations, facilitate a new way of looking at the affects involved and perhaps provide a new opportunity to integrate the experience, something that had initially been impossible. In the long term, there may be hope of re-symbolization and re-processing of those areas dominated by agony.[9]

In the remainder of his discussion, Ferenczi reaches the following interim conclusion:

> The question remains open whether there are not some cases in which the reunification of the traumatically split-off complexes is so unbearable that it does not fully occur and the patient retains some neurotic characteristics or sinks even deeper into a state of not-being or not-wanting-to-be [*Nichtseinwollen*]. [1932, p. 40]

This extract clearly shows Ferenczi's extraordinary clinical acumen: he remarks on the importance, for the prognosis, of negative aspects that may be operating in the patient's mind and in the analysis as a whole.

The "pre-primal trauma scar": Ururtrauma

The question that next fell to be dealt with was that of defining the mental *locus* where the trauma and the imprints it leaves are originally registered. Ferenczi clarified this in a clinical note dated 10 April 1932:

> . . . the question arises whether the primal trauma is not always to be sought in the primal relationship with the mother, and whether the traumata of a somewhat later epoch, already complicated by the appearance of the father, could have had such an effect without the existence of such a pre-primal-trauma [*ururtraumatischen*] mother–child scar. Being loved, being the centre of the universe, is the natural emotional state of the baby, therefore it is not a mania but an actual fact. The first disappointments in love (weaning, regulation of the excretory functions, the first punishments through a harsh tone of voice, threats, even spankings) must have, in every case, a traumatic effect, that is, one that produces psychic paralysis from the first moment. The resulting disintegration makes it possible for new psychic formations to emerge. In particular, it may be assumed that a splitting occurs at this stage. [1932, p. 83]

It was by then already clear to Ferenczi that when the relationship with the primary object is dysfunctional, or when the object is unable to act as a container and a protective shield against stimuli (Winnicott would later refer to these phenomena as environmental failures typical of the non-facilitating environment), then the result is *ururtraumatisch.* This occurs when the object itself is over-seductive at a very early stage (when the object is either absent or present to an excessive degree). The term *Ururtrauma* is a reference to the *locus* in which disorders of symbol formation and thinking originate, together with ego-modification, primary violence (a derivative of primary love and hate), and auto-erotic disorders (weaknesses and deficiencies in auto-eroticism). These all set the stage for denial and for the splitting processes that lie at the heart of phenomena such as the passionate transference, anaclitic depression, and negative therapeutic reactions, all of which reflect the importance of the mental destructiveness that is taking place.

By way of conclusion

Ferenczi was a true pioneer in the study of the so-called difficult cases (borderline and non-neurotic states); he provided the impetus for other analysts to go on developing the idea of "trauma" as the "traumatic consequence" of "primary traumatisms". These interfere with the binding of the instinctual drives and create defects in the establishment of narcissism, which in turn generate major deficiencies in representation.

The ideas he put forward would thus foreshadow those that, in the decades that followed, would serve as the foundation upon which contemporary psychoanalysis would be constructed. Some points are worth mentioning here, all of which are particularly important:

- the role played by early object relations, by the imprints that the object leaves on the mind, and by the environment in general;
- the (primary and secondary) traumatic effects of the object's denial of or failure to acknowledge the infant's affects and feelings (affect invalidation), or failure to respond to the infant's distress;
  —for some patients in the course of their analysis, it is important to initiate and develop a primary relationship (a primitive symbiotic relationship) that will make for a better understanding of early mother–child fantasies;
  —primary love and hate: hate facilitates fixation more than does love;
  —the "splitting/trauma" pairing: "narcissistic splitting" is a consequence of early psychic trauma (especially trauma that occur before the acquisition of language):
  —the split between thought processes and the body (somatopsychic splitting);
  —"splitting of the ego", which may lead to fragmentation of the mind;
  —primitive defence mechanisms such as expulsion and ex-corporation when the individual fears that some constraint or other will be imposed from outside; these verge on an immeasurable and nameless kind of "mental pain" (despair, agony) that leads to the "terrorism of suffering".

All of these conceptual developments have since become generally accepted into mainstream psychoanalytic thinking and are an implicit part of every contemporary analyst's theoretical and clinical equipment as deployed in his or her daily work.

Notes

Translated by David Alcorn.

1. In his attempts to make direct contact with the "child in the adult", Ferenczi, after abandoning the "active technique", suggested some techni cal innovations such as "relaxation" and "neocatharsis". These were met with some considerable scepticism by Freud, who considered them to be a regression in theory and perhaps even indeed a deviation in the form of "seductive laxity" (Green, 1990).

2. Traumatism has as much to do with the absence of an adequate response by the object as with an inappropriate response—that is, one that was aimed at satisfying the adult's desires or overcoming the child's distress. Later, other analysts were to follow in Ferenczi's footsteps on this point, Winnicott in particular. Klein, who laid less emphasis on the effects of the mother's response, focused more on the endogenous sources of mental life.

3. In his letter (No. 139) to Fliess dated 21 September 1897, Freud writes: "*And now I want to confide in you immediately the great secret that has been slowly dawning on me in the last few months. I no longer believe in my* neurotica" (Freud, 1985c [1887–1904], p. 264).

4. "We give the name of *traumas* to those impressions, experienced early and later forgotten, to which we attach such great importance in the aetiology of the neuroses" (Freud, 1939a [1937–39], p. 72).

5. I am borrowing the term "clinical thinking" from André Green (2002).

6. Winnicott's debt as regards Ferenczi is hinted at in "D.W.W. on D.W.W." (the transcript of an address to the 1952 Club he gave in January 1967): "I never know what I've got out of glancing at Ferenczi, for example, or glancing at a footnote to Freud" (Winnicott, 1967, p. 579).

7. Although Freud had already sensed that splitting played a major role in certain mental states (especially in the psychoses and the perversions), he had yet to write his seminal paper on the subject: "Splitting of the Ego in the Process of Defence" (Freud, 1940e [1938]).

8. Ferenczi's description of these states of mind would later be taken up and further developed by Winnicott (1945) and by Klein (1946) in terms of the "unintegrated ego", "ego disintegration", and "falling to pieces".

9. This is close to what Winnicott would later described in his 1974 paper on "Fear of Breakdown", where he says: "Fear of breakdown can be a fear of a past event that has not yet been experienced" (Winnicott, 1974, p. 103). "The only way to 'remember' in this case is for the patient to experience this past thing for the first time in the present, that is to say, in the transference" (p. 105).

7

Splitting and trauma: their relationship with *après-coup* and historicization

Luis Kancyper

The concept of splitting of the ego is of great significance within psychoanalytic theory and leads to a profound restructuring of both metapsychology and clinical practice. Indeed, this concept has different meanings in the writings of Freud: at the beginning he uses it in a descriptive fashion and later, in his last essays, as a conceptual instrument.

Freud uses "splitting of the ego" as a descriptive term in particular in order to point to the fact that the psychic apparatus is divided into systems (unconscious, preconscious, and conscious systems) and psychic agencies (ego, id, and superego) and also to describe the case when one aspect of the ego observes while the other is observed.

In addition, Freud uses this term in order to point out the splitting between two different sexual currents in an individual's love life: the sensual current and the affectionate current. "The whole sphere of love in such people remains divided in the two directions personified in art as sacred and profane (or animal) love. Where they love they do not desire and where they desire they cannot love" (Freud, 1912d, p. 183).

On the other hand, Freud uses the concept of splitting as a conceptual instrument, in particular in the articles "Fetishism" (1927e), *An Outline of Psychoanalysis* (1940a [1938]), and "Splitting of the Ego in the Process of Defence" (1940e [1938]). In these articles he makes reference exclusively to the splitting of the ego and, on discussing a highly specific defence mechanism—disavowal—he alludes to the coexistence (and not the conflict) at the heart of the ego of two psychic attitudes towards external reality insofar as this stands in the way of an instinctual demand: the first of these attitudes takes reality into consideration, while the second disavows it and replaces it with a product of desire.

> The two attitudes persist side by side throughout their lives without influencing each other. Here is what may be rightly called a splitting of the ego. [Freud, 1940a (1938), p. 203]

> But Freud's intention in speaking of a splitting *of the ego* (intrasystemic) rather than a splitting *between agencies* (between ego ad id) is to bring out a process that is new in comparison with the model of repression and of the return of the repressed. In fact, one of the specific traits of this process is that it does not result in the formation of a compromise between the two attitudes present, but that it maintains them simultaneously instead, with no dialectical relationship being established. [Laplanche & Pontalis, 1967, p. 429]

In the same year, Freud points out in what was to be his last work, *Moses and Monotheism* (1939a [1937–39), that traumas have a split and paradoxical nature, as they take cover behind a narcissistic wall (Freud, 1916–17) while at the same time striving to become noticeable:

> that is to say that they have great psychical intensity and at the same time exhibit a far-reaching independence of the organization of the other mental processes, which are adjusted to the demands of the real external world and obey the laws of logical thinking. They [the pathological phenomena] are insufficiently or not at all influenced by external reality, pay no attention to it or to its psychical representatives, so that they may easily come into active opposition to both of them. They are, one might say, a State within a State, an inaccessible party,

> with which co-operation is impossible, but which may succeed in overcoming what is know as the normal party and forcing it into its service. If this happens, it implies a domination by an internal psychical reality over the reality of the external world. [1939a [137–39], p. 76]

Freud (1940e [1938]), on introducing the idea of splitting of the ego, is not certain whether "it should be regarded as something long familiar and obvious or as something entirely new and puzzling" (p. 275). It is my view that the notion of splitting, both as a concept and a descriptive term, leads to a major restructuring of metapsychology and clinical practice.

Indeed, I believe that this concept exercises a direct and decided influence upon our metapsychological understanding of traumatic situations and their effects on the structuring and de-structuring of oedipal, narcissistic, and fraternal dynamics.

We should bear in mind Willy Baranger's words: "Trauma does not lie. Trauma complains, demanding repetition. Trauma is in charge until it is made explicit. Trauma has its own memory" (W. Baranger, 1994, p. 460) Therefore, with my contribution and through the presentation of a clinical case, I shall try to develop the concepts of narcissistic mortification and of the wall of post-traumatic resentment and remorse. As will be seen in the clinical case I present, these affects had been caused by the surviving effects of certain early traumas, which had hindered the process of narcissization but had been masked by a "screen trauma".

The issues I shall develop have been arranged into the following sections:

1. The memories of horror, of pain, and of rancour and their relationship with splitting and trauma.
2. Resentment and splitting of the ego.
3. Screen trauma and historicization.
4. Traumas and their vicissitudes.
5. Re-signification of traumatic splitting within the analytic field.

The memories of horror, of pain, and of rancour and their relationship with splitting and trauma

D. W. Winnicott (1971) once said: "I am indebted to my patients for the ideas they have inspired in me" (p. 9). I could not agree more, as I owe the expression "memory of horror" to one of my patients, Eduardo.

The individual suffering from the memory of horror just cannot learn to let go. He is overwhelmed by traumatic reminiscences, which are controlled by fear blended either with horror or with fright, and he cannot forget in spite of himself. He remains trapped by the memory of a traumatic past, which he cannot separate, or keep at a distance, from his conscious life.

When repression is at work, the individual removes the less traumatic events from conscious life, but when, in contrast, the individual cannot forget horror, traumatic facts are more intolerable for the ego in terms of his *Selbstgefühl.* They are similar to foreign bodies, isolated from the associative flow within the rest of the ego. As they are unable to enter into the symbolic chain of meaning, they cannot be repressed and thus remain split off. And, as what has been split off is kept out of psychic circulation, in consequence these traumatic events cannot evolve while they remain unanalysed.

The memory of horror is, precisely, the memory of manifold traumatic situations, in which feelings and representations are repeated as if they were repetition automatism—that is, without being accompanied by an affective re-experiencing capable of being integrated within a different structure, and with a new perspective of time.

At the manifest level, the memory of horror presents itself as the absence of prospects. However, at the latent level this apparent senselessness of the future is blocked by the uncanny presence of a contradiction in terms: the individual wants to avert the pains of the past and fend off the horrific danger of a future that threatens with the repetition of an unbearable yesterday.

In fact, when the individual suffers from the memory of horror, he becomes a "sur-dying" individual, always in fright, always like a sentry on duty, in order to prevent the sudden appearance of imminent breakdown.

The "sur-dying" individual flees from castration-death. He lives in order to triumph over the winged persecution of Thanatos. However, in the attempt at avoiding death as the main objective of his life, he finally becomes, in contrast, "sur-dying" from the perspective of both the external and the psychic realities.

I am aware I am saying "sur-dying" instead of "surviving".

We normally use the term "survivors" to refer to "those individuals who had their days numbered, but who somehow managed—unlike their fellow men—to escape this inexorable destiny. Thus, someone is said to survive a cataclysm, certain age or some serious, life-threatening illness" (Schmucler, 2007, p. 20).

In contrast, the "sur-dying" individual, in a similar way to the biblical Cain, is doomed to remain nomadic forever, in order to escape a spectral persecution. He lives, all things considered, to save himself through a permanent reassurance in order not to suffer. But he pays his right to existence through a constant amount of suffering, *dolo ergo sum*; he prefers to avoid unpleasure rather than to seek pleasure, but he cannot stop suffering. And it is precisely this tension of uncertainty, which stems from the mortification caused by the action of uncanny anxieties, that protects him from the absolute lack of tension characteristic of the Nirvana principle. Paraphrasing the poets: "Dying life, living death" (Kancyper, 2004).

In fact, the "sur-dying" individual is always in a precarious state and lacks, in consequence, a sustained feeling of belonging, because he is overwhelmed by certain traumatic traces of the past. He is thus haunted by compulsive, split-off feelings of terror, guilt, and shame, which are beyond his control (*Bewältigungstrieb*).

The individual who is obsessed with the memory of horror is a "sur-dying" nomad. He is unable to establish, and to commit to, a trusting, lasting relationship with another, from neither the personal, the professional, nor the institutional perspectives.

He is, all things considered, a drifter who at the same time treasures the belief that he might find a safe haven and break free from the repetition of traumatic situations (situations he is unable to "deactivate", as it were, and to separate from the present). In consequence, he cherishes this secret, dark hope and, when the time comes, takes refuge there, believing that, in so doing, he might save himself from uncanny experiences—because the memory of horror is the memory of the enacted return of the past, which is ruled not by castration anxiety but, rather, by death and helplessness [*Hilflosigkeit*] anxieties. These make the individual feel shattered and devastated with "the horror to continue living" (Borges). At other times, these individuals could feel the Borgean "nostalgia for the present". The memory unchained by resentment and remorse establishes, in contrast, the addictive memory of rancour, which, in turn, should be differentiated from the memories of pain and of horror.

The memory of rancour is deeply entrenched in, and feeds itself on, the hope for pay-back time, whereas the memory of pain manages to come to terms with the castration of reality. The memory of pain is not based on the underestimation of the past or the amnesia of facts, nor does it promote a superficial absolution. Rather, it is based on the discovery that the castration of reality cannot be changed, and thus the individual has to come to terms with it and with the feelings caused by this discovery—that is, sorrow, pain, and hatred—in order to be able to carry out the passage towards other objects, all of which allows him to undergo a normal mourning process.

The memory of pain regards the past as experience, not as a burden. It does not expect to deny the pain caused by what the individual has gone through and what he is aware of. It operates as a structuring, organizing remembrance and, with the help of life-drives, also as an alarm system that prevents—and protects the individual from—the repetition of negative experiences, giving rise to transformation.

To put it in J. Hernández's words:[1]

Es la memoria un gran don,
Calidá muy meritoria,
Y aquellos que en esta historia
Sospechen que les doy palo
Sepan que olvidar lo malo
También es tener memoria

The memory of pain does not split off the past; rather, the past is remembered as a useful experience. In this way, the past is integrated within the configuration of the other dimensions of time—that is, the present and the future.

Repetition present in the memory of rancour, in contrast, establishes yet again, with the "help" of death drives, the repetitive, and even insatiable, compulsion of revengeful power, thus paralysing the process of normal mourning. When we are dealing with rancour we notice that temporality presents singular traits, manifestly a particular relationship with the dimension of the future.

Repetition is the basic way of interfering with the future and of hindering the capacity for change. The memory of rancour, unlike the memory of pain, is ruled not by the pleasure principle or by the reality principle but, rather, by the "torment" principle.

The resentful individual does not remain anchored to timelessness, or to the suspended time of art: a time outside time that breaks with the dimensions of the past, the present, and the future. Neither does he remain trapped in an experience of eternity, contemplating the internal, marvellous object in order to disavow the passage of schizoid time. Rather, he has an urgent need to feel vindicated, as he believes he has suffered an affront that deserves punishment. Hence, the present and the future are mortgaged, because the individual feels he must defend his honour, an honour he feels has been besmirched. Indeed, this particular fragment of the past has taken control of the three dimensions of time.

The experience of time sustained by the power of rancour is the constant brooding over an affront that never ends, an expression of insurmountable grief. This desire for revenge could not only be present in the individual himself and within the intersubjective relationship, but could even be perpetuated through its transmission between generations, with which an inexorable fate is sealed within group memory. For, when rancour appears, defensive disavowal of the perception of reality is revived. In consequence, the creation of a substitute reality takes place, the effects of which are the intrasystemic splitting of the ego as well as a serious setback in the normal process of mourning (Kancyper, 1987, 1991, 1995).

Resentment and splitting of the ego

The resentful individual remains waiting for an impossible provider. He is unable to acknowledge the castration of reality because, if he did, he would therefore find inexorable proof that he must accept his own vulnerability as he has confirmed that he cannot change the structure of the other (nor can he be changed by the other according to his wishes). This is the reason why the resentful individual disavows the genuine perception that has shown him the lack in the other and holds on to the omnipotent conviction that: "The other has [something I desire] but he won't give it to me. That's unfair. I'm just an innocent victim, because it's obvious I'm not getting what I'm entitled to."

With this belief the individual feels he has a right to legitimize his blind repetitive revenge. Indeed, this vain hope for vindication is sustained by the over-investment of the subject and the object, by aggression at the service of Thanatos, and by the disavowal of an unbearable reality that results in a splitting of the ego.

However, the aspect of reality that has been thus disavowed continues to exert influence on the resentful individual because it has not been entirely split off. In fact, the affronts the individual has suffered within the oedipal, narcissistic, and fraternal dynamics (Kancyper, 2004) continue to get "infected", as it were, with the seething memories of rancour and of horror and generate, in turn, another product of desire. The process is similar to what occurs in fetishism: "The creation of the fetish was due to an intention to destroy the evidence for the possibility of castration, so that fear of castration could be avoided" (Freud, 1940a [1938], p. 203).

In addition, the process is accompanied by anxieties of a more primitive nature: pre-phallic castration anxiety and helplessness anxiety (Kancyper, 2006).

The resentful individual is usually stuck in obstinate rancour because, on the one hand, it provides him with narcissistic satisfaction as it promotes the elation of self-esteem as well as the cohesion of the ego and, on the other, rancour fulfils defensive aims: it tempers the de-structuring effects of other uncanny affects that threaten the individual with mental breakdown.

In consequence, when we analyse the behaviour of the resentful individual, we can appreciate the coexistence, at the heart of his ego, of two psychic attitudes towards external reality insofar as this stands in the way of an instinctual demand. In "Neurosis and Psychosis" (1924b [1923]), Freud refers to the possibility "for the ego to avoid a rupture in any direction (i.e., with the id or with reality) by deforming itself, by submitting to encroachments on its own unity and even perhaps by effecting a cleavage or division of itself" (pp. 152–153).

In fact, for the resentful individual, splitting is a defence mechanism as well as a state of the ego. In addition, disavowal is usually only partial and, in consequence, two psychic attitudes are established within the ego, attitudes that oscillate between acknowledging and disavowing the reality of castration. In this sense, resentment usually has a defensive aspect in order to temper the disrupting effects of certain kinds of anxieties that pose the risk of breakdown.

The feeling of hope present in resentment and remorse frequently becomes interminable when it acts as a defence—that is, when accepting irretrievable loss becomes impossible. In those cases the interminable and pathological hope of rancour "usually represents the only, and the last, possible relationship with the primary objects; giving it up would entail the definitive shattering of illusion, and the acceptance that those objects are utterly and completely lost forever" (Amati Mehler & Argentieri, 1990).

In fact, when resentment establishes itself within the analytic situation, the analysand legitimizes a regressive will to master that aims at imposing the power of retaliation over the analyst and over the world. It is then that the analysand carries his pretensions to excess and, in fact, stops at nothing: he protests his innocence and demands justice, thinking that justice will vindicate him. In these cases, the analyst generally represents, within the transference, an age-old offender, and the analysand may even prefer to take it out on him, experiencing sadomasochistic triumph, even at his own expense: he would rather take his revenge than cure himself.

In fact, the narcissistic affront originates in the analysand a regressive and repetitive need for vindication, which establishes a sovereign and absolute state of exception. According to Agambén (1998), the Sovereign is the one who has the power to decide the state of exception and who stands, on the one hand, within the law and, on the other, outside the law since he has power to suspend it. His Majesty, the resentful individual, claims with sovereign decision that he does not require the law in order to create it and, setting his own standards, provides the foundations for new legality. The affective state of resentment is irrational, impulsive, and implacable. Its gloomy repetitive powers revive all that is violent in man.

Indeed, resentment moves forward rapidly and inexorably towards its destructive aims.

Paraphrasing Wiessel (2002): "Resentment does not know frontiers or boundaries: it devastates ethnic groups, religions, political systems and socials classes. Despite the fact that it is the work of human beings, not even God can put a stop to it. Blind and blinding at the same time, resentment is the dark sun that, under a leaden sky, hits and kills those who forget the greatness of humanity and its promise. In consequence, fighting resentment is paramount in order to strip it from its false glory, which has been granted by its scandalous legitimacy."

The hard technical problem thus presented to us in our praxis is how to combat resentment within the analytic situation, as both resentment and its implacable need for revenge are regressive and repetitive manifestations of thanatic narcissism. And this type of narcissism is, in turn, controlled by the blind arrogance of the combative and murderous ideal ego, which attacks the setting.

Steiner (1996) puts forward the idea that resentment constitutes a nucleus around which a psychic refuge is organized. He further claims that:

> psychic refuges are pathological organizations of personality that provide a kind of stability which is resistant to psychic change. When resentment revolves around traumatic experiences where the analysand has felt hurt and affronted it apparently is experienced, from the perspective of space, as a regressive safe haven where the individual can look for refuge from reality, and in consequence, from anxiety and guilt. [p. 174]

Memories of horror, of rancour, and of pain within the analytic situation

> There are many frightful things, but none as frightful as man
>
> Sophocles, *Antigone*, v. 395

The way in which these different kinds of memories intertwined in Eduardo's love life and external reality becomes plain in some of his sessions, which I shall describe in this section.

Eduardo consulted me when he was 59 because the mechanisms of disavowal and splitting implemented by him had failed in the end, as they could not indefinitely keep his split-off aspects (mainly in the affective and professional areas) completely detached.

When Eduardo first came, he said: "I need to put my life into perspective, Doctor. Duplicity has put me in an untenable position. I find it very hard to go on living like this. My life is full of intrigue, of lies and deception. I really don't think I can deal with this impossible situation any longer. I don't think this duplicity is right. Besides, it makes me suffer. I am, and I've always been, a professional sufferer."

The sessions I describe here belong to Eduardo's fourth year of analysis. However, I should stress that, throughout all these years, there was a traumatic scene that would appear repeatedly during our sessions together: his grandfather literally locked the door against him without giving an explanation, and Eduardo remained paralysed with shock.

Indeed, this repetitive scene belonged to a traumatic situation that had affected his whole family. Eduardo was the first grandchild of that unforgettable grandfather who adored him and used to play with him every day. Until then, his grandfather had lived with Eduardo, his grandmother, two unmarried aunts, and his parents. However, when Eduardo was 6 years old, his grandfather had suddenly left and gone to live in a neighbouring country with a new partner. This was certainly a highly disruptive event to home life, which caused pathological grief in both Eduardo's mother and his grandmother and, in addition, provoked a fracture in his own process of subjectivation.

The repeated scene of his grandfather (whom he never saw again) staring at him and locking the door against him without explanation operated at a certain moment of the analytic process as a screen trauma that was masking other traumatic situations that had taken place both before and after this episode.

I believe that in the session I shall now describe (which I have called "Fractures and crutches") both the de-structuring effects of trauma, which continued to live in his memories of horror and of rancour, and their consequent influence on object-choice become plain.

In this session we can appreciate how the traumas suffered by

Eduardo made him feel narcissistic mortification and acute distress. In addition, they severely damaged his affective and psychic life, as intrapsychic splitting took the place of the usual mechanism of repression, a defence mechanism that only puts distance between consciousness and conflictive psychic contents.

In the second session, "From the memory of horror to the memories of rancour and of pain", we can appreciate how Eduardo works through these three kinds of memory within the analytic session.

The dynamics between these memories is fairly smooth, and we all "switch", as it were, from one to the other. However, we could well ask ourselves:

- How could the oscillations between these three types of memories be detected?
- How do the boundaries between these memories disappear during the analytic process?

Natalia Ginsburg (1999) claims that, "When we are happy, our imagination prevails, but when we are unhappy the power of memory takes over" (p. 45). Indeed, in the case of Eduardo, memory had great power: it sometimes covered him with its protective layers, and nearly smothered him, or else it had a paralysing, almost predatory quality.

"Fractures and crutches"

"I see myself, my own structure, as a solid block of concrete and the trauma with my grandfather as a chisel and a hammer which split me in two. A trauma is a partition, a fracture, and, well, . . . from then on, you stop being a block. I am a fractured structure, unstable stuff, a building with fractured columns, about to collapse.

"And throughout all these years, the building was merely a façade, because the genuine foundations of the building—that is, the iron, the internal structure—were fractured and weak.

"With this original fracture I stood up the best I could. Perhaps one embellishes the building with marble and other decorative elements and it looks as it were strong, but it isn't, because it hasn't grown right. I think all this is in my unconscious. The fracture and fragility were operating there. I had it all bottled up, I am putting it into words only now.

"I was terrified of a new fracture—that's why I used to think that if I divorced my wife I would lose my structure once again. I was so used to drama and to tragedy, I thought that divorcing my wife would be a tragedy, and that prevented me from making up my mind. That is how I became a spectator of life and could not commit to anything: neither to my family, nor to my professional activity.

"This fracture prevented me from walking with my own legs. I couldn't walk, I was carried."

Analyst: "Carried by whom?"

"I was carried because that was what I wanted: my parents, my wife. They were the crutches I used so that I could walk. Now I can see that the crutches were not forced on me: I asked for them. I was so desperate to be on my feet that I asked for them. My wife and my parents were the crutches I chose so that I could walk, and I still look for them for support."

Analyst: "Perhaps you are taking analysis and myself as another pair of crutches?"

"No, you are the one who mends the fracture. Structures can also be repaired so that the buildings can remain standing. When a fracture mends, a callus formation develops, which is even harder than the bone. In fact, the bone can break somewhere else, but not in the same spot. If I manage to mend my fractures and develop a good callus formation, I'm sure I won't collapse again."

From the memory of horror to the memories of rancour and of pain

"I've a photo of my grandfather from when I was 6, and now that I'll soon turn 63, this photo has turned into a film. Now, although I can't see myself in the photo, I know that I'm in the film. There were a number of correlated situations which formed themselves into a kind of sequence. The photo stopped being a photo and started to have continuity throughout the time I've lived and suffered.

"The most important image I can recall is that of the crutches that no one gave to me, that I asked for. This helps me to not blame others." [*From the memory of rancour to the memory of pain.*]

"When I lost my grandfather I turned to my father for support, and later on I turned to my wife, who is the carbon copy of my father, with her ailments and her manipulation.

"I have a feeling that, during the days I was ill and had to stay at home, I withdrew. I didn't want to be in touch with anyone, and I have finally understood I must let go of the crutches. It seems that the things we have gone through have their consequences. But at least I've lived to grasp my traumas and my problems. I need to feel relaxed, not under pressure.

"During the last few days I've wanted to be alone. I don't know if you can really know yourself with introspection, but what I do know is that I have many questions about myself. I feel I am an enigma to myself. I don't reproach myself for anything, rather I feel I've been fooling myself." [*From the memory of rancour to the memory of pain.*]

"I want to pour my heart out; I want to be frank about my own self-esteem, about my own independence, about my own time to experience what I want to experience. I would like to have autonomy, to feel free to act. I'm looking for that time, for that freedom of movement, freedom of thought.

I think that until recently I've been living as if I was trapped, with nowhere to run, because of the situation generated by the crutches: I believed that using crutches was the same as to walk. And the truth is that I could move with the crutches but I couldn't walk. Now I have this feeling of freedom, which is independent from the situations that I might experience." [*From the memory of horror and of rancour to the memory of pain.*]

"I have a feeling that, when I die, I will have lived according to my own times, instead of following those of others, instead of being a prisoner of the crutches (*he pauses for a moment and relaxes on the couch*).

"I was thinking about my daughter, she used to have similar anxieties to those of my father and my wife.

"I think that throughout all these years I have merely relieved other people's anxieties. Well! At least I thought I was doing that.

"I was always distressed, always on the watch in order to sense where tragedy would strike. It's evident for me that some of my own family relationships have broken up. I don't know if it's that or the fact that I'm considering relationships from another perspective, but I've been feeling more relaxed in spite of the tension at the companies I run.

"I'm not feeling tense, or anxious, I just want to reflect upon the things that are happening to me."

Analyst: "Did you find support in the crutches, or was it perhaps the other way round?"

"With my broken personality I couldn't decide, I didn't have enough strength to make conscious decisions.

"I think that, in the end, living in terror of loss put me at a disadvantage. Back then, the crutches were so high that I missed my footing and remained pedalling in the air; I couldn't walk. Now here I am: trying to sort myself out. I admit I have serious difficulties with commitment, with love." [*From the memory of horror to the memory of pain.*]

"I think that after the traumatic situation I went through, I suffered a sort of fracture, and after that, it's as if I'd fallen into a trap. I feel I have only committed to my children and to my grandson, but never to women. I never committed to my wife or with other women. My wife is unbalanced. She's aggressive, she scares people off. And I didn't want to see it. I denied many things, perhaps because it was easier that way, or perhaps because I was absolutely terrified of suffering a new fracture. The fear of the picture I was telling you about, the fear of a new fracture, prevented me from seeing certain things." [*The memory of horror.*]

"I have harmed my own children—not in an active way, mind you, but because I passively put up with my wife's violent behaviour towards them. But, well, here is the film I was telling you about, here is the fracture that didn't allow me to see. And now that I can see, what can I do about this film? I would like to feel happier.

"Now that I can see, perhaps I can laugh about it a little bit. I should learn to see the funny side of tragedy."

* * *

The psychic work involved in constructing an account with all the situations that Eduardo had gone through (the "film" he had created) leads us to consider the importance of the process of historicization—that is, the recovery and readjustment of past, forgotten situations—within the analytic work.

In fact, Roussillon (2006) points out that:

> historicization, as a means of mastering psychic representation, as the ability to represent what one truly is, continues to be the royal road, the main road, to the understanding of the representative nature of what makes itself actual in the individual. Historicization is what opens the road to the essential transformational process that favours the subjective work of symbolization. [p. 203]

Screen trauma and historicization

Psychoanalysis attaches great importance to screen memories (Freud, 1899a), because they condense a good number of real or fantasized elements. To Freud, "Not only *some* but *all* of what is essential from childhood has been retained in these memories. It is simply a question of knowing how to extract it out of them by analysis. They represent the forgotten years of childhood as adequately as the manifest content of a dream represents the dream-thoughts" (1914g, p. 148).

Paraphrasing Freud, it could be said that, in general, screen traumas are unconsciously used by the individual in order to hide—and, at the same time, reveal—early traumatic situations, as well as to cover up traumas that have occurred at a later date.

The mnemonic "selection", as it were, of a traumatic situation that is repeated unabated during the analytic process has great historical significance. Indeed, its viscous stickiness to the memory of horror usually condenses a plethora of different traumatic situations: pure traumas (Baranger, Baranger, & Mom, 19987), cumulative traumas (Khan, 1963), and early traumas. They all fail to be transformed into memories because the situations that caused them took place at a time when the psychic apparatus lacked the capacity for representation and language. In consequence, the effects of all these early traumas are usually enacted within the transference relationship.

From the phenomenological perspective, screen traumas appear throughout the analytic process with alarming frequency and are, in addition, cut out from the individual's conscious control.

As Eduardo made progress in his analysis, we found out that the repetition of the traumatic situation he had experienced with his grandfather condensed the effects of other traumas and defensively operated as a screen trauma, so that other situations—which had been even more disrupting for his psychic structure—would remain hidden. And in fact, Eduardo's narcissistic trauma (Freud, 1939a [1937–39]) appeared later on, as we shall see in the next section ("Traumas and their vicissitudes"). It is my opinion that this early trauma could well have affected his process of narcissization. In addition, the effects of it became visible through a defensive mechanism: his identification with the objects involved in the traumatic situation. Indeed, Eduardo, in identifying himself with the object-mother from the early traumas he had endured, used to get involved in sadomasochistic relationships in which he became the traumatizing agent. In this way, Eduardo—like his mother before him—was unable to perceive others as such, used to put his own needs above all else, and compulsively ill-treated women. On the other hand, he used to shut women out of his life, as his grandfather had done with him, leaving them overwhelmed and in a sudden state of helplessness (*Hilflosigkeit*). In this way, he did to others what he himself had suffered as a boy, when his grandfather had suddenly put an end to his relationship with him.

Likewise, this screen trauma from his childhood covered up his unsolved identity conflicts, which became noticeable in the tormented relationships he used to establish with women. Indeed, in these relationships, the narcissistic traumas Eduardo had suffered—traumas that had not been worked through and, in addition, had affected his psychic structuring—became signified *après coup*.

According to Chasseguet-Smirgel (1987), narcissistic traumas

> tend to appear early on in development, succumb to infantile amnesia and are connected to impressions of a sexual or aggressive nature and, undoubtedly, with narcissistic wounds that, in turn, cause narcissistic mortification. These traumas are caused by a failure, on the part of the mother, to counteract infantile helplessness by means of the narcissistic and object investment of the newborn. The mother also fails to establish a relationship between her own psychic apparatus and that of her child: in this

> way, the child is at risk of suffering yet other traumas later on. These conditions, among other things, could greatly disrupt the relationship between aggression and sexuality, on the one hand, and aggression and narcissism on the other. This is how sexuality could become the fundamental means through which self-respect is preserved, in a triumphal victory, flooded with hatred, over the primary object. [p. 778–779]

Eduardo used to engage in hyper-sexualized relationships with certain women and felt that he gained a sexual triumph over them. However, I believe that what he was in fact trying to do was to make up for the lack of maternal narcissistic confirmation.

Through his "sexual marathons" he discharged the tension caused by the profound narcissistic wound he had suffered early on (i.e., by transforming it into sexual arousal). In this way, he avoided working this tension through, a tension that would have caused intolerable consequences if it had remained linked to the early affront he had suffered at the hands of his mother.

Screen traumas are failed attempts at assimilating—and at coming to terms with—traumatic situations, because temporality remains frozen, thus giving place to false historicization. This, in turn, originates a circular temporality, which is opposed to "analytic historicization, operating by a retroactive movement, [which] tends to replace this false history with a truer one and, at the same time, to re-open temporality while future, present, and past dimensions interact dialectically" (Baranger, Baranger, & Mom, 1987, p. 133). Trauma cannot be separated from the process of historicization.

The process of historicization places traumatic events within a diachronic perspective of time and allows the individual to give the succession of isolated occurrences a place within a historical calendar. What is more, the incomplete and enigmatic aspects of certain traumas become restructured through historicization. And then, at a given time, as is usually the case with insight, these aspects acquire new meaning and, in reordering themselves within a new structure, reopen temporality.

In fact, in contemporary psychoanalysis there is a growing tendency to push back, as it were, traumatic situations to their origin, in order to give new meaning to the processes of splitting that the individual had implemented as a means of survival.

Traumas and their vicissitudes

Trauma usually has different vicissitudes. One of them could be the identification of the traumatized individual with the objects that were involved and lost in the traumatic situation: "and the ego makes a partial alteration in itself after the model of the lost object" (Freud, 1921c, p. 114).

This unconscious object relation, which is ruled not necessarily by the shadow of only one lost object, but by a complex interaction between different objects, is based on the model of "the relation between someone with superior power and someone who is without power and helpless—which may afford a transition to the hypnosis of fright which occurs in animals" (Freud, 1921c, p. 115). The hypnotic relation "is . . . a group formation with two members. . . . Out of the complicated fabric of the group it isolates one element for us—the behaviour of the individual to the leader" (Freud, 1921c, p. 115).

This process of identification, which is unchained by the effects of traumas, presents different defensive moments in the intrapsychic and intersubjective dimensions.

From the intrapsychic perspective, the traumatized individual usually identifies with the aggressor and/or with the victim, but he might also oscillate between these alternatives. Within the transference—that is, from the perspective of intersubjectivity—he places one of these forms of identification onto the other in an exclusive and tenacious fashion.

When we are dealing with intersubjectivity, we should analyse the way in which the response of the other is working—that is, if the other takes on what the traumatized individual has split and projected on to him. In consequence, in this relationship characterized by mastery, both agents—the one who controls, the individual controlled—contribute to the configuration and crystallization of certain perverse situations.

In fact, in certain cases, the individual, in order to defend himself from the disrupting effects of traumas, tends to take up the place of the aggressive agent, while the other is identified as, and turned into, the victimized and humiliated object. Thus, he is forced to tolerate all the suffering and humiliation that the traumatized individual once endured in a passive way.

In contrast, in other cases the contrary situation is created: the traumatized individual, stuck in the position of suffering object, splits off, projects, and places in the other the role of victimizing agent, thus suffering the effects of trauma all over again.

This situation is frequently encountered in couples, or in the relationship between parents and their children. In cases such as these, masochistic parents tend to "create", as it were, victimizing children—that is, ill-treating, rapacious, cruel, and sadistic children—in order to bring to fruition morally and/or erotogenically their own masochistic fantasies stemming from "a child-parent is being beaten".

Throughout the "time of generations" (Baranes, 1991), the enactment of the uncanny memory of horror is transmitted. It is characterized by the presence of the pair—victimizing agents/victims—within the dynamics of intersubjectivity, made possible by complex processes of identification that, in turn, have been caused by split-off traumatic situations.

This master–slave relationship necessarily becomes re-enacted within the analytic situation, and, in consequence, a perverse field between the patient and the analyst is established. The analyst unconsciously plays the role both of victim and of victimizing agent, according to the particular transference–countertransference moments of the analytic process.

I recall that Eduardo had once been ill with a pulmonary viral infection, and I had called him on several occasions in order to inquire after him. He had been unable to take any of my calls and had not called me back. Throughout that weekend I remained very concerned for him and was, quite naturally, eager to hear from him. At the same time, I found myself overwhelmed by countertransference reactions, feeling abandoned in the same way he himself could well have felt during his childhood, when faced with his grandfather's and his parents' thoughtlessness.

Once I had offered him this interpretation, Eduardo remembered, for the very first time, that as a child he frequently climbed trees at home in order to hide from his mother and that she would frantically search for him. This infantile situation of a cruel mother–child relationship was re-enacted, without his awareness, let alone his understanding, in his relationship with his wife and female lovers. Likewise, he re-enacted and re-experienced his traumatic past with me within the analytic situation; he identified me with the hurt object, whereas he identified himself with a resentful, aggressive agent who continued to take retaliatory action against present objects because he had been unfairly treated by his early ones.

Although Eduardo used to ill-treat women, what in fact predominated in him was the masochistic fixation described by Freud in "A Child Is Being Beaten" (1919e): Eduardo mainly identified with the victim and, at the same time, with the one who came to the aid and redeemed his fellow-men. This connection between narcissism and masochism operated as a narcissistic trap through which he brought to fruition masochistic-narcissistic *jouissance*, establishing, in this way, a redeeming identification.

The revengeful *Fort-Da* game, where the victimizing agent constantly victimizes the other, and vice versa, should be understood as a field phenomenon. In addition, the working-through of the effects of these identifications in the structuring of the intersubjective field dynamics is complex and depends on the interplay between different and intricate factors.

I believe that the interpretation, construction, and historicization of these kinds of identifications, which were originated in traumatic situations, as well as their progressive rearrangement thanks to their having been re-signified during the analytic process, open up for the individual a hopeful possibility of change that will prevent traumas from becoming fixed and split-off as "a State within a State" (Freud, 1939a [137–39]) or hidden behind the impregnable resistance of a "narcissistic wall" (Freud, 1916–17, Lecture XXVI).

Re-signification of splitting within the analytic field

The instrumentalization of the concept of *a-posteriori*, of deferred action (*Nachträglichkeit*), allows us to carry out fertile theoretical and technical considerations when we work with the mechanism of splitting caused by traumas.

Deferred action activates a particular memory—a memory that is linked to the traumatic scenes of the individual's cryptic history. And, in addition, while this history is repressed and split-off, it is at the same time intertwined with the unconscious and hidden, repressed, and split-off histories of the parents and siblings of the analysand. These are, in fact, intertwined histories and memories that have been part of the genesis and continuance of certain processes of identification.

The memory of *après-coup* suddenly opens up the gates of oblivion, and a chaotic sea of traumatic scenes—which had been kept suppressed and bereft of meaning through years and even generations—gushes out.

The re-signification of traumatic situations takes place throughout all the stages of life, because traumas have a memory of their own, but it "cries out", as it were, mainly during adolescence and menopause because these stages in particular are characterized by chaos and unavoidable crises. In addition, it is precisely during these stages that the re-signification of traumatic events (events bereft of meaning and from previous stages) is precipitated. In this way, the individual becomes capable of restructuring his identifications, with which the process of identity—a process that never ends—is confirmed (Kancyper, 1985).

Re-signification is not the deferred discovery of an event that had been forgotten; rather, it is the attempt (made possible by interpretation, construction, and historicization) to gain an understanding of the meaning carried by those enigmatic and hidden events.

> *Nachträglichkeit* [re-signification] is the attempt to constitute the trauma as such within a new historicization— that is, to make it comprehensible. In the two times of the trauma, the first time remains latent until the second time binds it and makes it appear as trauma. The first time of the trauma (we could say pre-traumatic) acquires its aetiological value from the second time through its reactivation by an event, perhaps trivial but nevertheless datable and nameable, and through the *analytic historicization* that links together the two times. The first time of the trauma remains mute until the *nachträglich* allows it to speak and to become trauma. [Baranger, Baranger, & Mom, 1987, p. 134]

In fact, retroactive re-signification, *Nachträglichkeit,* "goes beyond the polarity between historical reality and psychic reality. It is the moment when the traumatic, incomprehensible elements from the past are bound with the help of sensations, affects, images and words from the present. In this way, what has been split off becomes integrated to psychic reality and then can, in consequence, be repressed and forgotten" (Kunstlicher, 1995, p. 700).

This is the time when the mysterious, repetitive, and incomprehensible past suddenly becomes a clearer, more audible reality; in addition, in being integrated and restructured within psychic reality, it allows the individual to rewrite his own history and acknowledge his identity.

To finish, I would like to stress that the aim of our clinical work is not to bring back the past in order to re-experience it, but to rewrite it within a different structure. It is not so much about remembering; it is about rewriting. The emphasis is on the work of rewriting, rather than on re-experiencing the past.

Important as the re-experienced past may be, it certainly is not enough: it is only the starting point, whereas the finish line is the restructuring of the past. The individual's identity is defined according to the way in which his own biography is restructured in order to transform it into his own personal history.

Note

1. "Memory is a great gift/And has great merit/And those who feel that/Are much criticised/In this story/Should know that forgetting the bad/Also means to have a memory."

8

Notes for a theory of generalized splitting

Raul Hartke

According to his biographer Ernest Jones (1957), Freud began writing the article "Splitting of the Ego in the Process of Defence" [*Die Ichspaltung im Abwehrvorgang*] during Christmas 1937, but he left it unfinished and unpublished. It was only published in 1940, just over a year after his death. Jones believed that this may have occurred because a few details of the clinical case reported might have revealed the identity of the patient, a well-known public figure of the period.

The German term *Spaltung*, in the sense of a division of the mind, had already been used in psychiatry since the end of the nineteenth century, as pointed out by Laplanche and Pontalis (1967). The papers on hysteria and hypnosis in those days, for instance, as these authors remind us, used the notions of "dissociation of personality", "double consciousness", and "dissociation of psychological phenomena". Bleuler also used this term to designate the fundamental disturbance in schizophrenia, a term that means precisely split, divided, or cleaved mind or spirit.

Already in their *Studies on Hysteria*, Breuer and Freud referred to the "splitting of consciousness" [*Bewusstseinsspaltung*] (Freud, 1895d). It is known however, that the two authors differed as to the origin of this coexistence of two groups with contradictory, independent, and even mutually excluding phenomena in the mind of a person. Breuer attributed it to what he called a "hypnoid state"—that is, a state of consciousness equivalent to that generated by hypnosis. The psychic contents that occur during this state would remain split from the rest of psychic life. For Freud, on the contrary, this split of consciousness would be caused by a psychic conflict that would activate the mechanisms of repression and would separate psychic contents from consciousness, thus rendering them unconscious.

To begin with, in this general sense, the notion of splitting of the mind is at the very origin of the psychoanalytic theory of psychopathology, as well as of psychic functioning in general (Laplanche & Pontalis, 1967).

In the work of Freud, Strachey (1964b) includes the phenomenon of splitting in the broader theme of what the creator of psychoanalysis called "ego alteration", always generated by the defensive processes. In this sense, Strachey (1961c) sees very early signs of this notion already in the first article on defence psychoneuroses, of 1894, as well as in the manuscript sent to Fliess on January 1, 1896, known as Manuscript K. Strachey (1964a) supplies precious indications for the examination of the evolution of this idea of "ego alteration" in his introductory comment to Freud's article "Analysis Terminable and Interminable". Following this trail that he marked, I consider it possible to say that, in general, this refers to accommodations or even subjugations of the ego during its work of attention and conciliation of conflicting demands of the id, the external world, and the superego. The intention is to avoid contradictions within its own territory, in agreement with the synthetic tendency of its functioning. However, the split that Freud will describe years later surprises him precisely because it contradicts that synthetic function. Despite this, in "Neurosis and Psychosis" (1924b [1923]), Freud states that the ego can avoid collapsing towards one of these three demands, "by deforming itself, by submitting to encroachments on its own unity, and even perhaps by effecting a cleavage or division of itself" (pp. 152–153). Strachey (1961b) notes here—rightly in my opinion—an early allusion to the specific concept of ego splitting.

Be that as it may, and once again according to Laplanche and

Pontalis (1967), in most of his work Freud used the term *Spaltung* to refer to the separation of the psychic apparatus into systems (unconscious and preconscious/conscious), instances (id, ego, and superego), or even the division of the ego into a part that observes and another that is observed. At this level it was not a concept proper, and much less an operational concept (Le Gaufey, 1993).

It is only from 1927 onwards, in the article on fetishism, that splitting is raised to the category of a concept and is connected specifically to the ego. Thus, he begins to refer to an intrasystemic division and not between instances or systems in general.

Strachey (1964b) observes, once again in my opinion rightly, that the article "Splitting of the Ego in the Process of Defence", the central object of this book, can be considered a continuation of the other about fetishism. In this, however, splitting becomes the paper's title. Consequently it is inferred that this would be its central theme had it been completed. Furthermore, it appears to me that the final part of chapter VIII of the *Outline of Psychoanalysis* (1940a [1938]) not only includes but also expands, goes further into, and provides a better systematization of this issue. It is known that the latter work mentioned also remained unfinished and was only published posthumously. Yet, that chapter appears complete in itself, thus constituting an important reference for the study of ego splitting. It should not be ignored that it is a sort of epilogue of the writing by the founder of psychoanalysis (Strachey, 1964c). It was written a few months after the work on ego splitting, in May or July 1938 (Strachey, 1964c). I would not ignore the possibility that it contains, in its essence and even with improvements, what Freud would have said had he finished the one he wrote during Christmas 1937.

Be that as it may, it is based on what we might call this "triptych" that I will try to locate the centre of gravity of the concept involved, whose limits of outreach vary in the work of its own creator and even more under the pen of other analytic authors.

It is a "triptych" whose parts are, incidentally, unequal, as mentioned. The first, perfectly concluded, presents fetishism as a title, highlights the mechanism of disavowal [*Verleugnung*] of the absence of a penis in the woman, and shows ego splitting as a consequence of the latter. The second, clearly unfinished, is called "The Splitting of the Ego . . .", and, as a model to study it, it uses a case of fetishism. The last part should constitute a final schematic overview of psychoanalysis, but it also was not finished, although at least seven sections are apparently completed.

Next I examine each of the parts of the aforementioned "triptych" in further detail, so that later I can present general considerations about the basic subject of the present work. I do this because I believe that if I were to examine exclusively the article on ego splitting it would not be very productive, and, above all, it would be subject to the risk of a very limited, out-of-context appreciation.

The central theme of the work "Fetishism" (1927e) is the Freudian thesis that the fetish replaces the penis that is lacking in the woman (the mother), in whose existence the boy believes up to a certain time and to which—in these cases—he does not manage to renounce because this would be a demonstration that he himself could be castrated. But instead of a complete blanking out of the perception of absence of a penis in the woman, what happens is what Freud calls a "disavowal" [*Verleugnung*]. This concept, as informed by Strachey (1961a), had already been insinuated in 1911, in "Formulations on the Two Principles of Mental Functioning", but began to occupy a growing space from 1923 onwards, in the paper "The Infantile Genital Organization". In the 1927 article, Freud remarks that there is, and still persists, the perception of lack of a penis, but that at the same time it is the object of an energetic contrary action by the ego, for the purpose of disavowing it (1927e). However, at this point, Freud does not yet consider it necessary to create a new term for this mechanism, including it within the already known process of repression [*Verdrängung*]. But he suggests the possibility of designating repression as the destination of affect, and as disavowal that of the representation. Be that as it may, the result, in the case of fetishism, is a compromise, enabled only by the primary processes, by which part of the ego accepts the perception of lack of a penis in the woman, and part goes on believing in the infantile sexual theory that all human beings have it. For this purpose, it creates the penis substitute in the woman represented by the fetish. The latter situation—that is, the persistence of the two currents inside the ego, one that accepts castration, the other that disavows it—creates the conditions for the emergence of what Strachey (1961c), in the introduction to the article studied, considers as constituting "a fresh metapsychological development"

(p. 150), beginning with disavowal but ending in its inevitable consequence—that is, ego splitting. The latter, as we shall see further on, will undergo other developments, in addition to an exclusive connection with disavowal. Anyhow, it involves the general issue of ego functioning under the pressure of external reality. Indeed, to introduce the topic in the 1927 article, Freud writes—suggestively, in my opinion—that "the explanation of fetishism had another point of theoretical interest as well" (1927e, p. 155). He refers then to the cases of two young people he analysed, in whom it was found that both had disavowed a crucial fragment of reality—the death of their father when they were children—but that this did not cause them to develop a psychosis. This condition contradicts his previous thesis that the essential difference between neurosis and psychosis would be that in the former, the ego refuses a fragment of the id to fulfil demands of reality, and that in the other, part of the reality is refused to fulfil demands of the id. In the two patients mentioned by Freud, the same disavowal found in fetishism had occurred, just as the same ego splitting, but the disavowal was directed at the painful perception of the father's death.

> It was only one current in their mental life that had not recognized their father's death; there was another current which took full account of that fact. The attitude which fitted in with the wish and the attitude which fitted in with reality existed side by side. In one of my two cases this *split* had formed the basis of a moderately severe obsessional neurosis. The patient oscillated in every situation in life between two assumptions: the one that his father was still alive and was hindering his activities; the other, opposite one, that he was entitled to regard himself as his father's successor. [1927e, p. 156, emphasis added]

Freud adds that, in psychosis, the current according to reality would not be effectiveness.

Let us then retain the following, as additional information for later general considerations on the topic of this contribution. In this first part of our "triptych" ego splitting is considered a passive and inevitable consequence of disavowal, by the ego, of a fragment of reality, to respond to demands from the id. It is exemplarily present in fetishism, in this case resulting specifically from a disavowal of the lack of a penis in women. But it can also be found in neuroses and may thus derive from the disavowal of other aspects of external reality. In psychoses, the current that acknowledges perception would be maintained without effectiveness.

The beginning of the central piece of our "triptych" is marked by a doubt of the creator of psychoanalysis. He does not know whether the peculiar behaviour of the ego in situations of infantile psychic trauma that he is going to describe (i.e., splitting) is something already known and evident, or, on the contrary, something completely new and surprising. He is, however, inclined to the second possibility. I think it important to underline this initial hesitation, because a few months later, in chapter VIII of the *Outline of Psycho-Analysis*, he will say that "the facts of this splitting of the ego, which we have just described, are neither so new nor so strange as they may at first appear" (p. 204). I believe that this change of opinion expresses a modification—in this small time interval—of his conception of splitting in the general context of theorization on the defensive processes of the ego, as I argue later when discussing the contributions of chapter VIII.

In order to study this peculiar ego functioning, Freud cuts out and highlights, in the texts started during Christmas of 1937, one of its possible causes, but not the only one, as he stresses. Thus, faced with a conflict between a powerful demand of the drive and the fear that its satisfaction would result in a real, unbearable danger, the ego responds with two contrary reactions, simultaneous, independent from each other, but both effective.

"On the one hand", says Freud, "with the help of certain mechanisms he rejects reality and refuses to accept any prohibition; on the other hand, in the same breath he recognizes the danger of reality, takes over the fear of that danger as a pathological symptom and tries subsequently to divest himself of the fear" (p. 275).

The inevitable and important consequence is a fissure, a slit, a crack [*ein Einriss*] in the ego, which will not cease to grow over time. The persistence of this split surprises Freud, as already mentioned, because it goes against his ideas about synthetic ego function. This function, he says now, requires certain specific conditions to subsist, and it is subject to various disturbances.

Next, Freud presents a brief clinical example, once again of a case of fetishism (without specifying the fetish), in order to illustrate that process. This time he underlines that dread of castration, which triggers the disavowal of the absence of a penis in the woman and the consequent splitting and related symptoms, is a result of the necessary conjunction of two events: the view of the female genitals and the later verbal threat of castration. He also remarks that, despite the continuation of drive satisfaction (in this case, masturbation), enabled by disavowal, the boy all the same developed an intense fear of being devoured by the father, a regressive oral substitute for castration. He also began to show a displaced symbolic expression of castration itself, in the form of anxious sensitivity to contact with either of his two little toes. In other words, the disavowal and splitting resulting from the ego did not prevent the formation of expressive and defensive symptoms.

Summing up, in this small and unfinished (but even so, important) central panel of our "triptych", splitting becomes the central theme (this is the title of the article), and everything points to the fact that not only would it remain postulated for other psychopathological situations in addition to fetishism, as already occurred in the 1927 paper, but it would begin to be detached from the specific mechanism of disavowal. However, the latter possibility will have to await the next piece of the "triptych"—that is, chapter VIII of the *Outline of Psycho-Analysis* (1940a [1938])—to be explained and confirmed.

I would even consider that, in the latter text of the *Outline of Psycho-Analysis,* Freud clears the way and leaves us the first outlines for what we could consider "a conception of generalized splitting". He proposes that, when facing the conflicting impositions of the objective world and the id, the ego should defend itself from the instinctual demands via repressions [*Verdrängung*] and from the external demands by disavowal [*Verleugnung*] of the perceptions that report them. This disavowal is not the apanage of fetishism and always turns out to be incomplete as to the objective of disconnecting the ego from reality. In all cases it is seen that this disavowal is invariably accompanied by a concomitant recognition of the external reality. Thus two psychic attitudes, contrary to and independent from each other, are shown to be responsible for a psychic split. The final effect of this process will depend on the relative force of each of the psychic attitudes.

Freud postulates that this split is always present in the psychotic conditions. Psychosis is manifested when there is a predominance of the psychic attitude of disconnection of the ego from the external reality induced by the pressure of the id. The opposite attitude of keeping in touch with this reality persists simultaneously and silently. It may, for instance, be responsible for dreams that represent reality without any delusion. In the latter case, says Freud, it is as though a non-participating observer remained hidden somewhere in the mind, looking at the course of the psychosis. When the psychic attitude of preserving contact with objective reality preponderates, the delusion is expelled to the unconscious (where, in fact, it already was before the psychosis erupted), giving rise to an apparent cure.

But Freud once again broadens the outreach and implications of this phenomenon:

> The view which postulates that in all psychoses there is a *splitting of the ego* could not call for so much notice if it did not turn out to apply to other states more like the neuroses and, finally, to the neuroses themselves. [1940a (1938), p. 202; emphasis added]

In this sense, as to fetishism, he emphasizes that it simply constitutes an object that is particularly favourable to the study of ego splitting, and the first one that convinced him of this. He also states that in such cases there is not always ego splitting. It only exists in those in which the formation of the fetish—that is, for the purpose of avoiding castration anxiety destroying the proof of lack of a penis in the woman—does not prevent the development of this type of anxiety and the same reactions presented to it by the non-fetishists.

> Their behaviour is therefore simultaneously expressing two contrary premises. On the one hand they are disavowing the fact of their perception—the fact that they saw no penis in the female genitals; and the other hand they are recognizing the fact that females have no penis and are drawing the correct conclusions from it. The two attitudes persist side by side throughout their lives without influencing each other. Here is what may rightly be called a splitting of the ego. [1940a (1938), p. 203]

In other cases, Freud goes on, what happens after the fetish is formed is the compromise-formation that takes place with the help of a displacement [*Verschiebung*], following the lines already known from the study of dreams.

The issue of ego splitting in neuroses is not discussed very extensively in this writing. Freud had already supplied an illustration in 1927, with the case of the young man who, due to the disavowal of his father's death during his childhood, showed a splitting responsible for his obsessive neurosis. Furthermore, however—and in my opinion with important theoretical implications—in the last paragraph of the chapter he states that the presence of two opposite attitudes in the mind, contrary and independent from each other in relation to a given conduct, is "a universal characteristic of neuroses . . ." (1940a [1938], p. 204). In this case, however, one of these psychic attitudes will belong to the ego and the opposite one will be repressed in the id. In fetishism, on the other hand, both stay in the ego.

Thus, in the last instance, the difference would be, says the founder of psychoanalysis in this epilogue to his work, topographical or structural, and it is often difficult to decide which is the case in a specific clinical situation. And Freud goes on to say further:

> Whatever the ego does in its efforts of defence, whether it seeks to disavow a portion of the real external world or whether it seeks to reject an instinctual demand from the internal world, its success is never complete and unqualified. The outcome always lies in two contrary attitudes, of which the defeated, weaker one, no less than the other, leads to psychical complications. [1940a [1938], p. 204]

Grouping all the latter propositions would enable the following general consideration that, in my opinion, also includes and does not go against statements made by Freud about splitting the ego in the two previous papers.

Both the repressions of id drives and the disavowal of portions of the external reality provoke, as a *consequence*, a psychic splitting, a splitting that thus acquires a universal character in mental life. In any such cases, we will always be before two contrary and mutually independent psychic attitudes, both of them effective. The difference is only structural or topographical: in repression, splitting is between instances (between the ego and the id) or systems (unconscious and preconscious–conscious); the disavowal occurs within the ego itself. Under Freud's pen in this final writing, disavowal is not the apanage of fetishism (of perversions) and not every disavowal present in these cases would necessarily provoke a splitting of the ego. There is also disavowal in the psychoses (always associated with splitting) and in the neuroses. Thus, there is much left to be explained about the differences regarding the origins and effects of splitting in neuroses, psychoses, and perversions. In this sense Lacan's contribution proposing the foreclusion mechanism [*Verwerfung*] for the psychoses, disavowal [*Verleugnung*] for the perversions, and repression [*Verdrängung*] in the case of neuroses likely constitutes a tentative approach to improving the articulation of this whole issue (Roulot, 1993). Lacan postulates, in addition, a "splitting of the subject", distinct from Freud's splitting of the ego. This is the normal functioning of the subject, since this, in the words of Le Gaufey (1993), is "always represented by one significant to another, indefinitely split because of the functioning of the significant chain" (p. 84).

Based on all these propositions, could we not be dealing with what I call the concept of generalized splitting? If so, what are its implications for a general theory of defensive processes? Would it involve, as suggested by Green (1993), the need for a general review of the theory of defences? Regarding this matter, Green (1993) says the following:

> The perplexity of the 1938 article is, thus, explained by the question about the legitimacy of generalizing this mode of defence, i.e.—I believe, about the obligation, after the death instinct and the second topography were introduced, of a *general review of the concept of defence,* comparable to that which Freud had done about anxiety, a review whose need he appeared to have glimpsed. [emphasis added]

This statement by Green appears to me very pertinent and challenging in its general terms. I only question its classification of splitting as a defence mechanism in itself. I italicized the world "consequence" in the general considerations above because I agree with Laplanche and Pontalis (1967) that, in Freud, splitting is not a defence mechanism in itself, but an effect of the defensive processes. This splitting, they say, "is not properly speaking a defence of the ego, but rather a means of having two procedures of defence exist side by side, one directed towards reality (disavowal) and the other towards the instinct; this second procedure may lead to the formation of neurotic symptoms (e.g. phobic symptoms)" (p. 429).

The situation regarding this issue is different when we look at the fate of the notion of *Spaltung* in Melanie Klein's work (1946, 1952, 1957). Klein postulates the existence of a primary active splitting of the objects, and consequently of the ego, as one of the most primitive defence mechanisms, central in the so-called paranoid–schizoid position. For this very reason, it is a concept distinct from that of splitting of the ego proposed by Freud.

According to Klein (1946), the primary objective of the ego is, from birth, to deal with the anxiety generated by the internal action of the death instinct. Consonant with its lack of initial cohesion, the early ego tends to go to pieces under the pressure of this paranoid anxiety. Klein (1946), however, postulates that from the beginning, the ego also makes use of "active splitting processes" (p. 5) to defend itself from this anxiety: "As we assume, the early ego splits the object and the relation to it in an active way, and this may imply some active splitting of the ego itself" (p. 5).

Immediately after, still in the same work, she is even more emphatic, stating that the ego never manages to split the object without itself splitting: "I believe that the ego is *incapable* of splitting the object—internal and external—without a corresponding splitting taking place within the ego. Therefore the phantasies and feelings about the state of the internal object vitally influence the structure of the ego" (Klein, 1946, p. 6, emphasis added).

Splitting is associated from the beginning with other primitive mechanisms, such as introjection, projection, and projective identification. The latter consists of a combination of splitting off parts of the self with its projection into another person.

Klein emphasizes that this splitting of the internal and external objects, of emotions and ego, is part of normal development. She considers it "instrumental in building up the ego" (p. 6). It enables the separation between the frustrating good breast and the gratifying good breast, as well as the latter's introjection as a vital point of focus on the ego, which counterbalances the splitting and dispersion processes, thus providing cohesion and integration. Under certain conditions, above all when related to primary envy (Klein, 1957), it constitutes the base of pathological processes.

In the depressive position (Klein, 1952), the splitting (of the now complete object) begins to occur between a living, undamaged object and another damaged, threatened, dying, or dead object, and it serves as a defence against depressive anxiety.

As to the relations between splitting and repression, Klein (1952) says that splitting underlies the latter, and actually constitutes a primitive form of it. The most primitive splitting leads to states of disintegration of the self. This does not happen in the case of repression, because the division occurs between the conscious and the unconscious, both already more integrated internally. But the degree of working through or not of early, primary splitting decisively influences the later quality of the repression. The less it is overcome, the more intense will be the repression and therefore the greater the rigidity of the barrier between conscious and unconscious. The more it is overcome in primary splitting, the more moderate will be the repression, and the more porous the communication between the systems, thus enabling the unconscious contents to reach the ego and be processed according to their characteristics.

After all this, it can be said that in Klein's work, splitting is not only a defence mechanism in itself, primary and fundamental. It is also the resource underlying other important mechanisms such as projective identification (which implies splitting off) and repression (which would be a more evolved splitting). It is, moreover, the base from which other defences act (such as denial and idealization) as well as the instrument to build the ego.

It should be emphasized that, before Melanie Klein, Fairbairn (whom she quoted) already postulated that splitting constitutes the central mechanism in structuring what he calls the "basic endopsychical situation", to the extent of considering the "schizoid position" as main and fundamental for all psychic development (Fairbairn, 1952b).

The first step to structure the mind in this way is, in Fairbairn's final version, the incorporation of the partially unsatisfactory and partially satisfactory object, by an original ego that is still non-dissociated. An ambivalence of this ego as to the object then arises, and it therefore constitutes an ambivalent internalized object. In the next stage, the ego splits actively from the main body of the object the excessively exciting and excessively frustrating aspects, both of them unacceptable to it. From this splitting results an exciting object and a rejecting object, both soon also repressed, and what persists is a core of the original object. But the investment of the original ego in these objects continues, and, since it does not accept the exciting and rejecting objects, it is ultimately split too. The part connected to the exciting object will give rise to the libidinal ego and that connected to the rejecting object to the so-called internal saboteur. After this, a central core of the ego and a core of the original object remain. The latter, accepted by the ego, and therefore non-repressed, takes on the form of a desexualized and idealized object and, constitutes the core of the construction of the superego, which Fairbairn prefers to call the ego-ideal.

Thus, it is found that for Fairbairn, after the incorporation of the object (which in itself does not generate any psychic structure), the splitting constitutes, as I mentioned above, the central mechanism in the construction of the mind. Repression and externalization come later and are effected on its results. Once again, the first splitting (active as in Klein and different from Freud) is of the object (again as in Klein and without any reference in Freud). Splitting of the ego occurs later than that of the object (like Klein). But, both in Fairbairn and in Klein and Freud, splitting of the ego in itself is always a consequence of defensive processes. Freud, however (differently from Fairbairn and Klein), does not consider splitting a defence mechanism in itself, as was already highlighted previously.

Actually, each of the divisions mentioned so far would require its own metapsychological explanation, under pain of only making descriptive use of the term.

After all this, there is still a last expansion, which I consider possible, necessary and even required by a development that is increasingly accepted in contemporary psychoanalysis.

Up to this point in the present work, the phenomenon of splitting has been studied in an exclusively intrapsychic domain. However, the assumption has been increasingly adopted that all phenomena present, observable, and accessible to be worked on in the analytic space and process derive from an interplay between intrapsychic functionings of the analysand and the analyst. In other words, these are essentially intersubjective phenomena. Furthermore, for many analysts these phenomena are more than the sum of psychic functionings of the two participants. They transcend them, just as the phenomena of the group transcend the simple sum of the contribution of each of its members (Bion, 1961). In this sense, they are what we could call trans-subjective or suprasubjective phenomena, rather than simply intersubjective. They are conceptualized by the Barangers (M. Baranger, 2005; W. Baranger, 1979; W. Baranger & Baranger, 1969) within Willy Baranger's currently well-known "Theory of the Analytic Field". More recently, Ogden (1994b) includes them in his theoretical formulation about what he calls the "intersubjective analytic third", which would be in permanent dialectical tension with the two subjectivities that are also present in the setting. I believe that it would be equally possible to understand them beginning with the process described as the "emergent property" present in the so-called complex adaptive systems (Hartke, 2004; Honderich, 1995; Lewin, 1993). This is a global structure that, although it was generated by the interactions of individual elements, presents new characteristics of functioning that cannot be deduced from each of them singly. I consider that the phenomena that occur in the analytic space are always trans-subjective in the last instance. They will, however, appear as intrapsychic (in the analysand or in the analyst) or as belonging to the pair only because of the analyst's (or analysand's) observational point of view. In other words, only according to the vertex (Bion, 1965) adopted by the analyst or by the analysand when, thanks to a peculiar splitting in the ego, it is divided between an observing part and another that observes itself, the other, or the pair that they are forming. And further: using the notion of "complementary mode of description" postulated by Bohr (1958, p. 7) from what he called an "epistemological lesson" (p. 68) enabled by quantum physics, I believe that each of these vertexes always generates a different phenomenon. This results from the fact that the observational position will inevitably modify the functioning itself of the phenomenon observed (Hartke, 2007). At the same time, all vertexes are important and necessary so that the events present in the setting can be appropriately described and worked on.

Beginning with this basic positioning (epistemological, theoretical, and technical), the question is raised about which would be the intersubjective or trans-subjective equivalent of intrapsychic splitting examined so far. I consider that the Barangers (M. Baranger, 2005; W. Baranger, 1979; W. Baranger & Baranger, 1969) offer unique, precious contributions in this sense, summarized in the following passage:

> If, as Freud thought in one of his unfinished papers, every defence mechanism implies a certain "Spaltung", or a certain splitting inside the ego, all the pathological formation in the field will imply splitting one of its sectors, which escapes the general dynamics and creates a more or less pronounced paralysis. Even though a certain mobilization of the field is produced, it works leaving aside the split sector, in such a way as to keep it out of the dynamics of the situation. This splitting does not correspond to a repression, certain parts of the split sector are conscious or may easily become conscious. Other parts, on the contrary, are repressed and correspond to much more archaic splittings which support current splitting.
>
> In the bipersonal situation, this process becomes really prejudicial when the analysand's splitting assay finds unconscious complicity or a blind spot in the analyst. Then we see a partialization of the analytic process. Events continue to happen, part of the material continues to be worked through, but something important escapes the process and remains crystallized. [M. Baranger & Baranger, 1964, p. 8]

At these times, or in pathological situations in the field, there is formed what Willy Baranger (1979) calls the "bulwark" [*baluarte*], using the metaphor of an advanced defence to the approach to the central part of a fortress (M. Baranger, 2005). This is a peculiar formation of the analytic space, an area of defensive resistance created and maintained by both participants, and which sometimes escapes the possibilities of mobilization, verbalization, and working through that are specific to the analytic process.

The considerations carried out on the intrapsychic splitting, at all its levels and in all its forms, would thus also need (or rather, first need) to be recognized, conceptualized, and worked through technically in this inter- or trans-subjective scope.

Overcoming splitting in the field, which generates the bulwark, is made possible by the specifically analytic insight, also understood by the Barangers (1969) as a phenomenon necessarily in the bipersonal field: "The act of analytic insight is the formulation of the interpretation of the current state of the field, done by the analyst and shared by the analysand" (p. 163). It enables the reintegration, in the general dynamics of the therapeutic process, of those aspects of the field that were excluded, isolated, and paralysed in the bulwark. In addition to realizing what was happening, both participants can discriminate what belongs to each of them. It is obvious that the field will then immediately be restructured in another pathological form that will have to be overcome by a new insight, in a process characterized by Willy Baranger (1979) as "in a spiral". But what matters most for the purposes of the present work is the remark by Baranger that this type of insight requires and implies what he described as a "second look" (p. 55) or "a second-degree look" (p. 56). I quote him again to a certain extent, because I consider that this notion once again involves a peculiar process of splitting, extended thus not only to the pathology of the analytic field, but also to the instrument that is characteristic of and essential to the therapeutic process—that is, work aiming at insight:

> This division of the analyst's function in the field is expressed in a dual vision, or second look, and although this is a well-known phenomenon, little has been done to examine it further because it leads to countertransference, which is what most analysts would like to avoid. There are in any analytic session two different looks: a first, simple one, which focuses on the associative material rendered by the analysand: we analyse a dream, for example, connecting the elements of the manifest content with the associations, uncovering the day's residues that went into the making of the dream, establishing connections with previous dreams, with memories brought by the patient earlier, with his present situation related to other people, and so forth. While this work proceeds without problems, we stay within this look. Yet if some kind of difficulty arises, if something strange comes up in us—a definite feeling, a corporal reaction, an odd fantasy—we feel the need to change the direction of our look and to focus not only on the analysand but on the whole field, including ourselves. This second look includes the analyst's self-observation. [pp. 55–56]

The observing ego or the ego in its observation function, in the insight process, is differentiated by the Barangers (1964) from that present in the situations where the bulwark predominates, in which it works with the objective of defensive wakefulness and protection in relation to the other.

As I have already mentioned, I think that the "second-order look" can be directed to the functioning, in the session, of oneself, of the other, or of the pair, generating in each case a different phenomenon, but always with a trans-subjective origin and base. The fundamental aspect to be emphasized, however, is that this "second look" or "complementary vertexes operation" requires, in all cases, a splitting of the ego in the analytic field. And I consider that the use of the term *Spaltung* for this case is not merely descriptive, without any conceptual value, insofar as it supports and demands explanations as to its specific characteristics (examined by the Barangers in the articles of 1961–62 and 1964), conditions of possibility, and, perhaps, peculiar anxiety. In the first place, as to its unique characteristics, this division does not derive from a psychic conflict, nor does it result in a pathological situation. Both split parts (observer and observed) remain in the ego, conscious and recognized as one's own, but, contrary to the splitting of the ego mentioned by Freud, they generate the feeling of totality that belongs to insight. And there are certainly several other specificities as to this division, and in this case we also have the persistence of the possibility that this is simply the consequence of another process. Or, on the contrary, could we be dealing here primarily with a splitting of the ego, without necessarily implying any division of the object?

Ogden (1994b) and Britton (1989), based on different theoretical lines, comment on the development of the individual capacity of self-observation, which likewise implies a division of the ego and which, in my opinion, is applied equally to the conditions necessary for the psychic process involved in the "second look" in the analytic field. For both authors, this egoic function involves the acquisition of a thirdness. Thus, based on Winnicott, Ogden (1994b) says the following:

> The infant's observation of himself (as Other to himself) in the mother's reflection of him generates the rudiments of the experience of self-consciousness ("self-reflection"), that is, the awareness of observable me-ness. In other words, the mother, in her role as mirror, provides thirdness (Green, 1975) that allows for the *division* of the infant into an observing subject and a subject-as-object with a reflective space between the two. [p. 49, emphasis added]

Britton (1989), in turn, proposes that this thirdness can only be achieved with the elaboration of the depressive position and the oedipal complex, one depending on the other. The recognition, by the child, of the genital and procreative relationship between its parents (different from its own with each of them) creates what he calls a "triangular space" (p. 86)—a space delimited by the three participants in the oedipal situation, each in his own position—and this creates the possibility for different object relations:

> A third position then comes into existence from which object relationships can be observed. Given this, we can also envisage *being* observed. This provides us with a capacity for seeing ourselves in interaction with others and for entertaining another point of view whilst retaining our own, for reflecting on ourselves whilst being ourselves. This is a capacity we hope to find in ourselves and in our patients in analysis. [Britton, 1989, p. 87, emphasis added]

Finally, I think that Bion (1963) offers an interesting contribution regarding a peculiar anguish about this psychic splitting present in the insight process. He says that there is need for detachment in the intimacy of the analytic relationship (a splitting?) so that this can be examined during its course. In the object being examined this generates a painful feeling of solitude, of being abandoned; in the examining object, an also painful feeling of detaching from the base on which its existence depends—that is, from the "primitive animal mental inheritance" (p. 16).

> The apparently abandoned object of scrutiny is the primitive mind and the primitive social capacity of the individual as a political or group animal. The "detached" personality is in a sense new to its job and has to turn to tasks which differ from those to which its components are more usually adapted, namely scrutiny of the environment excluding the self; part of the price paid is in feelings of insecurity. [Bion, 1963, p. 16]

The relations between splitting and capacity for self-observation (necessary for insight, as well as to carry out correlations) are quite explicit in Bion's thinking (1965), in the passage below. Here also relations of splitting with vertexes of observation and with what he calls "binocular vision" are shown, as well as acknowledged normal or problematic (perverse) uses of it:

> Patients can be observed to change their attitude to an object by changes in view-point which may be perverse or analogous to change of position that a surveyor, terrestrial or astronomical,

> uses to estimate the range of a distant object. The procedure involves *splitting in time and space* and, depending on the nature of the intention, may aid the solution of a problem by providing a substitute for "binocular vision" when "binocular vision" is not available, or hinder a solution by destroying "binocular vision" when it is available. The immediate relevance of this lies in the use of *splitting* as a method of achieving correlation. [Bion, 1965, p. 66, emphasis added]

Splitting that is crucial for the process of seeking knowledge, perverse use of splitting, splitting in time and in space . . . more and more generalized splitting . . .

At this point, however, I consider at an end the path I intended to take in this long walk through the theme discussed by Freud in his unfinished article about splitting. Beginning with a merely descriptive use of the term *Spaltung*, we arrive, still with Freud, at the concept of splitting of the ego, initially connected with disavowal, but then considered a consequence (not a defence in itself) of defensive processes also against internal demands (repression). With this, the perspective of a conception of the generalized splitting insinuated in his final outline of psychoanalysis was opened. Fairbairn and Klein extended it to a defence mechanism in itself, directed primarily at a splitting of the object, and consequently giving rise to a splitting also of the ego—a mechanism that they considered fundamental for psychopathology as well as for the normal constitution of the mind. It should be emphasized that, both in Freud and in the later two authors, ego splitting in itself remains a consequence of defensive operations. Until this point, it was essentially an intrapsychic phenomenon. The Barangers expanded the concept to also include phenomena in the analytic field, of the analytic pair. In other words, they broadened it to an intersubjective dimension (I would say, also trans-subjective), which was, once again, present both in the pathology (bulwark) and in the characteristic process of the psychoanalytic insight.

In brief, we could say that, for the authors reviewed in this chapter, splitting of the ego in itself is always the consequence of defensive processes, whether they be directed against a fragment of external reality (disavowed), against some internal instinctual demand (repression), or in relation to the internal or external objects (splitting according to Fairbairn and Klein). "The outcome", as Freud already said, "always lies in two contrary attitudes . . ." (1940a [1938], p. 204)—that is, in a splitting of the ego. It is in this sense that, in my opinion, we can talk of a concept of generalized splitting.

This does not prevent the following and last general elucubration. The final result of any defensive process is always one or another form of division and, thus, separation between parts of the mind. There are different ways in which this division can be achieved, as well as different possible destinies for the resulting parts. This division and separation may even constitute the final objective of such processes. It is also possible that the mind, as such, can only structure itself and acquire operationality by functional divisions and separations between structures and contents. In all these cases so far mentioned, the separate structures or contents persist, all with psychic effectivity, requiring later mental work. In the beginnings of psychic development, the division would be effected thanks to an active, direct mechanism of splitting of the objects and, consequently, of the ego. The painful part of the resultant contents would suffer, in fantasy, the action of omnipotent annihilation processes, or alternatively, expulsion from the mind (foreclusion, projective identification). The accepted contents could in turn be idealized.

Later in development, this division would take place between or even within structures or psychic systems already separated functionally from each other, each of them more organized internally. Besides, it would be carried out by mediate, indirect (i.e., not directly by a division), and psychologically more sophisticated processes, directed against internal contents or against perceptions of the external world. The resultant contents, in turn, could remain within the ego itself, could be repulsed to the unconscious, or could once again be expelled to the exterior (projection).

When preserved within the ego, both conflicting parts could be maintained conscious and effective (splitting of the ego, *stricto sensu*). But the separation could, in this case, occur also thanks to, for instance, isolation [*Isolierung*] of a thought or behaviour of its associative connections with the rest of the mind or correlated affect (Freud, 1926d [1925]), or even by a logical process of negation [*Verneinung*] of contents that returned from the unconscious (Freud, 1925h).

In a special form, splitting would be in the normal origin itself of the subject, as in the development of the capacity for self-reflection. The latter situation, necessary (although not sufficient) for psychoanalytic insight, would appear to involve primarily a splitting of the ego.

These different modalities and levels of psychic splitting also occur in the inter or trans-subjective sphere.

These elucubrations (as all the other considerations presented during the course of this chapter) are simply suggestions of points of departure for the challenging line of research opened by Freud in his last writings and which had increasingly interested him: a possible review of the general theory of defences and, more specifically, the perspective of a theory of generalized splitting, which is the creditor of a corresponding metapsychology.

9

Splitting of the ego and perversion

Louise Carignan

Freud's views on perversion evolved through successive stages. In the *Three Essays* (1905d) he conceived of perversion as the persistence in adult life of untamed components of childhood, or "pregenital" sexuality, at the expense of adult genital sexuality. Perversion was contrasted with neurosis, in which these pregenital or perverse impulses were censored. By the 1920s, however, he had modified his views, seeing perversions as regressive defensive formations in relation to the Oedipus complex (Freud, 1919e). Finally, in his late works on fetishism and the splitting of the ego in the process of defence (Freud, 1927e, 1940a [1938], 1940e [1938]), he described *disavowal*—a mechanism that allows the fetishist to maintain his belief that his mother has a penis and negate the perceptual reality, side by side with acknowledging the fact of sexual differences and drawing the correct conclusions from it. The disavowal of female castration protects the fetishist from the fear of losing his own penis. Rather than hallucinating the missing female penis as would a psychotic, he only transfers the importance or value of the penis onto another part of the female body or another object called a fetish, which then renders the woman tolerable as a sexual object. Freud noted that the "*artful*" way of dealing with reality at work in disavowal, where two contradictory attitudes co-exist without influencing each other, was, however, achieved at the price of a *rift in the ego*, which persists or increases over time.

Our understanding of perversions has evolved since Freud's original formulations, with the discovery of the importance of pre-oedipal factors and of the central role played by early trauma, aggressive and vengeful impulses, and superego defects in perversion (Gillespie, 1956; Greenacre, 1953; Stoller, 1975). In addition, the multitude of perverse acts, scenarios, or fetishistic objects that have been described and the recognition that a perversion usually involves a combination of diverse perverse elements (fetishistic, sadomasochistic, exhibitionistic, and voyeuristic) have led workers in the field away from characterizing perversions according to sexual behaviour, and towards a conceptualization of perversion in terms of defensive organization, psychic strategy, mechanism, or form of relationship. The formulations of the French school, of Stoller (1975), Khan (1979), Etchegoyen (1978, 1991), and Steiner (1993), fall within this more current approach to perversion.

Disavowal holds a central place in the formulations of French analysts Aulagnier (1967), McDougall (1972, 1986), and Chasseguet-Smirgel (1981, 1984), who have sought to define the psychic structure underlying manifest perversions. They extended Freud's notion of a disavowal of castration in fetishism to include the disavowal of sexual and generational differences and of otherness. McDougall proposed that the sight of female genitals was terrifying for the "future pervert", not only due to castration fears, but also because it demanded that he recognize the father's role in the genital relationship between his parents and therefore abandon his omnipotent illusion of being the sole object of his mother's desire. Unwilling to relinquish his omnipotent hold on his mother, unable to tolerate his exclusion from his parents' genital relationship and to negotiate the fears and mortifications entailed in the passage through the Oedipus complex, he disavows the genital primal scene and replaces it with an alternative sexual scenario. This new scenario reduces the genital primal scene to a pregenital one, in which the differences between the sexes and the generations are abolished. Chasseguet-Smirgel stressed the role of anal-sadistic regression in the elaboration of the "perverse solution".

Khan (1979) implicated an early disturbance in the anaclitic relation to the mother who is unable to provide a "good-enough" holding environment and who idolizes her infant-child as her "thing-creation" rather than treating him as an emergent person in his own right. This results in a failure in the development of transitional objects and phenomena that usually provide a temporary and evolving area of illusion between inner and outer reality and facilitate symbolization and the separation from the actual mother (Winnicott, 1951, 1960). Instead, there is a turning to perverse relations with human and non-human objects or fetishes (Winnicott, 1965). While both the transitional object and the fetish are props whose presence brings current anxiety-provoking situations under the illusory control of the individual, the use of the transitional object aids psychic differentiation, whereas the use of the fetish on the other hand appears to be a fixed (addictive) solution that must be compulsively repeated (Greenacre, 1969, 1970). The disavowal of sexual and generational differences and of otherness found in perversion impedes psychic growth by allowing the individual to circumvent the elaboration of the oedipal situation and of the depressive position (Chasseguet-Smirgel, 1981, 1984; McDougall, 1986). Instead of a "structural disavowal", which determines the psychic space of fantasy,[1] one finds a pathogenic disavowal associated with a splitting of the ego (Britton, 1995; Casas de Pereda, 1997).

The notion that patients with sexual perversions reproduce a special type of relation in analysis, so that a transference perversion may be created and resolved, was put forward by Etchegoyen (1978, 1991). He was partly inspired by an earlier classic case study by Joseph (1971), showing how a rubber fetishist lived out his perversion in the analysis and how he could begin to be satisfactorily helped only when she could locate its main aspects in the transference. Joseph stressed the way in which her patient provoked her to act out by giving exciting sadistic pseudo-interpretations, which led to a silent or hidden sadomasochistic erotization of the transference that was not only a defence by means of which he sought to relieve himself of his impulses and painful feelings and withdraw from emotional contact, but also an attack upon the analyst and an attempt to pervert the transference by sexualizing it. Indeed, a common observation found in clinical reports is the pressure these patients put on the analyst to become a partner or an accomplice in perverse enactments, creating an ever-present danger of treatment impasse or failure (Baker, 1994; Chasseguet-Smirgel, 1981; Clavreul, 1967; McDougall, 1978). Etchegoyen (1991) and Ogden (1996) stated that the analysis of perversion necessarily involves the elaboration and analysis of a perverse transference–countertransference.

Khan drew attention to the quality of relatedness to the partner in perversion. His observations are important to grasp the nature of the relatedness at play in the perverse transference. His principal thesis is that "the pervert places an impersonal object between his desire and his accomplice: this object can be a stereotyped fantasy, a gadget or pornographic image. All three alienate the pervert from himself, as, alas, from the object of his desire" (1979, p. 9). The partner is depersonalized and occupies an intermediate place in perversion: he is accepted as separate on the one hand, but treated as a subjective object on the other. Khan thought that the perverse partner had the value of a transitional object, but it might more accurate to describe him as a fetish-object (Carignan, 2003, 2005). His paradoxical expression "the technique of intimacy"[2] captures how perversion is, at the same time, an attempt at intimacy and a defence against it.

The following clinical material describes the unfolding of a perverse transference during the initial four years of treatment of an overtly bisexual man. Throughout his marriage, this patient had maintained a "secret" homosexual life consisting of compulsive and anonymous encounters in saunas or public toilets. He re-enacted within the transference the pattern of leading a "double life" that had been present before with his wife, and his secretiveness about his homosexual sorties became the locus of a prolonged transference–countertransference engagement.

"Albert" showed signs of a split in the ego, between a quasi-neurotic (rather obsessional) part, and a part that created a "neo-sexuality" (McDougall, 1986) to preserve omnipotent illusions and disavow painful, unwanted, or threatening realizations. His superego attitude was also split: while a side of him was quite moralistic and upheld traditional family values, another side idealized sadism and the subversion of sexual barriers and taboos. His perverse[3] acting out within and outside the transference formed a complex erotized defensive/reparative/vengeful manoeuvre permitting the disavowal and magical reversal of perceived threats to his personal or sexual identity.

Clinical material[4]

The patient, a man in his forties I shall name Albert, identified bisexuality as the reason why he sought analysis. Throughout a marriage lasting two decades, he had engaged in compulsive anonymous homosexual liaisons in public toilets or baths. He thought that his homosexual sorties were connected with a need to fend off his wife's domination. She eventually requested a divorce because of his homosexuality. He had felt betrayed by her decision and had been unable to get on with his life ever since. He saw in his former difficulties with his wife a replica of his earlier struggles against submitting to his mother's will and becoming "*her thing*", as he put it. After the violent temper tantrums and open defiance of his childhood, his warfare with his mother had taken a more passive and self-defeating turn, as when, for example, he called her from the boarding school where she had sent him against his will to announce with vengeful glee that he had failed his academic year.

His mother reportedly told him that she had "discovered love" only after giving birth to him. She abandoned her career to look after him. He could recall no zone of comfort or pleasure with his mother, an anxious and overbearing woman, only his sustained battle against being "crushed" by her. Albert had always perceived that his mother covertly despised men. His father had been an apparent exception only because she controlled him entirely, and reduced him to being a provider of money and sperm (for procreation only). His father had, in fact, successfully climbed the corporate ladder up to the position of director in a large firm. When at home, however, he had been a remote and neutral bystander who was occasionally called on by the mother to discipline the children when she was at her wits' end. Emotionally, he was a stranger to Albert, who despised his father.

He said he remained prudish and uninformed about sexuality until his late teens. His first erections at puberty occurred shortly after he cut his penis accidentally on some sports equipment. The superficial cut had bled. He recalled feeling that his erections were abnormal, connecting them with this injury and being very nervous about them. Of his own volition, he consulted a male therapist when he was 19 because he felt that his sexual life was abnormal. Within six months of therapy, he had his first homosexual experience and dropped out of treatment.

Albert's only sibling, a brother three years younger, had settled with a homosexual partner some years before. Albert did not "believe in coming out of the closet", and he found his brother's open homosexuality objectionable because "he believes that his homosexual relationship is equivalent to a heterosexual one, making a travesty of heterosexuality". When I voiced my puzzlement over the contradictions implicit in his attitude towards homosexuality, Albert retorted that his homosexuality had value precisely in so far as it was a "transgression".

Feeling sexually attractive to men only, he was taken aback when his future wife pursued him, even though she knew of his previous homosexual relation. He described an "unbridled sexuality" in his twenties and thirties. Both spouses had affairs (his were mostly but not exclusively homosexual), and they also engaged briefly in a *ménage à trois* with a man. His wife, most likely as a result of the analysis she undertook later on during their marriage, eventually grew intolerant of his homosexual infidelities. He appeared to have remained quite tied to her despite several years of separation, but he related to her in a very removed and passive way. He had otherwise felt at sea since his divorce.

Opening phase

In the beginning sessions on the couch, he professed at length his fascination with Sade's *One Hundred and Twenty Days of Sodom*, for the tortures depicted in Bosch's paintings, and his admiration for the unrepentant Don Juan who opted to fry in hell rather than surrender to moral authority. I experienced his declarations as an opening gambit, in which he flaunted a perverse side of himself, as well as his determination to triumph through self-destructiveness rather than being made to submit. I told him my impression that he felt analysis posed the threat of a surrender to me, a danger he seemed resolved to overcome, through self-defeating means if need be. He responded by alluding to the crushing power of women. He subsequently tried to ascertain my views on homosexuality and, *pari passu*, the nature of my interest in treating him. After perusing the Catholic Church's recent position on homosexuality, he taunted me with the notion that analytic neutrality on that matter was by definition "amoral". Reporting that an analyst agreed to take a homosexual friend in treatment with the understanding that his friend did not wish to change his sexual orientation, he opined that the analyst had "capitulated".

I felt him trying to manoeuvre me into forbidding his homosexuality, unless I otherwise became an object of contempt for being as spineless and easy to deceive as the "other analyst". An interminable anal struggle or an impasse would soon have resulted. I told him my thought that he did not know me yet and was testing to see whether I was overbearing and moralizing like his mother or, alternatively, weak and maybe uninterested like his father, but what he feared the most perhaps was that I may not be genuinely concerned about treating him. He responded by saying that his previous analyst had not charged for missed sessions, feeling that this was weak and excessively compromising.

The first two years evolved at a snail's pace. Progress made in the occasional productive session seemed subsequently to evaporate into "nothingness". I experienced pronounced difficulties with attentiveness, was often overtaken by an intense sleepiness or torpor during sessions, and feared that the analysis was coming to a standstill and would fail. Attentive to my countertransference (to disturbances in attention and somnolence particularly), I focused my interventions on elucidating how, under the cover of a hollow cooperativeness during sessions, he "anaesthetized" painful feelings, retreated into his shell, and rendered himself unreachable. Any relaxation of his guard or movement forward evoked fears of getting closer to me or needing me, thus exposing himself to the danger of my deceptively exploiting any closeness subtly to mould him into my "thing" or a "little saint" (like his mother). It eventually became possible to identify and bring out into the open the surreptitious hostile and defiant component in his passivity and undoing and, later, envious and vengeful intentions to defeat me by making the treatment fail.

Middle phase

By the end of the second year, Albert's narcissistic withdrawal and feelings of deadness had lessened considerably. I was aware that he only very rarely alluded to sexual encounters with men, and then always with a great deal of vagueness. I became (unduly) preoccupied by my inability to know anything about his "hidden" homosexuality. My predominant feeling was that he was having frequent homosexual contacts and keeping me in the dark about them, although I sometimes thought his sexual life was non-existent, since he never mentioned any heterosexual relationships either. At times, I wondered if his homosexuality was too completely split-off to be brought into the treatment situation. I had gradually assembled a hazy mental picture-puzzle from his scattered and fragmentary allusions to "sordid" anonymous pickups in public lavatories, "pure sexual discharge", erotic scenarios of being bound and sodomized, and so forth. His occasional anecdotes about his homosexual life portrayed him as the dominating, if not sadistic or degrading, partner. His contacts were impersonal, his partners interchangeable, dehumanized anal objects, or "things" that were used and discarded afterwards. He had reportedly dismissed a suitor pining for further contact by telling him that he did not keep "scum" in his bed, and urinated into another man's mouth. I had also gathered that he had felt castrated when his wife insisted that he give up his homosexual infidelities, from his account that he subsequently stopped performing sexually with her. These considerations eventually led me to ask him if his vagueness about his homosexuality came from a need to keep secret a "hidden source of power" (my thought at the time was that he was concealing an anal phallus from me in the transference). He brushed me off, saying that he had never given much thought to his homosexuality.

The father imago

A week or so later, however, he reported the following dream:

> *I am in my office and have five minutes of calm to read the paper prior to meeting a female client. When the client arrives she says that there may be something missing or incorrect in a document I had given her.*

I tell her that I will go downstairs and check, in case. There is a store downstairs where I buy an enormous Santa Claus in white chocolate, holding a hockey stick behind his back, and a piece of cheese. I go on to the street. There are mountains of snow everywhere that I must walk around. To gain some strength, I take a bite of the chocolate hockey stick on the Santa Claus. At that moment, I find myself facing a black Labrador dog, with part of its tail missing. It looks half-dead, as though not yet fully alive. I think I must go back to the office to see this client who is waiting for me. We talk of the document I had given back to her. I was dissatisfied with the terminology she used.

The preceding week he had dealt with a difficult client, an "enraged feminist" who insisted upon changing the standard terminology, which used the generic masculine form, to include the feminine form in a document. He had felt infuriated by her "politically correct terrorism" and was thinking of ways to hold his own without causing an explosion. The black Labrador belonged to a lawyer whose office I had moved into (from another office located on the top floor of the same building), after he left a few months before. On his way up to my former office, Albert had often looked at the lawyer, finding him likable and particularly attractive and virile, and thought it would be pleasant to be his dog, who looked contented and well cared-for (the lawyer kept his dog in his office). He connected biting into the chocolate hockey stick on the Santa Claus with his need to incorporate some masculine strength before he faced the client in the dream, and to his looking at the lawyer (whose office was on the ground floor) before coming up for his session. I said that it sounded as if the lawyer had provided a fortifying masculine presence he had taken in before seeing me, and I asked him if the lawyer had meant something of a nourishing father. He answered that he had sometimes thought of the lawyer as a kind of ideal father and asked me what had become of him.

As I was telling him what little I knew, I suddenly felt very tangibly the absence of the lawyer whose office I was now occupying: the office felt intensely vacant as I thought with regret of the lawyer who had been obliged to leave it. I shared with Albert my feeling that we were both talking about an absent man and that his absence seemed to "weigh in the air" at the moment. He sank into a sad silence (quite unusual for him) and recalled a particularly frightening evening when his father was away while the family had to evacuate their home. He remembered having acutely missed his father then. This had a profound impact on him. It opened the door to the gradual recovery of memories of a more caring, protective, and competent father, who had tried to engage him but was actively excluded and disqualified by Albert's collusion with his mother's possessiveness and had capitulated long before his son's adolescence.

Secrecy . . . and other perverse enactments

I was increasingly troubled by the suspicion that he was turning the analysis into a sham by concealing his homosexual life (I learned later that he had visited saunas many times a week since the beginning of analysis). At one point I asked him how he thought I could be of help if he never discussed his sexuality. He was quite taken aback by the question. We came to understand that he was recreating within the transference the illusion of a collusive relationship with a mother who disavowed his sexuality: in his mind's eye, he was seeing and showing me only the (false) image of the precious passive and asexual child he had always believed his mother wanted him to be.

Subsequently, on a Monday after I had with advance notice cancelled the previous week's last session, Albert reported (for the first time) having picked up two men in the public baths over the weekend. He gave no details but said that he had thought at the time: "if only Dr C could see me!" He did not respond when I asked him what he thought I would have felt had I seen him, or if there could be a link with my cancellation. The Tuesday session was taken up with a boring enumeration of all the reasons why he could not talk about the homosexual encounter. A dream he brought on the Wednesday enabled me to interpret his wish to stall the analysis and frustrate me with an endless monotonous repetition of meaningless words, like a drone:

> *I am in your office during a session. You ask me to look at a drawing on the floor. There is something written over the drawing that I must repeat: "Even if I talk a lot, I have nothing to tell you". I repeat this as many times as it is written. I have the impression that I will continue*

repeating it for ever, like a kind of perpetual motion. As I was not paying attention to the drawing, you ask me to look at it more closely. What you wanted me to see appears. It is a fresco showing three men and a woman. The men have erections and are intensely excited. It is not clear if the woman shares this excitement.

The fresco with the three men and the woman brought to mind that he had not told me what he had done with the men in the baths. He thought the woman could be me. He feared I would find him disgusting for having sexual relations with two men. "Why two men?" I inquired. He replied that there was less risk of intimacy in a threesome than a twosome. When it became apparent that he felt I had explored the homosexual episode out of voyeurism, I pointed out to him how, within the context of his own perspective, he had tantalized me by dropping hints, only to frustrate and exclude me afterwards. I said that he seemed to take a malicious pleasure in teasing me with "I have a perversion but I am keeping it a secret". He recalled that with his wife, also, he had alluded to but concealed his homosexual activities, and he reflected that by betraying her with men, he had excluded her in a way that made it impossible for her to compete sexually. He began, bit by bit, to reveal the homosexual sorties he had kept under a veil of secrecy for over two years.

Over time, it became clearer that although a side of him apparently accepted the constraints of the analytic situation, another side did not (could not). He then retreated into perverse enactments, often accompanied by homosexual acting out, which served as a defence against experiencing painful emotional states and contained elements of magical repair, undoing, reversal, and triumph. The following enactment took place in the fourth year of treatment, after the working through of the malevolent maternal transference and the analysis of his defensive phallic woman fantasy had progressively enabled him to experience a sexual attraction towards me. After reporting at the beginning of the Monday session a weekend dream in which he was lying in bed beside a woman condensing features of both his mother and myself, he related picking up on the Saturday a young French man whose accent reminded him of mine and inviting him to have sexual relations in his apartment; he said that throughout the sexual encounter I had been in his mind, as though he could see me looking at him (the look was indeterminate). Seeing also a younger version of himself in the youth, who was approximately the age he had been early on in his marriage, Albert said that his homosexual life had lost some of its attraction since then.

The next day he reported this dream:

> *I am in a very large and beautiful house belonging to my ex-wife, during an evening with many guests. A guest asks me whether I like living in this house. In front of the whole company, I declare that this house leaves me completely indifferent. Among the guests there is a young man who is naked except for a belt from which are suspended alcohol flasks, serving as a sort of ambulatory bar. He had the lewd, worrisome air of a satyr. No one else seemed to notice him. He looked like a wolf in a flock of sheep with his non-conformism and his Dionysian appearance.*

His comment about his ex-wife's house reminded him of his former displays of indifference about their home. There was an intention to shock in his attitude, his cynicism. The satyr looked like the young man in Pasolini's film *Teorema,* who introduces himself into a family, causing its downfall. The mother falls in love with him, he acts as a catalyst for the son's homosexuality, sleeps with the daughter, and drives the father to the brink of madness. The satyr's debauched appearance contrasted with the conformism of the female guests, casting women in the role of guardians of order. He said that he was fearful of getting closer to his ex-wife (they had recently rekindled their relationship). He felt like running away. His mother's rule had been a stifling yoke, and she had turned his father into a slave.

A: You seem to feel that your mother castrated your father. I think you also worry about my making you conform to my norms and maybe give up homosexuality, which would feel like a castration of sorts. I think the satyr in your dream personifies a side of you who wants to subvert a process which you interpret as an enterprise to make you comply.

P: I am terrified of being castrated. I will not let myself be castrated. Pasolini led a life of debauchery until his death. . . .

He rebelled against society but also against the conformism of gay lobby groups. He found them nauseating. He was well aware that homosexuality was becoming "politically correct".

A: Losing some of its subversive punch?

P: He saw homosexuality as the ultimate rebellion. In a way, I do feel that if I resolve my homosexual problem, I will be falling in with the virtuous. . . . There are two sides to me: I would like to find some peace, but I also have a fierce will to defy what is expected from me. I have a strong will not to conform, as though I could lose my soul.

A: I think you are also afraid of losing your "masculine soul", that you feel that homosexual relations provide you with an important link to manhood.

P: That's true . . . but (*correcting my interpretation*) I also think I have more difficulty in desiring women than men. I can respond to a woman's desire if it's obvious. I am passive, I need to be wooed. This happens with men: I have the man. This reminds me of the "sexualization" you were speaking of . . . (*he became silent*).

A: You "have the man", whereas perhaps you felt rejected when I said that you were sexualizing the relation with me? (*I remembered using this technical term rather clumsily in a session the week before, after he voiced a fear of having an erection during the session and said that he usually did not talk about sex, he "did it"*)

P: I felt you were reproaching me for being a sexual being, capable of desiring women. Maybe I want to show you that I am not asexual . . . (*end of session*).

It was only towards the end of the session that I realized how this last enactment was triggered by my distancing comment of the preceding week (in retrospect, I would view it as a countertransference reaction to his incestuous wishes/fears and identification with his fear of his own erections). Albert's sexual acting out with the French man enabled him to reverse feelings of injury and rejection, repair his body image through his partner, take omnipotent control of him ("I have the man"), and exclude me in turn (as in his proclamations of indifference towards his wife's house [/body] in his dream). His satyr dream revealed underlying wishes to subvert sexual and generational boundaries and have access to unlimited oral supplies (the satyr serving as an ambulatory bar).

The role of family dynamics and early trauma

Trauma experienced in the relationship with his mother, the influence of her covert messages and attitudes, and the influence of the family dynamics appeared to be important factors in this case. The disqualification and withdrawal of his father, combined with his mother's negating response to his masculinity and sexuality, left Albert with a precarious masculine body image, showing in difficulties in integrating his erections at puberty (Greenacre, 1953). This occurred against a background of continuous disturbance in his relationship with his mother. Cumulative moments when he served as her prized but helpless fetish object or "thing", at the cost of his own personal and sexual identity, had constituted a core trauma. His fixation on, flight from, and desire to reverse and triumph over these past traumatizing experiences with her were central elements in his psychopathology, which were also replayed in the transference.

He had established a deeply dependent although ambivalent tie to his wife while maintaining a "secret" homosexual life on the side, and a complex interplay between heterosexual and homosexual relations enabled him to maintain some heterosexual functioning and counteract any accompanying sense of threat, frustration, or injury through perverse acting out with sexual partners.

Homosexual partners stood for narcissistic doubles who were induced to surrender through a "technique of intimacy" while he remained in control. Sexual behaviour included fellatio, mutual masturbation, and, less frequently, sodomy and sadomasochistic practices. He said that "gay saunas cater to the 'cult of the penis'", and the man's erect penis, the size of his erection, as well as his excited admiration for the patient's own erection were central elements in these rapports, serving as visual and sensory supports for the narcissistic restoration of his body image and, particularly, of the deficient image of his penis. He had no wish for affection or intimacy with his anonymous partners, who were reduced to "things" and discarded afterwards. Elements of his past traumatic relationship with his mother were clearly replayed and mastered in these encounters (Stoller, 1975). Not only was his passive childhood experience of being his mother's fetish-object now brought under his control and inflicted upon his partner, but it also became a source of erotic gratification and thus a means of triumph over her attacks on his masculinity, all the more so given the narcissistic reinforcement of the imago of the penis ensured by the actual presence of a homosexual double.

Perverse transference–countertransference

The prospect of engaging or changing in analysis was from the outset extremely threatening for Albert because it evoked the perspective of an emotional surrender to the analyst, reminiscent of his submission to the will of his early caretaker, which entailed a painful loss of personal and sexual identity by becoming the dehumanized "thing" of the other. Consequently, he covertly undermined analytic work by destroying insight and perverted the process by turning it into an erotized sadomasochistic struggle and keeping his homosexuality a walled-in and tantalizing secret for over two years, and the threat of impasse was always present. His perversion of the analytic process thus formed an ongoing negative therapeutic reaction to change.

Perverse transference enactments were often surreptitious and were picked up initially or mainly through countertransference feelings of malaise, a sense of being deceived, provoked, manipulated into playing a role, or a measure of induced excitement. Some enactments occurred punctually, when transferential reactivations or analytic constraints evoked intolerable affects, and a more drawn-out perverse transference–countertransference engagement was created by his secrecy about his homosexual life. They were defensive manoeuvres enabling him to rid himself of intolerable feelings provoked by his analysis, and they contained elements of revenge, magical repair, and triumph. At their core was a need to use the analyst as a partner (a sort of puppet) in his perverse scenarios, so as to triumph over his fears of having his personal and sexual identity annihilated by surrendering to her and becoming her "thing". The perverse acting-out seemed to have acquired some autonomy from its infantile roots, operating like a "ready-made" solution to ward off any emotional disturbance. The analytic task became clearer: to detect the dissociated acting-out taking place within and outside the transference and interrelate it with the vicissitudes of the analytic relationship, so as to help him elaborate emotional experiences within an analytic dialogue.

Psychic change

The detection and working through of the perverse transference was in my view a chief factor that enabled his analysis to move forward and eventually permitted an integration of his inner psychic split and the relinquishment of perverse sexual acting out. He underwent HIV testing in the fifth year of treatment, which fortunately tested negative, and abandoned anonymous homosexual sorties afterwards.

The father was excluded from the analytic stage (dominated by the pre-oedipal mother), until the session in which I shared with the patient my sense of loss about the lawyer/father's absence. This allowed him to acknowledge a previously denied attachment to his father and to recover memories of a more caring and competent father, reopening a path towards masculine development that was obstructed by his compliance and collusion with his mother's possessiveness and with her negation of the father. Access to the "second object" also promoted his emancipation from the orbit of the traumatizing pre-oedipal mother within the transference, which evolved a more openly acknowledged dependency and a fondness for me.

Conclusion

The evolution of the theory of perversion is evidently subject to the progression of psychoanalytic theory as a whole. Freud's late formulations on disavowal and the splitting of the ego in perversion remain valid today, but the core of perversion seems to be increasingly understood in terms of a defence against intimacy with a differentiated other, rather than as a defence against castration anxiety (Carignan, 1999; Parsons, 2000; Stein, 2005). The partner's "otherness" or "personhood" is disavowed. Perversion thus functions as a powerful, aggressive sexualized narcissistic defence that inevitably finds its way into the transference.

Notes

1. Freud (1911b) proposed that, with the introduction of the reality principle, one species of thought activity was "split off". It was kept free from reality-testing and remained under the sway of the pleasure principle alone. "This activity is *phantasizing*, which begins already in children's play, and later, continued as *day-dreaming*, abandons dependence on real objects" (p. 222). Later on in the *Outline*, he assigned a place to disavowal, alongside childhood repression, in psychic structuring (1940a [1938], p. 204).

2. This expression was used by Khan (1979) to describe the talent of the pervert to create the emotional climate in which another person is seduced and willingly coerced into becoming an accomplice in the shared enactment of his perverse sexual fantasies. Khan thought that the perverse partner was made to play his part through a mixture of manipulation, play, make-believe, and omnipotent control (implying projective identification). He stressed the important function of perverse acting out in transforming passive traumatic intrapsychic states into active, ego-directed, "play-action object relations", a view close to Stoller's.

3. The words "perverse" and "perversion" are used to refer to the function of the patient's sexual behaviour and to the aggressive dehumanization of sexual partners.

4. This case was originally published in greater detail in Carignan (1999).

10

Splitting and psychosomatics: on a third topography

Rubén Zukerfeld

> "I consider splitting a fundamental psychic activity because it is precisely that which gives rise to differentiation."
>
> André Green, 1998

1 Freudian logic: from the pathologic to universals

Roussillon (2007) says, "it has to be possible to remove the concept of the splitting of the ego from the simple clinical concept of the fetish, it will thus be given a higher theoretical status". This statement is based on psychoanalytic research into borderline states, which was also intensely carried out by Green (1975), who lays emphasis on the structural value of the psychic operation known as "splitting" or "cleavage". He points out that "in repression, the relation between the ego, as representative of reality, and drive demands, as representatives of pleasure, is *vertical* . . ., in splitting this relation is *horizontal.* The reason for the ego and the reason for drive demands *coexist* within the same psychic space" (emphasis added). These statements show that there exists a tendency to construct a global conception of psychic functioning starting from borderline pathology.

The point of view in this chapter is based on pondering over the splitting proposed by Freud (1927e, 1933a [1932], 1940e [1938]) within an "author's logic", which becomes evident in his work as the classic sequence: clinical characterization of an observable psychopathologic phenomenon, characterization of other observable psychopathologic phenomena, and, finally, characterization of the observable as a universal feature of mental functioning. This was the case with repression: first, the defence mechanism of female hysterics; then, the defence mechanism of obsessive neuroses and phobias; and, finally, a universal structuring mechanism. And we think this also occurs in splitting. Here, the sequence would be: the defence mechanism of fetishism, the defence mechanism of psychosis, the habitual mechanism of neuroses—*a universal mechanism?*

It is not a question of making Freud say what he did not say, but it is indeed a question of evaluating a typically Freudian style of revision and development—from clinical practice (e.g., fetishism, psychosis), towards a first theorization, and then a posthumous and unfinished second theorization, where he states that splitting "would not be worthy of such importance if it were not only confirmed in neurosis-like states but finally, in neuroses too" (Freud, 1940a [1938]). There is logic in discovering human and universal questions having pathologies as their starting point; furthermore, as is well known, it is from the theory of dreams that Freud initiates the study of normality, where the repressed unconscious is part of habitual daily life. The question that now comes up is whether what is split is *also* part of that daily life and not just a defence mechanism as described by different psychoanalytic currents. Actually, primitive defence mechanisms described by the English school—schizoid mechanisms—have a structuring value, but they are presented from a psychopathological perspective, as occurs in the mechanism of disavowal associated with splitting and trauma.[1]

However, it should be taken into account that the Freudian conception has been understood as a motivational theory of memory, starting from the dynamic unconscious functioning under the rules of repression. But nowadays the canonical conception of memories as different and *dissociable* systems, some of them explicit or declarative (semantic and episodic) and others implicit (procedural, emotional, priming), has turned problematic the homogeneous conception of a single unconscious system resulting from repression. As Pally (1998) points out, it is quite clear to the neurosciences that there is a *double* circuit of emotional processing composed of one circuit that goes through the cortex and involves the hippocampus and another that goes through the amygdala and is capable of producing emotional reactions without the ability to consciously recall them (emotional memory). Bucci (2001) affirms in the multiple code theory that there is "a subsymbolic, systematic and organized process that operates *in conjunction with* symbolic systems throughout normal, rational, adult life" (emphasis added).

On the other hand, the most serious criticism of psychoanalytic theories of the unconscious comes from cognitive neuroscience, where it is pointed out that "the existence of the cognitive unconscious[2] does not clearly support, and even throws some doubt upon, the existence of Freud's psychoanalytic unconscious" (Grünbaum, 2007). But cognitive theories of the mind also evolved from the computational conception in series towards the connective conception in parallel. This conception was received with wide support as a result of extensive research into procedural memory. As Díaz Benjumea (2002) points out, "we now see that there is a whole area of psychic functioning that functions through the automatism of the memory itself and is not caused by any motivation". Nevertheless, she adds,

> some authors champion the need for a *double level* to explain the subsymbolic processes which characterize connective systems on the one hand, and *another functioning level* to explain logical and rational thinking, and this poses some difficulties. It seems evident that the mind functions not only in the way connective systems describe, nor does it possess only procedural memory. [emphasis added]

That is to say, the hypothesis can be set forth that implicit memories (automatic) answer to a type of the unconscious, and declarative memories (motivational) and their cognitive derivatives answer to another type of unconscious functioning, and that both operate *simultaneously*. In this sense, if splitting can now be understood not only as a defence mechanism subsidiary, in the last analysis, to the rules of repression (the avoidance of unpleasure), but also as an *original and permanent* moving away from declarative representation, it is possible to think of the existence of what can be referred to as the *split unconscious,* correlative to implicit memories, which in their turn include different types of processing and neural networks. If this is the case, psychoanalysis is confronted with an interesting problem—topographical, dynamic, and economic—that would require a metapsychological revision of the last Freudian model of instances referential only to repression.

The objective, then, of this chapter is, first, to present a model of the psychic apparatus built on the notion of structural splitting, and, second, starting from there, to review the notion of "psychosomatics", since the concept of the mind–body relation has undergone crucial changes over the last three decades.

2 The structuring value of splitting: the split unconscious and a third topography.

2.1 Throughout the history of psychoanalysis there have been numerous kinds of conceptualization of what we understand as the split unconscious and its productions. In Freud's own works, this problem is outlined in all phenomena that cannot be explained by the theory of repression. Later on, the problem is set out in a sophisticated way in non-Freudian models of psychic functioning—for example, that of Bion (1963), who describes the elements and the beta screen as a *non-integrated* agglomeration—and in Lacan's notion of the Real (1975) as outside language, *inadmissible in symbolization.* Furthermore, this problem is in the clinical, terrifying fear of collapse (Winnicott, 1974) and in Aulagnier's development (1972) of a three-space topography, where she adds the primal or originating process and the pictogram to Freudian primary and secondary processes. Moreover, I think there is a relation with what we define as the split unconscious in archaic hysteria and the theatre of the impossible (McDougall, 1991), essential splitting (M'Uzan, 1994), structural splitting associated with narcissistic deficiency (Bayle, 1992), parallel dynamisms (Marty, 1990), the non-representable (Missenard et al., 1989), the unknown and unknowable (Rosolato, 1989), archaic and radical negativity (Kaës, 1989), the primal *non refoulé* unconscious (Dejours, 1986), the pre-repression unconscious (Roussillon, 1991), the unrepresentable delegation and the "other country" (Botella, 2006), and the notion of the "prepsychic", the work of the negative, and the developments on splitting (Green, 1998).

This list should not be viewed as exhaustive, nor does it try to simplify notions that ought to be studied in their referential contexts; however, it mentions various considerations in the psychoanalytic literature of what is functioning in an order that is not that of word representation and *cohabits* with classic representational formations of the unconscious.

It is now necessary to synthesize the theoretical starting points used to formulate a model of the psychic apparatus and its functioning that will account for what has been set out so far. There are four concepts, which come from articulations and non-reductionist correspondences between psychoanalysis, disciplines of subjectivity, and the neurosciences:

1. The notion of the *heterogeneity* of the unconscious: there are several functioning or operating systems having different characteristics, so that it is not possible to speak of *one* homogeneous unconscious. Examples of this notion are Bleichmar's developments (1999, 2001) of different unconsciouses, as well as his modular-transformational model.
2. The notion of *coexistence*: the different functioning systems operate simultaneously, and final productions always include variable aspects of them, so that any clinical manifestation is always mixed. This notion implies that of *predominance* and gradient and therefore entails the questioning of the idea of psychopathological structure.
3. The notion of *complexity*: functioning possesses recursiveness; therefore, there is no cause–effect determinism. All mechanisms described—for example, from a psychoneuroimmunoendocrine perspective—have this characteristic.
4. The notion of *restructuring* linkage: the restructuring potential of secondary bonds is added to classic perspectives of the structur-

ing value of primary bonds. This notion is associated with the modern conception of neuroplasticity[3] and the idea that new bonds build new subjectivities.

It is by taking into account these notions that we have made a revision of the last model of the Freudian psychic apparatus, because we believe that it is natural to Freudian logic—and scientific thought in general—to reconsider the different metapsychological categories in the light of new developments within the psychoanalytic corpus, and the contributions from other disciplines. This revision led to what we understand as the *third topography*.[4]

2.2 The third topography constitutes the metaphorical, graphic representation of the heterogeneity and coexistence of unconscious psychic functioning, which have a representational structure (thing-presentation and word-presentation) and a non-representational one. *It is a model of the psychic apparatus, understood as the construction of psychism between soma and the other, characterized by introducing splitting into the second Freudian topography as a universal and structuring mechanism that allows the universal coexistence of two large modalities of psychic functioning, both of which can be separately studied from different perspectives* (Zukerfeld, 1992, 1993, 1994, 1996, 1998, 1999; Zukerfeld & Zonis Zukerfeld, 1989, 1999, 2001, 2005).

Structuring splitting is topically represented in Figure 10.1 as a vertical bar perpendicular to a horizontal bar that metaphorically represents repression in the second topography and, together with which, regulates the meeting of two work demands, one of a biological character (I), the other of a cultural character (IIa and IIb). This means that the model tries to integrate drives theories and relational theories without establishing a hierarchical order, so that *in all psychic functioning there is something from a somatic order and something from an intersubjective order.*

2.2.1 From the *economical* point of view there are two derivations [(a) and (b) in Figure 10.1]:

(a) This derivation implies cathexis that will be bound to the thing- or word-presentation offered by the linkage to the other. In the first case, the first links are those of primary repression

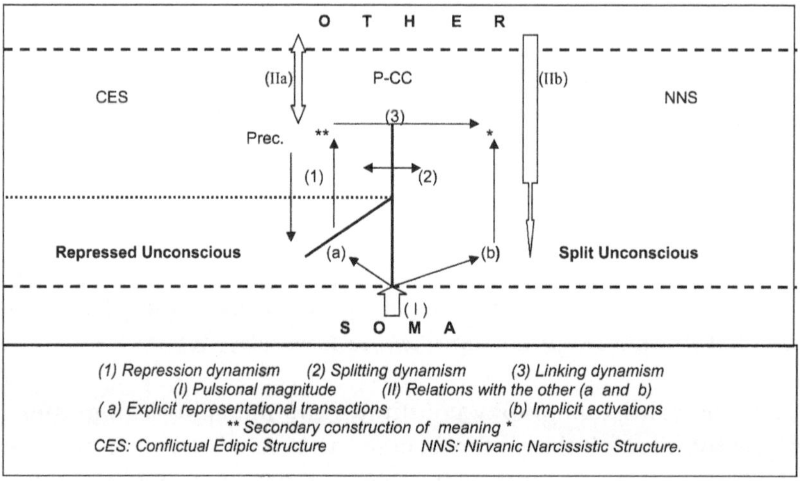

Figure 10.1. Third topography

and fixations, the starting point for representational transactions that follow the rules of the Freudian pleasure-unpleasure principle. Green (1975) clearly states that "thing-presentation captures, limits and transforms drive energy . . . '*it cannot link by itself all* that is part of the psychic representative" (emphasis added).

(b) This derivation corresponds precisely to *unlinked* cathexis, which generates traces that can be activated but not recalled,[5] corresponding to non-representable magnitudes both from the drive source and also from the relationship source (IIb in Figure 10.1). Part of them may imply the effect of what is traumatic (intrusion, pathogenic identification) associated with what Green (1975) specifies as "the well-known effects of affect on the body (or of the body on affect). Also, from there, the discharges due to somatic reactions or the passage to the act." Likewise, the notions of "the introduct" (Benyakar & Lezica, 2005), "passive primary identification" and "ungovernable trace" (Marucco, 1999), as well as "imposition" (Berenstein, 2001) are theorizations closely related to the vicissitudes mentioned. Other parts of these sources are associated with procedural memory and priming.

2.2.2 From the *dynamic* point of view, three dynamisms are described in this model [(1), (2), (3) in Figure 10.1]:

(1) That of *repression* and its processes of investiture and decathectization, progressive and regressive, inherent in the conflict ("vertical" movement), which implies fluidity of displacements and condensations and orders what does or does not become conscious with greater or lesser masking, according to the legalities of wish and interdiction.

(2) That of *splitting*, which determines *predominance* with fluidity[6] and alternatives in perception-consciousness (P-CC) in representational processes and/or trace activation (swinging or sweeping movement); thus it orders the differentiated interplay of all manifestations that acquire the quality of consciousness, and not necessarily that of word.[7]

(3) That of *linking*, which relates transactions (a) to activations (b), constituting *tertiary processes* (Zukerfeld & Zonis Zukerfeld, 2002). These processes were described by Green (1972) as "those processes that relate primary and secondary processes in such a way that primary processes limit the saturation of secondary ones and secondary processes that of primary ones", and that "they merit being isolated as relation processes at the conceptual level", so that "[thought,] focusing on exercising secondary processes, continues to be open to some primary processes which guarantee the irruption of creative intuition at exactly the same time as the most rigorous rationality is being exercised". Within our conception, we think that, in addition to the relation between primary and secondary processes, which give rise to preconscious creative richness, tertiary processes add a secondary sense to the nonrepresentable through an intersubjective bond (IIa), which is the *mechanism of the creation of newness* (Figure 10.1, from ** to *).

2.2.3 From the *topic* point of view and according to the foundational myths of psychoanalysis, an intersubjective production space is described, with its differentiations and instances, making up a conflictual edipic structure (CES) where the ego ideal is found, and another space where the ideal ego is rooted as part of a nirvanic narcissistic structure (NNS), the seat of radical disavowal, duplication, and discharge. Marty (1990) points out that

> the ideal ego represents immoderation . . . being perceived from the outside as a feeling of omnipotence of the subject with regard to himself, or with regard to the outside world, if that is the case, . . . it is not the little kid of repression . . . clinically it shows it is a powerful feature of character and behaviour. . . . In representing invulnerable *wholeness* or *nothingness* . . . it becomes essentially lethal. [emphasis added]

Thus a new topic of narcissism and ideals comes up where, in Green's terms, trophic aspects are part of the problem coexisting with split thanatic aspects. This point of view assumes the notion of "structure" only in a metapsychological sense, not in a psychopathological sense, since every symptom, disorder, or characteristic includes something from both structures or modes of functioning.

In this way, the final Freudian psychic apparatus becomes a mode—also universal—of psychic functioning that coexists with another corresponding to the *split unconscious*. This last notion constitutes the "hard nucleus" of the third topography, and we believe it is the one that best explains this functioning, for three reasons:

1. It hierarchically upgrades the splitting mechanism as *a primeval, global, and persistent moving-away or separation,* which correlates with that research in neuroscience that demarcates and studies articulations between systems when they are proved dissociable, as happens in the hippocampus and cerebral amygdala circuits (Bechara & Damasio, 1995).
2. It emphasizes its structural dimension, which, to our way of thinking, in the Freudian trajectory follows the same pathway as repression: first it was a hysterical defence, and then a universal mechanism. As Green (1998) points out in the epigraph to this chapter, splitting *implies a differentiation,* which is even a need from an evolutionary point of view.[8] According to the Freudian principle of constancy, it is clear that in order to articulate affect and representation, the psychic apparatus should not be overwhelmed by the high magnitude of energy that would occur as a consequence of traumatic events. This implies a discharge "space" so that the articulation becomes possible, which justi-

fies the "expansion" of the space as a result of traumatic events. Note that in Figure 10.1 this "expansion" would be graphically represented as a "moving towards the left" of the splitting bar, which would "crush" the preconscious.[9]

3. It dissociates the notion from any emphasis on what is pathological, since it is a constitutive, permanent, and economically necessary system, as Bateson (1972) had already stated when, in considering habits and skills, he said that "no organism can allow itself to be conscious of matter with which it can deal on an unconscious level". And these are "matters" that are not part of a conflict, although they are not absolutely autonomous because they may secondarily be caught up in conflictual dynamics. In fact, they belong in the whole area of what is understood as that of "implicit memories", and an important aspect to be determined is the relation between these unconscious processes not only with more or less automatic or procedural behaviour, but with neurovegetative mechanisms. In this sense, the unconscious we call split takes in modes of functioning typical of the amygdala–hypothalamus circuits that are at the basis of the psychoneuroimmunoendocrinologic answer. In metapsychological terms, we speak of magnitude unlinked to representations that are discharged and channelled through motor behaviour and somatic responses, or eclosion, of a different level.

In brief, we put forward that what we call the split unconscious—that is, what is *structurally separate* from the representational composition set by repression—may be characterized in different ways according to different psychoanalytic theories, research in neuroscience, cognitive psychology, and subjectivity disciplines. Within psychoanalysis, drive theories would correlate splitting with the area of the discharge, the thanatic or the negative; narcissistic theories, with the field of the *Theatre of the Impossible* (McDougall, 1991) and the seat of the ideal ego or the immortal double (Aragonés, 1999); identification theories, with passive primary identifications (Marucco, 1999) and pathogenic identifications (Bleichmar, 2001). For subjectivity disciplines, splitting would correlate with the non-representable and the trans-subjective. For cognitive psychology, it would be the cognitive unconscious and the space of subsymbolic processes, and, for the neurosciences in general, the area of implicit memories (procedural, emotional, and priming) with their different neural networks.

3 The predominance of split unconscious: from psychosomatics to somatic vulnerability

3.1 I think that the term "psychosomatic" is still in use in psychoanalysis more out of respect for a strong tradition than as an expression of current clinical and theoretical reality. It does not have the specificity of its origins, and it alludes to a field that implies body involvement in symptomatic manifestations. At present this field is sometimes defined as that of the study of emotional and psychosocial factors, linked to the origin, onset, exacerbation, consequences, evolution, prevention, and cure of somatic disease and what psychiatry calls somatomorphic disorders. Among others, these include two large, universal mechanisms: conversion and somatization. The former, as is known, constitutes the major Freudian discovery of the unconscious repressed in conversion hysteria, and it signals the birth of psychoanalysis. It consists of the paradigmatic mode of neurotic production of symptoms. Its proverbial pregnancy in clinical practice and in theory minimized Freudian developments on actual neurosis and—despite certain post-Freudian developments—the model of conversion (body language translatable to words) became the central axis of what was called psychosomatic. Thus, it did not really form a differentiated field within psychoanalysis strictly considered (there are no differences in respect of neuroses)[10] until the Paris Psychosomatic School's research and publications. In principle, these developments postulate particular characteristics of psychic functioning that try to demarcate a specific category.[11] The now necessary differentiation regarding the field of neurosis makes the Lacanian current characterize these "psychosomatic" modes of functioning as expressions of a "phenomenon"—which is not a symptom—and which remains on an "edge" where it will encounter what is borderline, non-neurotic/non-psychotic, normopathic (McDougall, 1982). The same terminology—the word "edge" or eventually "frontier"—alludes to the existence of a "centre", which continues to be that of psychoneurosis transference.

We think that this "neurotic-centred" model became a Procrus-

-tean bed hindering the perception of coexistence and simultaneity of manifestations of different orders, as an early Freud had already perceived (all psychoneuroses have a nucleus of actual neurosis). That is why the model of the third topography based on two structuring mechanisms—repression and splitting—has neither centre nor edge, because every clinical manifestation is by definition a hybrid. Hence, predominance and eventually crystallizations will define clinical presentations. In this sense, predominance of the manifestations of one aspect of split unconscious—that which corresponds to a nonrepresentable, emotional memory[12]—may be expressed as a somatic eclosion (among other modes of expression), and it is to this predominance that we attribute a pathological potential—that is, a particular *vulnerability*.

3.2 In earlier publications (Zukerfeld & Zonis Zukerfeld, 1999), we have defined this predominance and crystallization of split unconscious as *vulnerability*—that is, as a mode of psychic functioning and/or a subjective condition the more frequent manifestations of which are clinically expressed as some deficit in fantasmatic activity, a certain scarcity of ego resources in dealing with vital experiences and elaborating mourning, and a tendency to behavioural and/or somatic act-discharge.

That is why, if we now had to demarcate what is traditionally called "psychosomatic", we would centre this around the notion of somatic vulnerability, so that this field would be defined as the one studying *how and why the vulnerability of a subject to fall ill increases or diminishes—that is, how a mode of psychic functioning, in which what we understand as split unconscious predominates or is crystallized, has been built and operates*. Insofar as the model of the third topography is a coexistence model, starting from a structuring and universal splitting, the predominance cited above *always coexists* with the characteristic manifestations of what is repressed; thus we can generically describe two large modes of falling ill, with various vicissitudes. The first is defined in terms of the existence of a psychic transaction, and in a regressive manner it corresponds to what Freudian and post-Freudian psychoanalysis—even with manifest differences—have traditionally described as the *conversive* form of symptomatic production. It is known that the representations of one's own body and concomitant affects are processed regressively here according to the rules of psychoneurotic functioning—that is, as part of a *repressed conflict* governed by the Oedipus complex and acquiring a symbolic value. Its predominance is shown through an intense fantasmatic activity typical of the vicissitudes of unconscious wish and interdiction.

The second mode is defined through the absence of representational transactions and comprises what has traditionally been described by Freudian and post-Freudian psychoanalysis (allowing for differences) as the *somatization* manner of symptomatic production. This manner implies the activation of traces that cannot be recalled, which are metapsychologically split off. The splitting may also be defensive and may imply the non-repressive dismantling of the ideo-affective structure expressed, for example, in the notion of alexithymia. We are here within what is now usually considered as the "psychosomatic", which is functioning where there exists a deficit of fantasmatic activity, which we would rather call *somatic vulnerability*, where what predominates is split unconscious. From the viewpoint of the neurosciences, it is interesting to point out that the deficit mentioned (as the notion of alexithymia, too) could be thought of as the missing or inadequacy of what Damasio (1994) described as "a somatic marker". These markers are a special kind of feelings, generated from secondary emotions and connected, through learning, to certain decisions, the neural base of which is located on the connections between the amygdala and the prefrontal cortex.[13]

It should be noticed that, in reality, we replace the prefix "psycho-" by the construct "vulnerability" insofar as this is the term we use to name the predominance of certain *psychic functioning*. Consequently, the "psychosomatic" patient is, in reality, a patient with "somatic vulnerability"—that is, with a certain potential for somatic pathology facilitation, what M'Uzan (1994) called "quantity slaves". In conclusion, both manners coexist, starting from structural splitting, as the answer to deficiency or excess,[14] and they both manifest themselves through different types of cognitive constructions and behaviours when facing reality.

3.3 That is why, it has currently become relevant to determine the existence of *vulnerability*—that is, psychic functioning where split unconscious predominates. It should be observed here that the construct "vulnerability" is not strictly synonymous with fragility or predisposition (habitual uses of the term); it is, rather, the opposite of the notion of mentalization.[15] Hence *the psychoneurotic symptom does not express any vulnerability*. We understand the greater or lesser vulnerability as directly associated with an intricate combination (Figure 10.2, a) between historical and actual adversity and the existence or non-existence of a bond network that provides support and identifying models. Thus, the more persistent the traumatic is and the less support capacity the bond network has (Figure 10.2, b, c), the greater the vulnerability will be and also, consequently, the probabilities of exacerbation and complication of pre-existent pathology, or inclusively the unspecified generation of illness. On the other hand, predominance of the functioning mode ordered by repression entails the notion of re-significance, the development of defence mechanisms, and the symbolic value of corporal manifestation. However, what is interesting to underline is that the clinical notion of vulnerability—insofar as it concurs with the theoretical notion of the split unconscious—is universal and does not mean pathological in the medical sense of the term. Thus it refers only to the predominance of psychic functioning that may turn pathological but may also be reintegrated in a homeostatic state (Figure 10.2, d) or may even evolve into a resilient development (Figure 10.2, e).[16] We are not going to deal here with the biological (genetic, etc.) and social (quality of life, cultural ideals) variables

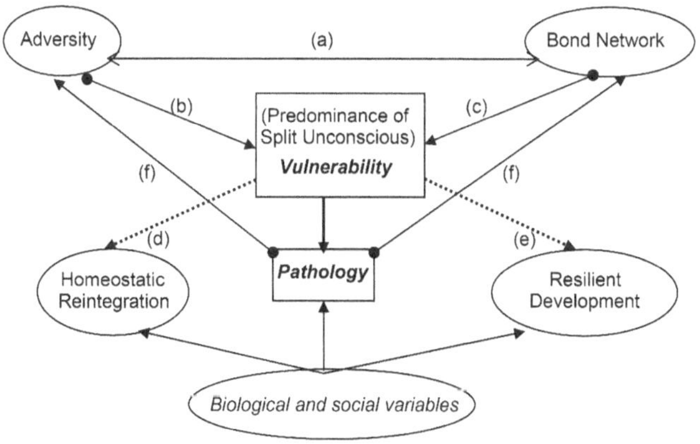

Figure 10.2. The clinical concept of split unconscious: the vulnerability notion

that intervene, but it is important to understand the recursiveness of the model, since if illness were to occur, this in its turn becomes adversity and alters the bond network of the affected subject (Figure 10.2, f), whose vulnerability may then increase.

It is clinically important to again underline the notion of coexistence, because the predominance of splitting and its vicissitudes (vulnerability) does not exclude the existence of neurotic symptoms. Therefore, the model put forward pertains to the logic suggested by Bernardi (2005): "a single body but sufficiently complex".[17] On the other hand, the construct "vulnerability" as we defined it *ut supra,* is rendered open to procedures of empirical research that may be contrasted with those of clinical research. Therefore, if the effects of adversity are studied in terms of traumatic experiences or stress-generating experiences according to the quality, presence, and interiorization of meaningful relationships, a gradient of vulnerability may be obtained as an indirect mode of evaluating the predominance of split unconscious.

Final reflections

"Entia non sunt multiplicanda sine necessitate."

William of Ockham, 1328

Theories and models intend to give an account of certain complex realities, assuming a reduction of the complexity. It is known that a "territory" is always more complex than any "map" of it, and that dialogic relations (Morin, 2001) take place there.[18] In this sense, the third topography is a Freudian-based psychoanalytic cartography designed for exploring this complexity, including the aim of integrating drive theories with relational theories and interdisciplinary findings.

But, fundamentally, I believe it is worth reconsidering certain of Freud's final concepts—such as that of splitting—in order to think not only of pathologies but also of global psychic functioning. This intention is founded on certain epistemologic parsimony, given that if a Freudian concept has not exhausted its heuristic and explicative power, it is convenient to use it before introducing neologisms ("prepsychic unconscious", "pre-repression", "unknown", "other country", etc.) or before setting it aside as an object of psychoanalysis (cognitive unconscious). On the other hand, the metapsychological notion of split unconscious, which lays the foundation of the clinical notion of vulnerability viewed as a universal and permanent condition, permits—to my way of thinking—the formulation of a more precise proposal, open to research and interdisciplinary contact, for the commonly named psychosomatic field. Therefore, it is in this field—which currently includes psychocardiology, psycho-oncology, and, in general, psychoneuroimmunoendocrinology—where modern psychoanalysis may regain the important position it held at the start of the last century.

Notes

Acknowledgments to Raquel Zonis-Zukerfeld, Beatriz Godoy, and Sol Szuchman.

1. The same also applies to the classic concept of "the psychotic part of personality".
2. M. Froufe (1997) has developed this notion exhaustively. What gives rise to some difficulty is the use of the adjective "cognitive", trying to legitimize—or not—the so-called psychoanalytic unconscious. I think it is better to say that there is important research into the notion of the unconscious in cognitive and psychoanalytic sciences, which shows convergencies and divergencies.
3. Understood as a certain liberation from "genetic determinism" or as "the mechanism through which each subject is singular and each brain unique" (Ansermet & Magistretti, 2004)
4. The term "third topic or topography" as used by Green (1975), Dejours (1986), Marucco (1999), Raggio (1989) and Merea (1994), Winnicottian authors (Accioly Lins, 1994), and those associated with psychosomatics (Rappoport de Aisemberg, 2001). Authors like Kaës (1999) and more recently Brusset (2006) promote this metapsychological revision from an intersubjective point of view.
5. These traces are clearly associated with Freud's automatic anxiety.
6. Permanent and fluid dynamics is that of normal-neurotic functioning associated with linking dynamics (point 3), whereas crystallized predominance (without fluidity), rigidity, or splitting break-up would represent pathologic configurations.
7. This last possibility is characteristic of trace activation (b) as ineffable sensations.
8. Certain conceptions from evolutionary psychology might explain this.

9. In the neurosciences it would correlate with hippocampus deterioration due to repeated-stress hormones.

10. The term "organo-neurosis" is an example. All the same, the problem of symbolization had already been discussed in depth by pioneers, as the schools of Boston and Chicago show.

11. It is not surprising that the members of the school define themselves as "psychosomatists" and not psychoanalysts. Green (1998), in his discussion with representatives of the school, points out the neglectfulness of Bion's and Winnicott's ideas on limit states.

12. The substratum of which would be the neuronal networks of the amygdala–hypothalamus circuits and their immunoendocrine integration.

13. To some extent, this would be a modality of subsymbolic "communication"—without word intervention. Besides, hope would exist that this "message" would be received and contained by someone, and it could even be supposed to form part of an "unconscious plan" (Weiss, 1993)

14. Where the *a posteriori* effects coexist with those of traumatic disarticulation.

15. Both the notion developed by Marty (quality, quantity, and availability of preconscious representations; 1990) and that put forward by Fonagy (the condition of the development of the reflective function—that is, to perceive one's own mental states and those of the other, capacity associated with secure attachment; 1999).

16. In this model, "homeostatic" is the recovery of a state before trauma and "resilient" is the transformation towards a different state, where the significative, intersubjective links have a decisive influence.

17. This author questions the classic division between "erogenous body" and "biological body", proposing a "living body" and an "incarnate psychism" with overlapping zones.

18. Understood as a complex unity between two supplementary, concurring, and antagonistic logics that feed on each other, are complementary, and are also opposed.

REFERENCES AND BIBLIOGRAPHY

Accioly Lins, M. I. (1994). "Terceira tópica?" Proceedings of the III Encuentro Winnicottiano, Gramado, Brazil

Agambén, G. (1998). *Homo Sacer: Sovereign Power and Bare Life.* Palo Alto, CA: Stanford University Press.

Amati Mehler, J., & Argentieri, S. (1990). *Esperanza y desesperanza. Un problema técnico?* [Hope and hopelessness: A technical problem?]. Lima: Libro Anual de Psicoanálisis.

Ansermet, F., & Magistretti, P. (2004). *A chacun son Cerveau. Plasticité neuronale et inconscient* [To each his own brain: Neuronal plasticity and the unconcious]. Paris: Odile Jacob.

APA (2004). *Diagnostic and Statistical Manual of Mental Disorders* (4th ed., text revision). Washington, DC: American Psychiatric Association.

Aragonés, R. J. (1999). *El narcisismo como matriz de la teoría psicoanalítica.* Buenos Aires: Nueva Visión.

Aulagnier, P. (1967). La perversion comme structure [Perversion as structure]. *L'Inconscient,* 1: 11–43.

Aulagnier, P. (1972). *La violence de l'interpretación. Du pictogramme à l'énoncé* [Violence of interpretation: From pictogram to statement]. Paris: Presses Universitaires de France.

Baker, R. (1994). Psychoanalysis as a lifeline: A clinical study of a transference perversion. *International Journal of Psychoanalysis, 75*: 742–753.

Baranes, J. J. (1991). Desmentida, identificaciones alienantes, tiempo de la generación [Disavowal, alienating identifications, time of the generation]. In: *Lo negativo* [The negative]. Buenos Aires: Amorrortu.

Baranger, M. (2005). Field theory. In: S. Lewkowicz & S. Flechner (Eds.), *Truth, Reality, and the Psychoanalyst*. London: International Psychoanalytical Association.

Baranger, M., & Baranger, W. (1961–62). The analytic situation as a dynamic field. 1961–1962. *International Journal of Psychoanalysis, 89* (No. 4, 2008): 795–826.

Baranger, M., & Baranger, W. (1964). Insight in the analytic situation, In: *The Work of Confluence: Listening and Interpreting in the Analytic Field*, ed. L. G. Fiorini. London: Karnac, 2009.

Baranger, M., Baranger, W., & Mom, J. M. (1987).The infantile psychic trauma from us to Freud: Pure trauma, retroactivity, and reconstruction]. In: M. Baranger & W. Baranger, *The Work of Confluence: Listening and Interpreting in the Psychoanalytic field*, ed. L. G. Fiorini. London: Karnac, 2009.

Baranger, W. (1979). Spiral process and the dynamic field. In: M. Baranger & W. Baranger, *The Work of Confluence: Listening and Interpreting in the Psychoanalytic field*, ed. L. G. Fiorini. London: Karnac, 2009.

Baranger, W. (1994). La situación analítica como producto artesanal [The analytic situation as a handcrafted product]. In: W. Baranger, R. Zak de Goldstein, & N. Goldstein (Eds.), *Artesanías psicoanalíticas* (pp. 445–461). Buenos Aires: Kargieman.

Baranger, W., & Baranger, M. (1969). *Problemas del Campo Psicoanalítico* [Problems of the psychoanalytic field]. Buenos Aires: Kargieman.

Bateson, G. (1972). *Steps to an Ecology of Mind*. New York: Chandler.

Baudrillard, J. (1995). *The Perfect Crime*, trans. C. Turner. London/New York: Verso, 1996.

Bauman, Z. (2000). *Liquid Modernity*. New York: Polity Press.

Bayle, G. (1988). Traumatismes et clivage fonctionnels [Trauma and functional splitting]. *Revue Française de Psychanalyse, 52* (6): 1339–1356.

Bayle, G. (1992). La carencia narcisista. *Revista de Psicoanálisis, 49*: 3–4.

Bayle, G. (1996). Les clivages [Splitting]. *Revue Française de Psychanalyse, 60*: 1303–1547 [special Congress issue].

Bechara, A., & Damasio, A. (1995). Double dissociation of conditioning and declarative knowledge relative to the amygdala and hippocampus in humans. *Science*, 269 (5227).

Benyakar, M., & Lezica, A. (2005). *Lo traumático. Clínica y paradoja*. Buenos Aires: Ed. Biblos.

Berenstein, I. (2001). *El sujeto y el otro. De la ausencia a la presencia*. Buenos Aires: Paidós.

Bernardi, R. (2005). Un único cuerpo pero suficientemente complejo. El diálogo entre el psicoanálisis y la medicina. In: A. Maladesky & Z. López Ozores (Eds.), *Psicosomática. Aportes teórico-clínicos en el siglo XXI*. Buenos Aires: Lugar Editorial.

Berners-Lee, T. (1999) (with Fischetti, M.). *Weaving the Web: Origins and Future of the World Wide Web*. London: Orion Business.

Berners-Lee, T. (2005). *Berners-Lee on the Read/Write Web*. Available at http://news.bbc.co.uk/1/hi/technology/4132752.stm

Bion, W. R. (1957). Differentiation of the psychotic from the non-psychotic personalities. In: *Second Thoughts: Selected Papers on Psycho-Analysis* (pp. 43–64). London: Heinemann, 1967; reprinted London: Karnac, 1984.

Bion, W. R. (1959). Attacks on linking. In: *Second Thoughts: Selected Papers on Psychoanalysis* (pp. 93–109). London: Heinemann, 1967; reprinted London: Karnac, 1984.

Bion, W. R. (1961). *Experiences in Groups*. London: Routledge.

Bion, W. R. (1962). A theory of thinking. In: *Second Thoughts: Selected Papers on Psycho-Analysis* (pp. 110–119). London: Heinemann, 1967; reprinted London: Karnac, 1984.

Bion, W. R. (1963). *Elements of Psychoanalysis*. London: Heinemann; reprinted London: Karnac, 1984..

Bion, W. R. (1965). *Transformations*. London: Heinemann; reprinted London: Karnac, 1984.

Bion, W. R. (1970). *Attention and Interpretation*. London: Tavistock.

Bleichmar, H. (1999). Fundamentos y aplicaciones del enfoque modular transformacional. *Aperturas Psicoanalíticas, 1* (April) (available at www.aperturas.org).

Bleichmar, H. (2001). El cambio terapéutico a la luz de los conocimientos actuales sobre la memoria y los múltiples procesamientos inconscientes. *Aperturas Psicoanalíticas, 9* (November) (available at www.aperturas.org).

Bohr, N. (1958). Essays 1933–1957 on atomic physics and human knowledge. In: *The Philosophical Writings of Niels Bohr, Vol. 2*. Woodbridge, CT: Ox Bow.

Bokanowski, T. (1996). Freud and Ferenczi: Trauma and transference depression. *International Journal of Psycho-Analysis, 77* (3): 519–536.

Bokanowski, T. (2005). Variations on the concept of traumatism: Traumatism, traumatic, trauma. *International Journal of Psychoanalysis, 82* (2): 251–265.

Bolognini, S. (1997). Empathy and empathism. *International Journal of Psychoanalysis, 78*: 279–293.

Bolognini, S. (1998). Compartir y malentender. *Revue de Psicoanalisis, 55*: 7–20.

Bolognini, S. (2002). *Psychoanalytic Empathy*. London: Free Association Books, 2004.

Borges, J. L. (1941). *The Garden of Forking Paths*. In: *Collected Fictions*, trans. A. Hurley. Middlesex: Penguin, 1999.

Borges, J. L. (1981). *Nostalgia del presente* [Nostalgia for the present]. Buenos Aires: Emecé.

Botella, C. (2006). "Sobre el trabajo de figurabilidad". Paper presented at the Conferencia en Sociedad Psicoanalítica de Porto Alegre (September) (www.sppa.org).

Brenner, I. (1994). The dissociative character: A reconsideration of "multiple personality" and related phenomena. *Journal of the American Psychoanalytic Association, 42*: 819–846.

Brenner, I. (1999). Deconstructing D.I.D. *American Journal of Psychotherapy, 53*: 344–360.

Brenner, I. (2001). *Dissociation of Trauma: Theory, Phenomenology and Technique*. Madison, CT: International Universities Press,.

Brenner, I. (2002). "Trauma, Transmission and Time." Paper presented to P.A.N.Y./Melitta Shmidberg Lecture.

Brenner, I. (2003–2004). Remembering, forgetting and keeping separate: Reflections on the "gospel" according to Freud. *Journal of the Indian Psychoanalytical Society, 57*: 25–35.

Brenner, I. (2004). *Psychic Trauma: Dynamics, Symptoms and Treatment*. Lanham, MD: Jason Aronson.

Britton, R. (1989). The missing link: Parental sexuality in the Oedipus complex. In: J. Steiner (Ed.), *The Oedipus Complex Today: Clinical Implications* (pp. 83–101). London: Karnac.

Britton, R. (1995). Reality and unreality in phantasy and fiction. In: *On Freud's "Creative Writers and Day-dreaming"*. New Haven, CT: Yale University Press.

Britton, R. (2001). Beyond the depressive position: Ps(n+1). In: C. Bronstein (Ed.), *Kleinian Theory: A Contemporary Perspective*. London: Whurr.

Britton, R. (2003). *Sex, Death. and the Superego*. London: Karnac.

Brusset, B. (2006). Metapsicologia dos vínculos e "terceira tópica"? *Revista de Psicanálise, 13* (2).

Bucci, W. (2001). Pathways of emotional communication. *Psychoanalytic Inquiry, 21* (1): 40–70.

Buzzati, D. (1940). *The Tartar Steppe*, trans. S. C. Hood. Edinburgh: Canongate, 2007.

Cahn, R. (1983). Le procès du cadre ou la passion de Ferenczi [The issue of the framework, or Ferenczi's passion]. *Revue Française de Psychanalyse, 47*: 1107–1133.

Carignan, L. (1999). The secret: Study of a perverse transference. *International Journal of Psychoanalysis, 80*: 909–928.

Carignan, L. (2003). Exotica: Unravelling a perverse solution to trauma. *Canadian Journal of Psychoanalysis, 11*: 493–506.

Carignan, L. (2005). "Aspects of 'Mad Love' in the Analytic Situation." Unpublished manuscript.

Casas de Pereda, M. (1997). Disavowal: Structural effect and pathogenic dimension. *International Journal of Psychoanalysis, 78*: 379–384.

Chasseguet-Smirgel, J. (1981). Loss of reality in perversions—With special reference to fetishism. *Journal of the American Psychoanalytical Association, 29*: 511–534.

Chasseguet-Smirgel, J. (1984). *Creativity and Perversion*. London: Free Association Books.

Chasseguet-Smirgel, J. (1987) Intento fallido de una mujer por encontrar una solución perversa [A woman's vain attempt to find a perverse solution]. *Revista de Psicoanálisis, 44* (4).

Clark, A. (2000). *Natural Born Cyborgs?* Available at http://www.edge.org/3rd_culture/clark/clark_index.html

Clavreul, J. (1967). The perverse couple. In: S. Schneiderman (ed.), *Returning to Freud: Clinical Psychoanalysis in the School of Lacan* (pp. 215–233). New Haven, CT: Yale University Press, 1980.

Cobo Romaní, C., & Pardo Kuklinski, H. (2007). *Planeta Web 2.O. Inteligencia colectiva o fast-food media*. [Planet Web 2.0: Collective intelligence or fast-food media]. Available at www.planetaweb2.net

Damasio, A. (1994). *Descartes' Error: Emotion, Reason, and the Human Brain*. New York: Putnam.

Dejours, C. (1986). La troisieme topique. In: *Lecores entre biologie et psychanalyse*. París: Gallimard.

Díaz Benjumea, M. D. J. (2002). Lo inconsciente psicoanalítico y la psicología cognitiva. Una revisión interdisciplinar. *Aperturas Psicoanalíticas, 11* (July) (available at www.aperturas.org).

Dickes, R. L. (1965). The defensive function of an altered state of consciousness: A hypnoid state. *Journal of the American Psychoanalytical Association, 13*: 365–403.

Donnet, J. L., & Green, A. (1969). *L'enfant de ça. Psychanalyse d'un entretien: la psychose blanche* [The child of the id. Psychoanalysis of an interview: Blank psychosis]. Paris: Editions de Minuit.

Duras, M. (1964). *The Ravishing of Lol Stein*, trans. R. Seaver. New York: Pantheon, 1986.

Escoll, P. J. (2005). Man's best friend. In: *Mental Zoo: Animals in the Human Mind and Its Pathology* (pp. 127–159). Madison, CT: International Universities Press.

Etchegoyen, R. H. (1978). Some thoughts on transference perversion. *International Journal of Psychoanalysis, 59*: 45–53.

Etchegoyen, R. H. (1991). *The Fundamentals of Psychoanalytic Technique.* London: Karnac.

Fairbairn, W. R. D. (1952a). *On Object-Relations Theory of the Personality.* New York: Basic Books.

Fairbairn, W. R. D. (1952b). *Psychoanalytic Studies of the Personality.* London: Routledge & Kegan Paul.

Febvre, L. (1946). *Marc Bloch et Strasbourg. Souvenirs d'une grande histoire.* In J. Le Goff, *La Nouvelle Histoire.* Paris: Editions Complexe, 1988.

Federn, P. (1952). *Ego Psychology and the Psychoses,* ed. E. Weiss. New York: Basic Books.

Ferenczi, S. (1931). Child-analysis in the analysis of adults. *International Journal of Psychoanalysis, 12*: 468–482. Also in: *Final Contributions to the Problems and Methods of Psycho-Analysis* (pp. 126–141), ed. M. Balint, trans. E. Mosbacher et al. London: Karnac, 1980.

Ferenczi, S. (1932). *The Clinical Diary of Sándor Ferenczi,* ed. J. Dupont, trans. M. Balint & N. Z. Jackson. Cambridge, MA : Harvard University Press, 1995.

Ferenczi, S. (1933). Confusion of tongues between adults and the child. In: *Final Contributions to the Problems and Methods of Psycho-Analysis* (pp. 156–167), ed. M. Balint, trans. E. Mosbacher et al. London: Karnac, 1980.

Ferenczi, S. (1949). Notes and fragments (1930–32). In: *Final Contributions to the Problems and Methods of Psycho-Analysis* (pp. 219–279), ed. M. Balint, trans. E. Mosbacher et al. London: Karnac, 1980.

Fleiss, R. (1953). The hypnotic evasion: A clinical observation. *Psychoanalytic Quarterly, 22*: 497–516.

Fonagy, P. (1999). "Transgenerational Consistencies of Attachment: A New Theory." Paper presented to the Developmental and Psychoanalytic Discussion Group, American Psychoanalytic Association Meeting, Washington, DC (13 May).

Freud, A. (1936). *The Ego and the Mechanisms of Defence.* London: Hogarth Press, 1937.

Freud, S. (1891d). Hypnosis. *S.E., 1.*

Freud, S. (1895d) (with Breuer, J.). *Studies on Hysteria. S.E., 2.*

Freud, S. (1899a). Screen memories. *S.E., 3.*

Freud, S. (1905d). *Three Essays on the Theory of Sexuality. S.E., 7.*

Freud, S. (1910a [1909]). Five lectures on psychoanalysis. *S.E., 4.*

Freud, S. (1910h). A special type of choice of object made by men. *S.E., 11.*

Freud, S. (1911b). Formulations on the two principles of mental functioning. *S.E., 12.*

Freud, S. (1912d). On the universal tendency to debasement in the sphere of love. *S.E., 11.*

Freud, S. (1914c). On narcissism: An introduction. *S.E., 14.*

Freud, S. (1914g). Remembering, repeating and working-through (Further recommendations on the technique of psycho-analysis, II). *S.E., 12.*

Freud, S. (1915c). Instincts and their vicissitudes. *S.E., 14*: 109–139.

Freud, S. (1915d). Repression. *Standard Edition, 14*: 141–157.

Freud, S. (1915e). The unconscious. *S.E., 14.*

Freud, S. (1916–17). *Introductory Lectures on Psychoanalysis. S.E., 16.*

Freud, S. (1917e [1915]). Mourning and melancholia. *S.E., 14*: 237–257.

Freud, S. (1918b [1914]). From the history of an infantile neurosis. *S.E., 17*: 1–122.

Freud, S. (1919e). A child is being beaten. *S.E., 17.*

Freud, S. (1919h). The uncanny. *S.E., 17.*

Freud, S. (1920g). *Beyond the Pleasure Principle, S.E., 18*: 1–64.

Freud, S. (1921c). *Group Psychology and the Analysis of the Ego. S.E., 18.*

Freud, S. (1922b). Some neurotic mechanisms in jealousy, paranoia and homosexuality. *S.E., 18.*

Freud, S. (1923b). *The Ego and the Id. S.E., 19.*

Freud, S. (1923c [1922]). Remarks on the theory and practice of dream-interpretation. *S.E.*, 19.

Freud, S. (1923e). The infantile genital organization: An interpolation into the theory of sexuality. *S.E., 19.*

Freud, S. (1924b [1923]). Neurosis and psychosis. *S.E., 19.*

Freud, S. (1924c). The economic problem of masochism. *S.E., 19.*

Freud, S. (1924e). The loss of reality in neurosis and psychosis. *S.E., 19.*

Freud, S. (1925h). Negation. *S.E., 19.*

Freud, S. (1926d [1925]). *Inhibitions, Symptoms and Anxiety. S.E., 20*: 75–174.

Freud, S. (1927e). Fetishism. *S.E., 21*: 152–157.

Freud, S. (1933a [1932]). *New Introductory Lectures on Psycho-Analysis. S.E., 22.*

Freud, S. (1937c). Analysis terminable and interminable. *S.E., 23*: 209–253.

Freud, S. (1939a [1937–39]). *Moses and Monotheism. S.E., 23*: 3–140.

Freud, S. (1940a [1938]). *An Outline of Psycho-Analysis, S.E., 23*: 139–207.

Freud, S. (1940e [1938]). Splitting of the ego in the process of defence. *S.E., 23*: 271–278.

Freud, S. (1985 [1887–1904]). *The Complete Letters of Sigmund Freud to Wilhelm Fliess 1887–1904*, ed. and trans. J. Masson. Cambridge, MA: Harvard University Press.

Froufe, M. (1997). *El inconsciente cognitivo. La cara oculta de la mente.* Madrid: Biblioteca Nueva.

Gabbard, G. (1994). *Psychodynamic Psychiatry in Clinical Practice* (4th ed.). New York: American Psychiatric Publishing.

Gay, P. (1987). *A Godless Jew: Freud, Atheism and The Making of Psychoanalysis.* New Haven, CT: Yale University Press,

Gillespie, W. H. (1956). The general theory of sexual perversion. *International Journal of Psychoanalysis, 37*: 396–403.

Ginsburg, N. (1999). *E difficile parlare di se* . Rome: Inaudi.

Green, A. (1972). Notes sur les processus tertiaires. *Revue Française de Psychanalyse, 36*: 407–410.

Green, A. (1975). The analyst, symbolization and absence in the analytic setting. In: *On Private Madness.* London: Karnac, 1996.

Green, A. (1990). *On Private Madness.* London: Karnac, 1996.

Green, A. (1993). Splitting: From disavowal to disengagement in borderline cases. In: *The Work of the Negative* (pp. 116–160). London: Free Association Books, 1999.

Green, A. (1998). Théorie. In: A. Fine & J. Schaeffer, *Interrogations psicosomatique.* Paris: Presses Universitaires de France.

Green, A. (2002). *La pensée clinique* [Clinical thinking], Paris: Odile Jacob.

Greenacre, P. (1953). Certain relationships between fetishism and the faulty development of the body image. In: *Emotional Growth, Vol. 1* (pp. 9–30). Madison, CT: International Universities Press, 1971.

Greenacre, P. (1969). The fetish and the transitional object. In: *Emotional Growth, Vol. 1* (pp. 315–334). Madison, CT: International Universities Press.

Greenacre, P. (1970). The transitional object and the fetish: With special reference to the role of illusion. In: *Emotional Growth, Vol. 1* (pp. 335–352). Madison, CT: International Universities Press.

Grinberg, L. (1976). *Teoria de la identificacion.* Buenos Aires: Paidos.

Grotstein, J. (1981). *Splitting and Projective Identification.* New York: Jason Aronson.

Grünbaum, A. (2007). Cien años de teoría y terapia psicoanalíticas. Examen retrospectivo y perspectivas (II). *Revista del Centro Psicoanalítico de Madrid* (6 December).

Halpern, J. (1999). Freud's intrapsychic use of the Jewish culture and religion. *Journal of the American Psychoanalytical Association, 47*: 1191–1212.

Hartke, R. (2004). "Criatividade e expansão psíquica no limite do caos. A mente como um sistema adaptativo complexo." Paper presented at the Bion 2004 Conference, São Paulo, Brazil.

Hartke, R. (2007). A evolução da teoria e prática psicanalíticas. Rumo a uma assintótica situação analítica total. *Revista de Psicanálise da Sociedade Psicanalítica de Porto Alegre, 14* (3).

Hernández, J. (1945). *Martín Fierro.* Buenos Aires: Araujo.

Honderich, T. (1995). *The Oxford Companion to Philosophy.* Oxford: Oxford University Press.

Janet, P. (1889). *L'automatisme psychologique.* Paris: Ballière.

Jones, E. (1953). *Sigmund Freud: Life and Work, Vol. 1.* London: Hogarth Press.

Jones, E. (1957). *Sigmund Freud: Life and Work, Vol. 3.* London: Hogarth Press.

Joseph, B. (1971). A clinical contribution to the analysis of a perversion. *International Journal of Psychoanalysis, 52*: 441–449

Joseph, B. (1989). *Psychic Equilibrium and Psychic Change: Selected Papers of Betty Joseph,* ed. M. Feldman & E. B. Spillius. London: Routledge.

Kaës, R. (1989). El pacto denegativo en los conjuntos trans-subjetivos. In: A. Missenard et al., *Le negatif. Figures et modalities.* Paris: Dunoch.

Kaës, R. (1999). *Las teorías psicoanalíticas del grupo.* Buenos Aires: Amorrortu, 2000.

Kancyper, L. (1985). Adolescencia y a posteriori [Adolescence and *a posteriori*]. *Revista de Psicoanálisis, 42* (3): 535.

Kancyper, L. (1987). El resentimiento y la dimensión temporal en el proeso analítico [Resentment and the dimension of time in the analytic process]. *Revista de Psicoanálisis, 44* (6).

Kancyper, L. (1990). Adolescencia y desidentificación [Adolescence and disidentification]. *Revista de Psicoanálisis, 47* (4): 750.

Kancyper, L. (1991). Narcisismo y pigmalionismo [Narcissism and pygmalionism]. *Revista de Psicoanálisis,* 48 (5/6): 1003. Also in: *La confrontación generacional.* Buenos Aires, Paidós, 1997. [Portuguese version: *Confrontacao de Geracoes.* São Paulo: Casa do Psicologo, 1999. Italian version: *Il confronto generazionale,* Milan: F. Angeli, 2000.]

Kancyper, L. (1995). "Resentimiento y odio en el duelo normal y en el patológico [Resentment and hatred in normal and pathological mourning]. *Revista de Psicoanálisis, APA, 52* (2).

Kancyper, L. (1998). Complejo fraterno y complejo de Edipo en la obra de Franz Kafka [Fraternal complex and oedipal complex in the work of Franz Kafka]. *Revista de Psicoanálisis, 55* (2). Also in: *El complejo fraterno* [The fraternal complex]. Buenos Aires: Lumen, 2004.

Kancyper, L. (2004). *El complejo fraterno* [The fraternal complex]. Buenos Aires: Lumen, 2004.

Kancyper, L. (2006) *Resentimiento y remordimiento* [Resentment and remorse]. Buenos Aires: Lumen. [Portuguese version: *Ressentimento e Remorso.* São Paulo: Casa do Psicologo, 1994. Italian version: *Il risentimento e il rimorso.* Milan: F. Angeli, 2003.]

Khan, M. (1963). The concept of accumulative trauma. In: *The Privacy of the Self.* London: Hogarth Press, 1974

Khan, M. (1979). *Alienation in Perversions.* New York: International Universities Press.

Klein, M. (1921). The development of a child. In: *Love, Guilt and Reparation and Other Works 1921–1945: The Writings of Melanie Klein, Vol. 1* (pp. 1–53). London: Hogarth Press, 1975; reprinted London: Karnac, 1992.

Klein, M. (1927). Symposium on child analysis. In: *Love, Guilt and Reparation and Other Works 1921–1945: The Writings of Melanie Klein, Vol. 1* (pp. 139–169). London: Hogarth Press, 1975; reprinted London: Karnac, 1992.

Klein, M. (1929). Personification in the play of children. In: *Love, Guilt and Reparation and Other Works 1921–1945: The Writings of Melanie Klein, Vol. 1* (pp. 199–209). London: Hogarth Press, 1975; reprinted London: Karnac, 1992.

Klein, M. (1932). Early stages of the Oedipus complex and of super-ego formation. In: *The Psycho-Analysis of Children: The Writings of Melanie Klein, Vol. 2* (pp. 123–148). London: Hogarth Press, 1975; reprinted London: Karnac, 1993.

Klein, M. (1933). The early development of conscience in a child. In: *Love, Guilt and Reparation and Other Works 1921–1945: The Writings of Melanie Klein, Vol. 1* (pp. 248–257). London: Hogarth Press, 1975; reprinted London: Karnac, 1992.

Klein, M. (1935). A contribution to the psychogenesis of manic-depressive states. In: *Love, Guilt and Reparation and Other Works 1921–1945: The Writings of Melanie Klein, Vol. 1* (pp. 262–289). London: Hogarth Press, 1975; reprinted London: Karnac, 1992.

Klein, M. (1940). Mourning and its relation to manic-depressive states. In: *Love, Guilt and Reparation, and Other Works, 1921–1925: The Writings of Melanie Klein, Vol. 1.* London: Hogarth, 1975; reprinted London: Karnac, 1992.

Klein, M. (1946). Notes on some schizoid mechanisms. In: *Envy and Gratitude and Other Works: The Writings of Melanie Klein, Vol. 3.* London: Hogarth Press, 1975; reprinted London: Karnac, 1993.

Klein, M. (1952). Some theoretical conclusions regarding the emotional life of the infant. In: *Envy and Gratitude and Other Works: The Writings of Melanie Klein, Vol. 3* (pp. 61–93). London: Hogarth Press, 1975; reprinted London: Karnac, 1993.

Klein, M. (1957). Envy and gratitude. In: *Envy and Gratitude and Other Works: The Writings of Melanie Klein, Vol. 3* (pp. 176–235). London: Hogarth Press, 1975; reprinted London: Karnac, 1995.

Klein, M. (1958). On the development of mental functioning. In: *Envy and Gratitude and Other Works: The Writings of Melanie Klein, Vol. 3* (pp. 236–246). London: Hogarth Press, 1975; reprinted London: Karnac, 1995.

Kohut, H. (1971). *The Analysis of the Self.* New York: International Universities Press.

Kunstlicher, R. (1995). "El concepto de *Nachträglichkeit*" [The concept of *Nachträglichkeit*]. *Revista de Psicoanálisis, 52* (3).

Lacan, J. (1953). Some reflections on the ego. *International Journal of Psychoanalysis, 34*: 11–17.

Lacan, J. (1954). Response to Jean Hyppolite's Commentary on Freud's "Verneinung". In: *Ecrits,* trans. B. Fink. New York: W. W. Norton, 2006.

Lacan, J. (1975). Le séminaire. Livre XXII. RSI. *Ornicar*: 2–5.

Lacan, J. (1982). *Female Sexuality.* New York: W. W. Norton.

Laplanche, J., & J.-B., Pontalis (1967). *The Language of Psychoanalysis,* trans. D. Nicholson-Smith. London: Hogarth Press, 1973; reprinted London: Karnac, 1988.

Le Gaufey, G. (1993). Clivagem. In: *Dicionário Enciclopédico de Psicanálise,* ed. P. Kaufmann. Rio de Janeiro: Zahar, 1996.

Le Guen, C., Anargyros, A., Bauduin, A., Bayle, G., Bonnel, J., Bouhsira, J., et al. (1986). Le refoulement (les défenses) [Repression (defences)]. *Revue Française de Psychanalyse, 50* (1): 23–335.

Lévy, P. (1997). *Evoluzione del concetto di sapere nell'era telematica* [Evolution of the concept of knowledge in the telematic era]. Available at http://www.mediamente.rai.it/home/bibliote/intervis/l/levy02.htm

Lewin, B. D. (1954). Sleep, narcissistic neurosis and the analytic situation. *Psychoanalytic Quarterly, 23*: 487–510.

Lewin, R. (1993). *Complexidade. A vida no limite do caos.* Rio de Janeiro: Rocco, 1994.

Lewkowicz, I. (2004). *Pensar sin Estado* [Thinking without a state]. Buenos Aires: Paidós.

Lichtenberg, J. D., & Slap, J. W. (1973). Notes on the concept of splitting and the defense mechanism of the splitting of representations. *Journal of the American Psychoanalytical Association, 21*: 722–787.

Marty, P. (1990). *La psicosomática del adulto.* Buenos Aires: Amorrortu.

Marucco, N. (1999). *Cura analítica y transferencia. De la represión a la desmentida.* Buenos Aires: Amorrortu.

McDougall, J. (1972). Primal scene and sexual perversion. *International Journal of Psychoanalysis, 53*: 371–384.

McDougall, J. (1978).The sexual scene and the anonymous spectator . In: *Plea for a Measure of Abnormality*(pp. 21–52). New York: Brunner-Mazel.

McDougall, J. (1982). *Plea for a Measure of Abnormality.* New York: Brunner-Mazel.

McDougall, J. (1986). Identifications, neoneeds and neosexualities. *International Journal of Psychoanalysis, 67*: 19–30.

McDougall, J. (1991). *Theaters of the Body: A Psychoanalytic Approach to Psychosomatic Illness.* New York: W. W. Norton.

Meltzer, D. (1967). *The Psychoanalytical Process.* London: Heinemann.

Meltzer, D. (1968). Terror, persecution, dread: A dissection of paranoid anxieties, *International Journal of Psycho-Analysis, 49*: 396–400. Also in: *Sexual States of Mind* (pp. 99–106). Strath Tay: Clunie Press, 1973; and in: E. B. Spillius (Ed.), *Melanie Klein Today: Vol. 1: Mainly Theory* (pp. 230–238). London: Routledge, 1988.

Meltzer, D. (1978). *The Kleinian Development, Part III: The Clinical Significance of the Work of Bion.* Strath Tay: Clunie Press.

Merea, C. (1994). *La extensión del psicoanálisis.* Buenos Aires: Paidós.

Missenard, A., et al. (1989). *Le negatif. Figures et modalities.* Paris: Dunoch.

Moreno, J. (2002). *Ser humano. La inconsistencia, los vínculos, la crianza.* [Being human: Inconsistency, bonds, upbringing]. Buenos Aires: Ed. Del Zorzal.

Morin, E. (2001). *L'identité humaine. La méthode 5. L'humanité de l'humanité.* Paris: Seuil.

M'Uzan, M. (1994). *La bouche de l'inconscient.* Paris: NRF, Gallimard.

Neumann, E. (1954). *The Origins and History of Consciousness.* London: Routledge & Kegan Paul.

Neyraut, M. (1995). *Les raisons de l'irrationel* [The reasons of the irrational]. Paris: Presses Universitaires de France.

Ogden, T. (1992). The dialectically constituted/decentred subject of psychoanalysis. II: The contributions of Klein and Winnicott. *International Journal of Psychoanalysis, 73*: 613–626.

Ogden, T. (1994a). The analytic third: Working with intersubjective clinical facts. *International Journal of Psychoanalysis; 75*: 3–19.

Ogden, T. (1994b). *Subjects of Analysis.* Northvale, NJ: Jason Aronson.

Ogden, T. H. (1996). The perverse subject of analysis. *Journal of the American Psychoanalytical Association, 44*: 1121–1146.

O'Reilly, T. (2005). *What Is Web 2.0? Design Patterns and Business Models for the Next Generation of Software.* Available at http://www.oreillynet.com/pub/a/oreilly/tim/news/2005/09/30/what-is-web-20.html

O'Shaughnessy, E. (1981). A clinical study of a defensive organization.

International Journal of Psychoanalysis, 62: 359–69. Also in: E. B. Spillius (Ed.), *Melanie Klein Today: Vol. 1: Mainly Theory* (pp. 293–310). London: Routledge, 1988.

O'Shaughnessy, E. (1999). Relating to the superego, *International Journal of Psychoanalysis, 80*: 861–870. .

Ostow, M. (1989). Sigmund and Jacob Freud and the Philippson Bible. *International Review of Psychoanalysis, 16*: 483–492.

Oxnam, R. B. (2005). *A Fractured Mind.* New York: Hyperion.

Pally, R. (1998). Emotional processing: The mind–body connection. *International Journal of Psychoanalysis, 79* (2): 349–362.

Parsons, M. (2000). Sexuality and perversion a hundred years on. *International Journal of Psychoanalysis, 81*: 37–49.

Prensky, M. (2004). *The Emerging Online Life of the Digital Native.* Available at http://www.marcprensky.com/writing/Prensky-The_Emerging_Online_Life_of_the_Digital_Native-03.pdf

Prudent, A. (1988). *Les enfants surdoués* [Gifted children]. Diploma dissertation, Dijon University, France.

Pruyser, P. W. (1975). What splits in "splitting"? A scrutiny of the concept of splitting in psychoanalysis and psychiatry. *Bulletin of the Menninger Clinic, 39*: 1–46.

Racamier, P.-C. (1992). *Le génie des origines. Psychanalyse et psychose* [The genius of origins: Psychoanalysis and psychosis]. Paris: Payot.

Raggio, E. (1989). Sobre la escisión del yo. Reflexiones sobre una tercera tópica freudiana. *Revista de Psicoanálisis, 46* (2–3).

Rappoport de Aisemberg, E. (2001). Revisión crítica de las teorías y de los abordajes de los estados psicosomáticos. *Revista de Psicoanálisis, 58* (2).

Rheingold, H. (2002). *Smart Mobs: The Next Social Revolution.* Cambridge, MA: Perseus Books.

Rizzuto, A. M. (1998). *Why Did Freud Reject God?* New Haven, CT: Yale University Press,

Rosenfeld, H. (1950). Notes on the psychopathology of confusional states in chronic schizophrenia, *International Journal of Psychoanalysis, 31*: 132–137.

Rosenfeld, H. (1952). Notes on the psycho-analysis of the superego conflict in an acute schizophrenic patient, *International Journal of Psychoanalysis, 33*: 111–131. Also in: *Psychotic States: A Psycho-Analytical Approach* (pp. 63–103). New York: International Universities Press; London: Karnac, 1965.

Rosenfeld, H. (1971). A clinical approach to the psychoanalytic theory of the life and death instincts: An investigation into the aggressive aspects of narcissism, *International Journal of Psychoanalysis, 52*: 169–178.

Rosolato, G. (1989). Lo negativo y su léxico. In: A. Missenard et al., *Le negatif. Figures et modalities.* Paris: Dunoch.

Roulot, D. (1993). Neuroses e psicoses. In: *Dicionário Enciclopédico de Psicanálise,* ed. P. Kaufmann. Rio de Janeiro: Zahar, 1996.

Roussillon, R. (1991). *Paradoxes et situations limites de la psychanalyse.* Paris: Presses Universitaires de Frances, 2005.

Rousillon, R. (2006). Historicidad y huella subjetiva, la tercera huella [Historicity and subjective memory]. In: L. Glocer Fiorini (Ed.), *Tiempo, historia y estructura* [Time, history, and structure]. Buenos Aires: Ed Lugar-APA.

Rousillon, R. (2007). "Configuraciones transferenciales 'límites'." Paper presented at the Conferencia Asociación Psicoanalítica Argentina (November).

Sarlo, B. (2000). *Siete ensayos sobre Benjamin* [Seven essays on Benjamin]. Buenos Aires: Fondo de Cultura Económica.

Schafer, R. (1968). *Aspects of Internalization.* New York: International Universities Press.

Schmucler, H. (2007). El dilema de las palabras [The dilemma of words]. *Diario Página, 12* (25 January).

Searles, H. F. (1965). *Collected Papers on Schizophrenia and Related Subjects.* New York: International Universities Press.

Segal, H. (1972). A delusional system as a defence against the re-emergence of a catastrophic situation. *International Journal of Psychoanalysis, 30*: 69–74.

Segal, H. (1993). On the clinical usefulness of the concept of the death instinct, *International Journal of Psychoanalysis, 74*: 55–61.

Shengold, L. (1989). *Soul Murder: The Effects of Child Abuse and Deprivation.* New Haven, CT: Yale University Press.

Silberer, H. (1909). Report on a method of eliciting and observing certain symbolic hallucination phenomena. In: D. Rapaport (Ed.), *Organization and Pathology of Thought* (pp. 195–207). New York: Columbia University Press, 1957.

Smith, H. (2006). Analyzing disavowed action: The fundamental resistance of analysis. *Journal of the American Psychoanalytic Association, 54*: 713–737.

Stein, R. (2005). Why perversion? *International Journal of Psychoanalysis, 86*: 775–799.

Steiner, J. (1993). *Psychic Retreats: Pathological Organizations in Psychotic, Neurotic and Borderline Patients.* London: Routledge.

Steiner, J. (1996). The aim of psychoanalysis in theory and in practice. *International Journal of Psychoanalysis, 78*: 580–582.

Sterba, R. (1934). The fate of the ego in analytic theory. *International Journal of Psychoanalysis, 15*:117–126.

Stoller, R. J. (1975). *Perversion: The Erotic Form of Hatred.* New York: Pantheon.

Strachey, J. (1934). The nature of the therapeutic action of psychoanalysis, *International Journal of Psychoanalysis, 15*: 127–159.

Strachey, J. (1961a). Editorial comment. In: S. Freud (1923e), "The Infantile Genital Organization" (p. 143, n. 4). *S.E., 19.*

Strachey, J. (1961b). Editorial comment. In: S. Freud (1924b [1923]), "Neurosis and Psychosis" (p. 153, n. 7). *S.E., 19.*

Strachey, J. (1961c). Editor's note. In: S. Freud (1927e), "Fetishism" (pp. 149–151). *S.E., 21.*

Strachey, J. (1964a). Editor's note. In: S. Freud (1937c), "Analysis Terminable and Interminable" (pp. 211–215). *S.E., 23.*

Strachey, J. (1964b). Editor's note. In: S. Freud (1940e [1938]), "Splitting of the Ego in the Process of Defence" (p. 274). *S.E., 23.*

Strachey, J. (1964c). Editor's note. In: S. Freud (1940a [1938]), *An Outline of Psycho-Analysis* (pp. 141–143). *S.E., 23.*

Surowiecki, J. (2004). *The Wisdom of the Crowds: Why the Many Are Smarter Than the Few and How Collective Wisdom Shapes Business, Economies, Societies, and Nations.* New York: Doubleday.

Watkins, J. G., & Watkins, H. H. (1997). *Ego States: Theory and Therapy.* New York: W. W. Norton.

Weiss, J. (1993). *How Psychotherapy Works.* New York: Guilford Press.

Wiessel, E. (2002). *La intolerancia* [On intolerance]. Barcelona: Granica.

Winnicott, D. W. (1945). Primitive emotional development. *International Journal of Psychoanalysis, 26*: 137–143. Also in: *Through Paediatrics to Psycho-Analysis* (pp. 145–156). London: Hogarth Press & The Institute of Psycho-Analysis, 1975.

Winnicott, D. W. (1951). Transitional objects and transitional phenomena. In: *Playing and Reality.* London: Tavistock, 1971.

Winnicott, D. W. (1960). Ego distortion in terms of the true and false self. In: *The Maturational Processes and the Facilitating Environment.* New York: International Universities Press, 1965.

Winnicott, D. W. (1965). *The Maturational Processes and the Facilitating Environment.* New York: International Universities Press, 1965.

Winnicott, D. W. (1967). D.W.W. on D.W.W. In: *Psycho-Analytic Explorations* (pp. 569–582), ed. C. Winnicott, R. Shepherd, & M. Davis, London: Karnac, 1989.

Winnicott, D. W. (1971). *Playing and Reality.* London: Tavistock Publications.

Winnicott, D. W. (1974). Fear of breakdown. *International Review of Psycho-analysis, 1*: 103–107. Also in: *Psycho-Analytic Explorations* (pp. 87–95), ed. C. Winnicott, R. Shepherd & M. Davis, London: Karnac, 1989.

Wittgenstein, L. (1953). *Philosophical Investigations.* New York: Macmillan.

Yerushalmi, Y. H. (1991). *Freud's Moses: Judaism Terminable and Interminable.* New Haven, CT: Yale University Press.

Zorn, F. (1982). *Mars.* Paris: Gallimard.

Zukerfeld, R. (1992). Tercera tópica y locuras públicas. De lo limítrofe a lo central. *Revista de Psicoanálisis, 46* (3–4).

Zukerfeld, R. (1993). "Acerca de la Tercera Tópica." Paper presented at the 38th IPA International Congress, Amsterdam (July).

Zukerfeld, R. (1994). Locuras privadas, locuras públicas. La tercera tópica. *Revista de Psicología y Psicoterapia de Grupo, 17* (2).

Zukerfeld, R. (1996). *Acto bulímico, cuerpo y tercera tópica* [Bulimic act,the body, and the third topography]. Buenos Aires: Paidós.

Zukerfeld, R. (1998). "Psicoanálisis actual. Tercera Tópica e interdisciplina." Paper presented at the 3rd Congreso Argentino de Psicoanálisis, Córdoba.

Zukerfeld, R. (1999). Psicoanálisis actual. Tercera tópica y contexto social. *Aperturas Psicoanalíticas, 2* (July) (available at www.aperturas.org).

Zukerfeld, R. (2002). "Psicoanálisis y procesos terciarios. Resiliencia y prácticas sociales transformadoras." Paper presented at the 1st Congreso Internacional de Salud Mental y Derechos Humanos, Universidad Popular Madres de Plaza de Mayo (UPMPM), Buenos Aires.

Zukerfeld, R., & Zonis Zukerfeld, R. (1989). "Acerca del inconsciente. La tercera tópica Freudiana." Paper presented at the 7th Encuentro y Symposio anual, AEAPG, Buenos Aires (1990).

Zukerfeld, R., & Zonis Zukerfeld, R. (1999). *Psicoanálisis, tercera tópica y vulnerabilidad somática* [Psychoanalysis, third topography, and somatic vulnerability]. Buenos Aires: Lugar Editorial.

Zukerfeld, R., & Zonis Zukerfeld, R. (2001). "Tercera tópica, sostén vincular y vulnerabilidad." Paper presented at the 42nd IPA International Congress, Nice, France.

Zukerfeld, R., & Zonis Zukerfeld, R. (2002). "Procesos terciários". Paper presented at the 24th Congreso Latinoamericano de Psicoanálisis, Montevideo (September).

Zukerfeld, R., & Zonis Zukerfeld, R. (2005). *Procesos terciarios. De la vulnerabilidad a la resiliencia* [Tertiary process: From vulnerability to resilience]. Buenos Aires: Lugar Editorial.

INDEX